THE FIRST
HUNDRED YEARS

A History of South Carolina Football

THE FIRST
HUNDRED YEARS

A History of South Carolina Football

By John Chandler Griffin

LONGSTREET PRESS

Atlanta, Georgia

Published by
LONGSTREET PRESS, INC.
2140 Newmarket Parkway
Suite 118
Marietta, Georgia 30067

Printed in the United States of America

1st printing, 1992

Library of Congress Catalog Number 91-77189

ISBN: 1-56352-032-X

This book was printed by Arcata Graphics/Kingsport, Kingsport, Tennessee.
The text was set in Goudy Old Style.

Book design by Laurie Shock.
Jacket design by Laurie Shock.

Dedication

To my wife, Betty, to my daughter, Alexis, and to those fine young men who have given so much over the past hundred years for the glory of the University of South Carolina.

Acknowledgments

I am deeply indebted to John Crew Carroll, Wendy Walton, Jelain Chubb, and John Heiting for the valuable assistance they provided on this project; to Kerry Tharp and Tom Price of the University of South Carolina's Sports Information Office; to the archives of the University's McKissick Library; and to the following additional sources: the *Garnet and Black*; the *Gamecock*; the *State* (Columbia); the Charleston *News and Courier*; the Charlotte *Observer*; *The Gamecocks* by Jim Hunter (Strode, 1975); *A History of the University of South Carolina* by Dan Hollis (Univ. of South Carolina Press, 1951); and *The Carolina-Clemson Game, 1896-1966*, by Don F. Barton (*State* Printing Co., 1967).

I also wish to express my fond gratitude to John A. (Pete) Arnold, Dean of the College at USC – Lancaster, for allowing me the freedom to write this book and for his encouraging words.

Photos courtesy of the *Garnet and Black* and the Athletic Department of the University of South Carolina.

Foreword: From A Hundred Years of Gamecock Memories

In their fifth season, the South Carolina College Jaguars hire their first coach, Dixie Whaley . . . Big Thursday Number One, 1896: Carolina 12, Clemson 6 . . . our first winning season, 1900 . . . Christie Benet and the Great Riot of 1902 . . . Coach Bob Williams goes 14-3, 1902-03 . . . Fritzie, Dutch, and the Blond Viking bring home the state championship, 1912 . . . the great "ringer" scandal of 1915 . . . Sol Metzger signs a five-year contract, Tatum Gressette ends the drought against Clemson, 1920 . . . our first victory over the Tarheels, 1924 . . . three straight shutouts over the Tigers, 1924-26 . . . "one of the biggest upsets of all time": USC over Amos Alonzo Stagg's Chicago, 6-0, in 1928 . . . the first sighting of the Gaffney Ghost, 1931 . . . and the last sighting, 1933, in a huge upset of Auburn . . . the arrival of Rex Enright, 1938 . . . Lou Sossamon, USC's first AP All-American, 1942 . . . sweet wartime memory: Carolina holds Clemson to one yard, total, in 1943 . . . Cary Cox, the only man in history to captain both the Gamecocks and the Tigers.

The Big Thursday bogus ticket scandal (and riot) of 1946 . . . dynamic duo: the Bishop and the Cadillac, 1948-50 . . . all-time great win over Army brings #15 national ranking, 1954 . . . Enright retires in '55 as USC's winningest and losingest coach . . . Warren "Ground Game" Giese, 1956-60 . . . Alex Hawkins and King Dixon lead the Gamecocks to #15 in final AP poll, 1958 . . . the end of Big Thursday, October 22, 1959 . . . Sigma Nu, dressed out like Clemson Tigers, pulls off prank of the century, 1961 . . . Deacon Dan and the dismal years, 1963-64 . . . Tyler Hellams' 73-yard punt return beats the Tigers, 1968 . . . Coach Dietzel leads the Gamecocks to their first-ever outright ACC championship, 1969 . . . All-American Jeff Grantz throws five TD passes to tame the Tigers in 1975 . . . George Rogers, USC's one and only Heisman Trophy winner, 1980 . . . The Man in Black comes to Columbia, 1983 . . . Black Magic on offense, Fire Ants on defense, 1984 . . . Todd Ellis rewrites the record book, 1986-89 . . . Sparky Woods takes the helm, 1989.

With 1992, the second century begins, and the great tradition of Gamecock football continues.

1

1892 – 1901

THE BEGINNING

Christmas Eve, 1892, dawned bright and cool, a perfect day for a football match. Kickoff was scheduled for 3:00 p.m. at the Charleston Base Ball Field. Special cars were provided to carry the fans to the park. Or, should they prefer, fans were permitted to drive their carriages through the gate and right up to the playing field.

The players of both teams were transported to the park in carriages provided by their respective Charleston alumni. Both teams wore uniforms of white duck material, the sleeves of which were dyed to reflect their team colors. Our South Carolina College boys also sported red caps.

Our best players in '92 were W. W. Wannamaker, William and Robert Moorman, and Melton Clark. Wannamaker was elected team manager, while Clark had the distinction of being Carolina's first team captain. In the absence of a coach, Professor A. T. Smythe volunteered to oversee the team.

The following lineups were provided to the referees just prior to kickoff:

South Carolina College		Furman
E. C. Parker, 170 lbs.	CTR	G. A. Jeter
E. S. Block, 180 lbs.	LG	R. J. Parker
J. M. James, 160 lbs.	RG	O. F. Going
G. K. Laney, 160 lbs.	LT	R. E. Burriss
W. W. Wannamaker, 148 lbs.	RT	W. O. Holland
J. D. Lawrence, 170 lbs.	LE	J. J. Nixon
Anderson, 165 lbs.	RE	W. E. Lott
M. Clark	QB	H. B. Young
W. Moorman, 170 lbs.	RHB	O. S. Lipscomb
R. Moorman, 140 lbs.	LHB	B. C. Holland
W. H. Lipscomb, 148 lbs.	FB	E. G. Stewart

Furman's Mountaineers were in their fourth year of intercollegiate competition, and they put their experience to good advantage, totally neutralizing the effectiveness of our wedge formation and repeatedly throwing our runners for losses throughout the day. Their offense, on the other hand, was irrepressible, and they scored with only five minutes elapsed in the game to take a 4-0 lead (touchdowns counted four points at that time, the kicked extra point counted two points, and a field goal five points.

Midway in the first half, Furman's quarterback, E. G. Stewart, went down with a head injury and lay unconscious for fully five minutes. But then he regained his feet, to the cheering of both squads, and resumed his position. A few minutes later, however, he received a kick to the head and again went down. The Mounties, to their credit, deemed both injuries unintentional and promised they would not retaliate against the young Jaguars.

Still, a few minutes after Stewart was replaced at quarterback, the Jaguars' fullback, W. H. Lipscomb, was found lying unconscious at the bottom of a big pileup. He too was suffering from a kick to the head and had to be replaced. The Furman boys smiled and said they were not responsible, and play continued.

At the end of the first half (thirty-five minutes) the score stood at 16-0, in favor of the Mountaineers. The second half went about as did the first, only worse, and the game ended with Furman holding the big end of a 44-0 shutout.

Our record stood at 0-1, true, but it was a beginning. Football had come to the South Carolina College.

1894

After a year's hiatus, the SCC came back in '94 grimly determined to make its mark on the gridiron. We were still coachless, but we did have a team. And on October 27 we received a letter from the powerful University of Georgia eleven, asking if we would be interested in a match for November 3. The team met, voted on the proposal, then sent back an enthusiastic yes.

This would be the first time in history that our Jaguars had played before a home crowd in Columbia, and enthusiasm was at a fever pitch throughout the city. The *State* reported, "Everybody you meet is talking football. In a word, Columbia is all in a flutter, the excitement extending into the most fashionable residences in the city."

The Georgia team, all seventeen members, led by their captain George Butler, arrived by train on Friday afternoon and were met at the depot by our young Jaguars. The players of both teams, by the way, were readily identifiable as football players because of their long unkempt hair. Players back then wore leather nose guards, but not helmets, so they wore their hair long as a sort of head protection. Oddly enough, hair pulling was considered a serious infraction, and a player could draw a 15-yard penalty were he foolish enough to bow to temptation and swing an opposing player around by the hair.

The game, the next afternoon at two o'clock, went pretty much as expected, with the larger and more experienced Georgia team running roughshod over the smaller Jaguars, finally winning by a score of 40-0. But it was reported that the SCC's halfback, Bryan, was a team unto himself, that much talent was shown by Laney, Green, and Moorman, and that the Jaguars were looking forward to the future with much optimism.

Eight days later, on November 11, the Jaguars played their second game of the season, this time against the Augusta YMCA. Most YMCAs at the time sponsored teams composed of young men of all ages, many of them former college players who admired the game and wished to continue to play. Their opponents were other Y teams and college teams.

Kickoff was slated for 4:00 p.m. in Augusta, and our boys were surprised to see that the Y team "played without orders," which is to say that they did not call plays between downs. But such play-calling was really unnecessary, since their only play was the wedge over center, which they ran repeatedly and successfully all day, battering the smaller Jaguars into submission. Green did score a touchdown for the Jaguars, the first ever scored by a SCC player, but the inevitable final score read Augusta Y 16, SCC 4.

1895

Both of Carolina's football games in 1895 were played in Columbia, and with good reason. The student body had petitioned the board of trustees to allow the football team to engage in intercollegiate activities, "under the direction of the Faculty," at out-of-town sites. But the board refused. Under no circumstances could the Jaguars travel outside the city limits of Columbia to engage in a football contest. Carolina, however, was not alone in this unfortunate situation. That same year the football team of Cornell University petitioned their president for permission to travel to Ann Arbor for a game with the University of Michigan. But their president refused, saying, "I will not permit forty of our young men to travel 800 miles simply for the purpose of agitating a bag of air."

As kickoff time approached on Friday, November 8, streetcars from all over Columbia began bringing fans to Shandon Park, while dozens of carriages bearing husbands, wives, and children began filling the park area surrounding the playing field. The Furman Mountaineers had rolled into town the day before, and it seemed that the whole city was ready for the spectacle.

The Jaguars had several returning veterans from the '94 team, and hopes ran high that this day would bring our first intercollegiate football victory in history. Captain Bryan, however, was sidelined with an injury suffered in practice that week, a real blow to our chances.

As it turned out, neither our fans nor our team was to be disappointed. The Jaguars, led by the magnificent running of Bass, who

replaced Bryan at left half, jumped off to a 10-4 halftime lead, then held on in the second half to win by 14-10.

It was our first victory, and it was said that sounds of revelry could be heard far into the night throughout Columbia. It was also sweet revenge for the shellacking Furman had given us back in 1892.

Just six days later, on November 14, we played our second and final game of the season. This time we faced the powerful Terriers of Wofford College, coached by William Wertenbaker, who would become coach of the Jaguars in 1898. It was State Fair week, but by 2:00 p.m. the crowd at the fair began to thin as devoted SCC fans mounted streetcars bound for Shandon Park. By kickoff it was estimated that more than a thousand men, women, and children filled the stands and the sidelines, the first time that the Jaguars had ever pulled such a crowd to a game.

Our smaller Jaguars could not keep their eyes off the big, strapping Terrier team during pregame warmups, and fans could see from their dejected expressions that the game was lost before it had begun. Such indeed was the case, as the Terriers won by a score of 10-0.

But we were 1-1 on the year, our first non-losing season.

1896

The student body of 1896, aware that football was the latest phenomenon in athletics and outraged that the SCC administration was not taking steps to remain competitive with such teams as Tennessee, Georgia, Georgia Tech, Alabama, and Auburn, finally made its shrill voice heard. As a result, the administration hired our first coach in history, Mr. W. H. "Dixie" Whaley, a former star player for the University of Virginia.

The 1896 Jaguars: (standing) Coach Dixie Whaley, team manager D. D. McCall, L. M. Haseldon, Professor LeConte Davis (for whom Davis Field was named), Franklin C. Woodward (president of the SCC, 1897 – 1902); (sitting) J. S. Verner, A. H. Brooker, J. Cantzon Foster, B. A. Bolt, Christie Benet, Lee Hagood; (on ground) J. G. Hughes, Mason Brunson, N. W. Brooker.

The hiring of Coach Whaley was also prompted by the news that our new neighbor to the west, Clemson Agricultural College, had not only assembled a steamroller of a team its very first year of existence, but had even hired a coach, Professor Walter M. Riggs, formerly captain of the Auburn Plainsmen.

A loss to Clemson of any sort at this point in our history was considered intolerable. Bad blood already existed between the South Carolina College and Clemson back in those early days — and for understandable reasons. Clemson had opened its doors only three years before, in 1893, thanks largely to the efforts of Governor "Pitchfork" Ben Tillman, who blamed what he called "the sorry plight of agriculture" in the state on the "pitiful and contemptible" agriculture department at

(what was then called) the University of South Carolina. As a happy afterthought Tillman added, "It is time the state have an institution the citizens can be proud of." The good folks at the University of South Carolina were hardly flattered by his remarks. Then in 1889, the year Clemson received its charter and became an unpleasant fact of life, insult was added to injury when we lost our status as the state university and again became simply the South Carolina College.

As though all that were not enough to raise the hackles of the most charitable among us, by 1896 Clemson could boast an enrollment of 446 students, while we, founded in 1801, were struggling along with an enrollment that had dwindled to only 164 students. What was more, while the SCC and Winthrop College were forced to go to the state legislature every year, hat in hand, and plead for operating capital, Clemson, thanks to the farsightedness of Governor Tillman, was supported by a special tax placed on fertilizer. In 1896 they received over $200,000, more than was received by the other two state institutions combined.

And now, on top of everything else, the administration discovered, to its horror, that someone had been foolish enough to challenge those ploughboy upstarts to a football match—the very first game of the season and we didn't even have a football coach. Thus came W. H. "Dixie" Whaley. On November 12, 1896, a great tradition was born. It was the first Big Thursday, staged during State Fair week, and on that fateful morning some two thousand fans paid twenty five cents for the pleasure of either sitting in the old wooden grandstand or standing along the sidelines during the contest. The big Tiger team trooped arrogantly onto the field that day dressed in orange sweaters, duck pants, and blue-and-orange-striped stockings. We Carolinians, on the other hand, wore our garnet sweaters and duck pants.

As for the game itself, Carolina won the toss and elected to receive. Clemson fullback A. M. Chreitzberg enjoys the distinction of being the first to kick off during this long series between two schools, while Carolina quarterback Vass was the first to return a kickoff, running it back to our own 40-yard line.

The only first-half score came when our N. W. Brooker achieved immortality by scoring our first touchdown against the Clemson Tigers. Captain C. H. McLaurin then kicked the extra point and the Jaguars took a 6-0 lead.

Only eighty-five seconds into the second half, Clemson's fleet J. A. Stone, a substitute for injured J. M. Bain, raced around end for sixty yards and Clemson's first score against the Carolinians. Chreitzberg kicked the extra

point and the score was knotted at 6-6. But then the Brooker brothers went to work, hitting the big Tiger line repeatedly for nice gains until we reached their 15-yard line. Then Cantzon Foster, on what was described as a "cross-cross," ran the remaining distance for another Jaguar score. Again McLaurin was true with the extra point, and we were back in the lead at 12-6. That's the way the first game ever between these blood rivals came to an end.

Our euphoria lasted for exactly one week, until November 19, when we squared off against the Terriers of Wofford College in a game modestly billed as "The Great Battle for the State Championship of South Carolina." Unfortunately, the Terriers left Columbia with the crown when McLaurin's extra-point kick, which would have tied the game, sailed just under the goal posts.

Our Jaguars played their final game of the season on November 26, 1896, in Greenville. We won the toss that day, but that was the only thing. Furman scored once in each half to take a 12-0 victory.

Following the game, Coach Whaley explained that the loss came about as the result of several factors: first, the team did not depart Columbia until 8:00 a.m. Saturday, then spent six hours in the cars, not arriving in Greenville until after two. At that time, the ravenous Jaguars were fed a pregame meal of raw oysters. Then they suited up and were driven two miles to the park by horse and wagon, where they arrived, totally exhausted, about five minutes prior to kickoff. By that time, lamented Whaley, the boys were beginning to feel a little green around the gills from their oyster luncheon. Everything considered, he concluded, it was a miracle that they could play at all.

Still, it wasn't a bad season. We'd won our first game ever with the Clemson Ploughboys, then barely lost the State Championship game, then came close to beating Furman. As for Dixie Whaley, he

The 1897 Jaguars and their second coach, Frederick M. Murphy (standing, top left).

returned to his home in Charleston following the '96 season to begin his practice of law. In later years he would become Speaker of the House of Representatives, then go on to Washington as Chief Justice of the Court of Claims.

1897

In 1897 we hired our second football coach, Mr. Frederick M. Murphy, a young medical student who, like Dixie Whaley, had played for the University of Virginia. Unlike Coach Whaley, he failed to lead us to victory over the Tigers in our season opener. We lost six fumbles that day, and came out on the short end of a 20-6 score. So we were now 1-1 with the Tigers, but we had no time for regrets. We had to tighten our nose guards and get ready for our big game with the Charleston YMCA on

Thanksgiving Day. Because of his outstanding play against the Tigers, Cantzon Foster was elected as a co-captain along with team captain Christie Benet.

The odd thing about this game was that Dixie Whaley, who had returned to Charleston to practice law, played left half for the Christians that day. He was only too familiar with both our plays and our signal calling, so he knew every play we called and immediately tipped off his teammates. Consequently, except for some fine runs by Cantzon Foster, we were totally stymied throughout the afternoon. In fact, it was Whaley who scored the Christians' only touchdown that day, and we finally lost by a score of 6-0.

1898

Coach William Wertenbaker took

From the 1898 squad: Boyd Evans, coach William Wertenbaker, captain Cantzon Foster.

charge of the Jaguars in 1898, our third coach in as many years, and our Carolinians defeated Bingham College of Asheville, North Carolina, by a score of 16-5 on October 18. Bingham, by the way, was actually more of a high school academy than a college, but at that point we'd accept victories wherever we could get them.

A month later came our second game of the season — our hated rivals, the Tigers of Clemson. They also came into the game with a favorable record, having lost to Georgia 20-8 but having beaten Bingham 55-0. On the morning of the game, November 17, we gathered as usual at the State Fairgrounds, where a crowd of some 2,500 jammed the old wooden bleachers and stood along the sidelines awaiting the kickoff.

Captains Cantzon Foster of the SCC and A. S. Shealy of the CAC met at midfield for the coin toss. We won and elected to receive the second half, a strategy which backfired. The Tigers took the kickoff, mounted a drive of some sixty-six yards, then scored with only five minutes elapsed in the game. Our boys held and the half ended with the score Clemson 6, Carolina 0, but Clemson had already established itself as the dominant force that day. Indeed, on the first play of the second half, our quarterback McIntosh fumbled the ball, and Clemson's Shealy picked it up and dashed untouched twenty-two yards for another Tiger score.

We could mount only one drive of any significance that afternoon, and even then we lost the ball on a penalty. Clemson scored twice more and finally won the game 24-0.

Our record now stood at 1-1 as we headed into the final game of the season against the powerful Wildcats of Davidson College at Latta Park in Charlotte, North Carolina.

The Jaguars of 1899. Coach I. O. Hunt is standing, left rear; captain Monroe Shand is holding the football.

An interesting highlight occurred early in the game when the Wildcats were called for being offsides and the ball given to the SCC. They, in protest of the call, left the field and refused to return. At that point the referee awarded the game to the Jaguars by default, but we insisted that the penalty be nullified and that play continue. We eventually lost by a score of 6-0, but no one could deny that we were gracious in defeat.

1899

In 1899, for the first time in our brief history, the Jaguars played a five-game schedule. And under new coach I. O. Hunt, a former footballer from Brown University, we jumped off to a winning start, defeating the Columbia YMCA 4-0 on our home field.

Then came the Clemson Tigers for the state championship, and it would truly be a Big Thursday for both teams. The entire student body from Clemson arrived Wednesday on a train covered with purple and orange bunting, and the two hundred fans who greeted them at the depot were similarly bedecked. Some of Clemson's players were returnees from their great team of '98, and one member had been a starter since 1896. It was said to be the Tigers' best team in history, and they appeared hearty and confident as they faced our smaller Jaguars on that bright Thursday morning.

During the first half Jaguar captain Monroe Shand and Harry Withers ripped off some nice gains, but as time ran out Clemson went to the sidelines holding a 11-0 lead. (Touchdowns now counted five points, by the way, extra points one point.) The Jaguars fared even worse in the second half. Shealy for the Tigers was unstoppable. He scored two touchdowns that day, to go with the two he'd scored the year before, and put us in a hole we'd never get out of. The final score was 34-0, our third worst loss in history.

But the season was far from over. We were 1-1 at that point and still had three games to play. On Wednesday of the next week we journeyed to Asheville to play good old Bingham again, and we surprised no one when we came home with an easy 11-5 victory. However, the next week we played good old Bingham again, and surprised everyone by going down in defeat 18-6. Which proved that we could not trust anyone, not even our whipping boy, Bingham College.

On November 30, in a game played at Latta Park in Charlotte, we lost our finale to Davidson 5-0. So we had suffered through another losing season, but despite our 2-3 record, we gave Coach Hunt a vote of

confidence and looked forward to his return.

1900

It was 1900, the last year of the nineteenth century, and we longed to end it on a winning note. For the first time we were playing a seven-game schedule, and we were playing some outstanding regional teams. We elected T. J. Bell our team captain that year, and on October 20 we traveled to Athens, where we met the powerful Bulldogs of the University of Georgia.

Throughout most of the game we surprised the experts by playing the Bulldogs to a standstill. Georgia led at the end of the first half by a score of 5-0, but we scored midway in the second, and the score was knotted at 5-5. Then with only four minutes remaining, Georgia had the ball, fumbled,

Team captain Ted Bell (holding ball) and the 1900 Jaguars.

and our Withers recovered. Referee Rowbotham initially signaled a recovery, but then when he saw that it was a Jaguar with the ball, he changed his mind and awarded the ball to Georgia. We left the field and refused to return, unless the referee would admit his error and give the ball to us, where it rightfully belonged.

The referee obstinately refused, and we declined to play. Instead, we commissioned Captain Ted Bell to extend our regrets to the captain of the Georgia team and explain that we could not, honorably, continue under the circumstances. Georgia's captain replied that he was disappointed but understood our position and looked forward to meeting us in the future. Thus, despite having played an excellent game, we departed Athens for Columbia accepting a 5-0 defeat by default, our honor intact.

We gained our first victory of the season by defeating Guilford College 10-0 in Columbia; then, on November 1, we again went up against the Clemson Tigers. A record crowd of some five thousand fans turned out for the game: one thousand seated in the grandstand, 2,500 standing along the sidelines, and another 1,500 jammed together on the upstairs plazas of the main buildings of the State Fair.

For SCC fans, it proved a painful spectacle. Led by Claude Douthit's three touchdowns, the Tigers laid a thrashing upon the Jaguars even more painful than the previous year's. To add to the insult of this 51-0 rout, even Jake Woodward, a hulking Tiger lineman, scored on a fumble recovery. (In our defense, it might be noted the Tigers of 1900, under Coach John Heisman, enjoyed their first undefeated season in history.)

The defeat was demoralizing, but we somehow managed to put it behind us as we prepared to receive North Carolina A&M (NC State) on November 10. To our credit, though the game was constantly interrupted

by both teams arguing with the referee and engaging in slugging matches with one another, we hitched up our nose guards and beat the Cadets by a score of 12-0.

The next week our streak continued as we defeated a strong Furman team 27-0, a victory we considered particularly sweet, considering the numerous indignities we'd suffered at the hands of the Mounties over the years. Several new players saw action in this game—Ryttenburg at fullback, Coburn at quarterback, and Gunter at end. They would help considerably in the years to come.

The next week we again experienced the "Carolina luck" and lost a close one to Davidson, 5-0, in a game played at Latta Park in Charlotte. But we finished the season on a winning note, taking our second encounter with North Carolina A&M by a score of 17-5. So, despite our disappointments this season, we had reached a milestone: with a 4-3 record, it was our first winning season in history.

1901

After our winning season in 1900, and now with a new coach coming aboard in the person of Byron W. Dickson, we had every reason to expect the best. R. E. L. Freeman had been elected team captain, while J. Nixon Stringfellow served as team manager. We split our first two games of the season. A tough loss to Georgia, 10-5, was followed by a big win over the Mountaineers of Furman in a game with an historic footnote. With only forty seconds remaining, and with Furman threatening our goal, tackle Ed Oliver grabbed the ball away from a Furman runner and dashed, untouched, a hundred yards for a touchdown. So, instead of a Furman touchdown and a tie, we won the game, 12-0. The record book confirms that Oliver's 100-yard touchdown run with a

R. L. Freeman, captain of the 1901 team.

fumble recovery was a record that would stand until Harry Skipper's 101-yard return against Pacific in 1982.

After the next four games, the record was still even. We beat the boys of Bingham, 11-6, then allowed Davidson to slip away from our own Fairgrounds with a 12-5 victory. A trip to Atlanta resulted in a 13-0 loss to Georgia Tech, but we rebounded by scoring more points than ever before in a 47-0 thrashing of North Carolina Military Academy.

Six days later, still flush from our great victory over the Tarheel Cadets, our Jaguars traveled to Spartanburg to play the Wofford Terriers in our final—and pivotal—game of the season. The record shows that Wofford was declared the winner, 11-6, but the final score does not tell the entire story.

For example, early in the game we scored a touchdown from Wofford's 20-yard line. The Terriers were offsides on the play, so the referee, citing what he termed a "new rule," brought the ball back, penalized Wofford ten yards, and declared no touchdown. A little later, however, he made the reverse decision in Wofford's favor, declaring a Terrier touchdown when we were clearly offsides on the play.

Also, early in the game, Cogburn scored a touchdown for us, but in doing so, according to the referee, he "willfully fell on a Wofford player's head." Thus the touchdown was disallowed, the ball was given over to Wofford, and we were penalized twenty yards. The referee also called Cogburn an uncomplimentary name and ordered him off the field.

So we finished 1901 with a somewhat disappointing 3-4 season. But C. R. Williams was about to be named our sixth head coach since 1892, and we hoped that under his direction our gridiron glory was at hand.

2

1902 – 1903

Two Superlative Seasons

The year 1902 marked another bright beginning for our young Carolina football team when Bob Williams, formerly a star player at the University of Virginia, was hired as head coach. Another first occurred when the athletic committee hired Christie Benet, a former Jaguar tackle and now a practicing Columbia attorney, as Coach Williams' assistant. It was also in this year that the traditional hijinks following the Clemson game erupted into what has come to be known as the riot of 1902.

What was to prove one of our finest seasons ever began with three straight shutouts: 10-0 over Guilford College, 60-0 over North Carolina Military Academy, and 28-0 over Bingham. In the rout over NCMA, by the way, Guy Gunter established two records which still stand today: he returned a kickoff for a 100-yard touchdown and scored five touchdowns in all.

Then came Big Thursday, October 30,

against the mighty Clemson Tigers of Coach John Heisman. We hadn't beaten Clemson since the series opened in 1896, and we wanted this one badly.

Some five minutes into the game, Guy Gunter scored for the Carolinians on a three-yard buck, and we took the lead 6-0. Just eight minutes later Gunter again scored, and the half ended with the Jaguars holding a 12-0 lead.

In the second half, with some twelve minutes elapsed, Clemson's Sitton went sixty yards for a touchdown and our lead was cut to 12-6. But then time ran out, and the Carolinians had won their fourth game in a row.

Yes, we'd won the game, cheered the Clemson team, and everyone, players and fans alike, were jubilant. The real trouble did not start until the following night. As always, the Clemson cadets—about four hundred strong—remained in Columbia

The four lovely coeds who served as sponsors for the 1902 Clemson game:

Miss Flinn

Miss Heyward

Miss Davis

Miss Baron

In 1902 the Jaguars became the Gamecocks. This sketch appeared in the Garnet and Black *that year.*

following the game to enjoy the State Fair. It was traditional for these cadets to parade about, celebrating their usual victory over the SCC by wrapping their shoes in garnet and black cloth. This year, however, having been beaten, the cadets were forced to behave in a more subdued manner.

But what truly antagonized them was this: A Main Street tobacco merchant, in celebration of the game, had hung a big transparency in his store window depicting a gamecock crowing over a bedraggled-looking tiger. It did not take our young Carolinians long to borrow this transparency and begin parading it around the Fairgrounds and later up and down Main Street.

The Clemson men informed the Carolinians that it would be poor judgment to display that insulting transparency in the big parade sponsored by the Elks on Friday evening. Law enforcement officials, alarmed at the Clemson threats and concerned for the peace and tranquility of the city, agreed. The Carolinians, however, refused to be intimidated. Christie Benet stated that to avoid the Elks parade with their transparency would amount to nothing less than conceding to threats of violence.

At the conclusion of the parade the four hundred Clemson cadets were dismissed at the foot of the State Capital on Main Street, just a short walk to the campus of the SCC. Armed with bayonets and sabers, the cadets quickly marched to the Sumter Street entrance to the Horse Shoe, where a band of some thirty irate Carolinians crouched behind barricades quickly thrown up to block the entrance of the Clemson students. The Carolinians, by the way, had taken time to arm themselves with pistols, shotguns, clubs, and anything else to defend themselves.

Professor Dan Hollis, in his fascinating History of the University of South Carolina, recounts that a senior called to freshman J. Rion McKissick (who would later become president of the University): "McKissick, are you armed?"

McKissick showed him a revolver. The senior grasped the freshman's shoulder in fervent appeal. "Make every shot count."

Finally, before blood could be shed, Christie Benet arrived on the scene and offered to fight any Clemson student chosen by the corps. When that idea failed, he suggested that committees be appointed to arbitrate. By then the police and officials from both schools arrived at the scene and threatened stern action against any student who moved against another. The matter was finally settled when a joint committee of six students reached a compromise and the transparency was burned between the two student bodies, who took turns cheering each other.

Clemson officials dismissed this event as a typical boys-will-be-boys sort of thing, but Carolina officials decided that in the interests of both institutions the Carolina-Clemson contest should come to an end. We would not see the resumption of this series until 1909.

Two weeks later, after a hard-fought, 5-0 victory over St. Albans College, we played our old nemesis, the Mountaineers of Furman University, on their inclined field in Greenville. It was here that our bubble finally burst, as the Mounties kicked a field goal in the first half, then added a touchdown in the second to capture the game 10-0. It was also here that our new nickname, which the press had bestowed upon us after the Clemson game, became unofficially official. Toward the end of the last half a Furman student ran the length of the field with a stuffed rooster, plucking out his tail feathers as he ran. At this, the Furman rooters began to shout, "Poor little gamecock, poor little gamecock." The name was here to stay.

Two weeks later our record-breaking season ended in fine fashion with a game against overmatched Charleston Medical College. We scored thirteen touchdowns that day, and the final score read USC 80, CMC 0, despite limiting the second half to only ten minutes. Coach Bob Williams had led us to a 6-1 record, an .857 winning percentage. It was our best year in history. In 1984 we would go 10-2, but still that was not as good as 6-1.

1903

It was a year of firsts. Not only did 1903 mark the first year we played a ten-game schedule; it also marked the first year that the Gamecock logo appeared in the Carolina yearbook, the *Garnet and Black*, in association with the football team. Coach Bob Williams, after his sensational 6-1 1902 season, was back for his second year, with the trusty Christie Benet again as his assistant.

What would prove to be our second most successful season in history began on a triumphant note as we defeated the Columbia Y by a score of 24-0, and then four days later ran up our highest score ever when we blanked the young lads of Hartsville's Welsh Neck Academy 89-0.

But both these teams were non-collegiate, and we were eager to see how the Gamecocks would do against tougher competition. We found out on October 10, the day following our workout with Welsh Neck, when the Tarheels of North Carolina came to town. They entered the game heavily favored, outweighing the Gamecocks fifteen pounds per man, and they took the measure of us, 17-0.

A week later, our Gamecocks went back to their old winning ways, defeating the Georgia Bulldogs for the first time ever. It was a hard-fought contest, played in ankle-deep mud, and frequently marred, the press said, by Georgia's team captain Ketron, who had to be repeatedly warned to stop kicking Carolina players.

After a routine, 29-0 win over Guilford it was time for yet another first. On November 8, we went up against those always tough Davidson Wildcats at Latta Field in Charlotte. We'd played them four times in the past without a single win to our credit, but today we were ready. In the first half we easily scored seventeen points, while they could not even muster a single first down. But the second half was different. We kicked off and Davidson's speedy left half, McCollie, ran it back 105 yards for a touchdown, cutting the score to 17-6. Then, moments later, their Bryan Setzer picked up a loose Carolina fumble and dashed sixty yards for a score, making the score now 17-12. But that was it for the Wildcats. We held them scoreless for the rest of the game, while adding another twelve points of our own.

It was a great win, and our sixth of the season, but it was no time for laurels. Six

The fleet Guy Gunter, captain of the 1903 Gamcocks.

days later, the Gamecocks took on one of the most formidable teams in the nation, the University of Tennessee. During the first five minutes of the game it appeared as though the vaunted Vols would take our Carolinians easily, but then the Gamecocks went to work. James Wyman again pulled his famous bootleg play and dashed an incredible ninety-five yards through the entire Tennessee team for a touchdown. Moments later, the speedy Guy Gunter, though still hobbled with injuries suffered against Guilford, managed to zing the Vols again with a 40-yard touchdown run. By game's end, the Gamecocks had pulled off a major upset, defeating mighty Tennessee 24-0.

On November 14, however, our fine win streak came to an end with a disappointing 6-5 loss to North Carolina A & M. Not only that, we would now have to face the always

tough men of the Charleston YMCA. In this game, for example, the Y team outweighed us fully ten pounds per man, and six of their players had played college ball. But today we were not to be denied. Oliver scored twice for us, while Wyman kicked a 25-yard field goal. Final score: SCC 16, Charleston Y 0.

We were now 7-2 on the year and looking forward to Wednesday when we'd journey down to Atlanta to play the Blacksmiths of Georgia Tech in the big Thanksgiving extravaganza planned by that city. It turned out that Thanksgiving 1903 was bitterly cold, and the players' hands were so numb that they couldn't hold the ball. Consequently, there were numerous fumbles that day. But eight minutes into the game Ed Oliver scored for Carolina, and we led 5-0 at intermission. Then in the second half, it was more Ed Oliver. He went over the Blacksmith goal twice more for USC touchdowns, and we finally won by a score of 16-0. It was a great win over an outstanding Georgia Tech team.

It turned out to be one of our finest seasons ever, as we won eight out of ten games. In fact, we would not win eight games in a single season again until 1979 when the Gamecocks went 8-4 under Coach Jim Carlen. Over the past two seasons under Coach Bob Williams we'd won fourteen games while losing only three, thus giving Coach Williams a .823 winning percentage, the best of any coach in the history of Carolina football.

Coach Williams, unfortunately, would not be returning for the 1904 season. In fact, we'd next see him again when he stood across the field from us at the Carolina-Clemson game in 1909.

3

1904 – 1908

THE CHRISTIE BENET ERA

It was widely suspected at the time that much of Coach Williams' success had been due to the efforts of his assistant coach, Christie Benet, so there was little disappointment when Benet became head coach in 1904. In fact, many players stated that it was Benet's inspirational pep talk just prior to kickoff that gave the team the motivation to go out and lick Clemson 12-6 in 1902. Benet had been an excellent player at both the SCC and the University of Virginia. Following his retirement from coaching, he would become a highly successful attorney. Oddly enough, in later years Benet would become chairman of the board of trustees at Clemson College.

The 1904 campaign looked promising. Eugene Oliver, the team captain, was one of ten returnees from our great 1903 team, and the season got off to a fast start with a 40-0 win over outmanned Welsh Neck Academy. A week later, however, in a game played in Chapel Hill, our Gamecocks went down in defeat to a much larger Tar Heel team. The team quickly rebounded against Guilford, 21-4, thus setting the stage for what would prove the most controversial game of the year.

We were now 2-1 and making preparations to entertain the big Georgia boys from Athens at noon on Wednesday, October 26, during State Fair week. However, bad news greeted the Gamecocks, now members of the newly formed Southern Intercollegiate Athletic Association, when they were informed that Horace Cogburn, who had played tackle for Clemson the year before, would be ineligible to play against Georgia or any other team sanctioned by the SIAA for another year.

At noon on Wednesday the playing of the game was thrown into doubt when wily Coach Benet (suspecting that it was Georgia who ratted on Cogburn) confronted

Coach Christie Benet (1904 – 05, 1908 – 09), one of the most admired coaches in Gamecock history.

Manager Hull of the Bulldogs concerning the eligibility of two Georgia players, William Black and Joe Rossiter. When Hull denied that either man was a professional player, as Benet charged, Benet asked him to sign an affidavit to that effect. But Hull declined to do so, saying that if Benet cared to bring charges against those players then they would sign an affidavit themselves. A lengthy dispute ensued, but finally Benet stated that he would prefer to proceed with the game than to disappoint the State Fair crowd.

(Benet was vindicated when it was later proven that both Black and Rossitor had been paid football players for the Savannah Athletic Club and thus ineligible to compete in college play under the new SIAA rules.) Their presence, however, did the Bulldogs little good, as they went down for the second straight year to the Gamecocks, this time by

a score of 2-0. Georgia had tried to punt, but the kick was blocked, then picked up by a Georgia player who was tackled behind the goal for a safety.

So now with a record of 3-1, we met the Cadets of North Carolina A&M a week later in Raleigh. The A&M team was heavily favored, and it was said that the gamblers at the game were freely betting that the Cadets would score at least thirty points on the Gamecocks. In fact, though, it was only with the greatest luck that the Cadets managed to hold the Gamecocks to a 0-0 tie.

After 6-0 losses to both Davidson and the Charleston Athletic Club, our record stood at 3-3-1, with the final game of the season to come five days later, on Thanksgiving Day, against the Generals of Washington & Lee. Carolina played its best of the season, and the game was decided before five minutes had elapsed. Much in evidence that day was the quarterback bootleg that Benet had invented and used so successfully in 1903. At the end of the first half, led by "The Blond Giant," halfback Bill Boyle, the Carolinians led 15-0. We scored 10 more in the second half, and the game ended, a Carolina win, 25-0, over a powerful Washington & Lee team.

With a winning season record of 4-3-1, Coach Benet's first season at the helm had to be considered a success.

1905

The 1905 season started out with a tougher-than-expected, 14-0 victory over Welsh Neck Academy, followed by a routine win over Bingham, 19-6. Coach Benet's record since coming to Carolina now stood at 7-2, but we were apprehensive about the next week's opponent, the big Cadets from North Carolina A&M. They would be our opponent on Big Thursday, during State

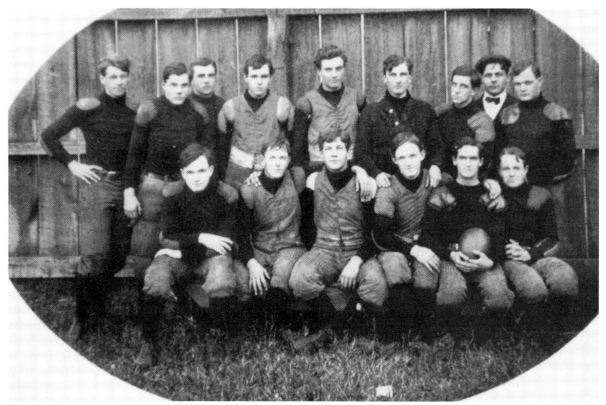

The 1905 varsity squad. Coach Benet is standing, third from left; holding the ball is (probably) team captain Doug McKay.

Fair week.

The Cadets averaged 175 pounds per man, while the Gamecocks averaged only 156, and that told the story of the game. As The State reported: "It was strength versus grit. The heavy Tarheel backs plunged over and through the little Gamecock line like the horses jump through the paper-covered hoops in the circus." The Carolinians were simply outclassed and went down in defeat 29-0, our first loss of the season.

But we had no time to mourn our loss, for nine days later, on November 4, we were to meet the powerful Wildcats of Davidson College at Latta Park in Charlotte. We surprised the experts that day, however, as the first half ended with the score tied 0-0. In the second half, Davidson took the lead, 4-0, on a 20-yard field goal, but on the ensuing kickoff, Foster took the ball at the fifty and darted through the entire Davidson team for a touchdown. He was hit time after

time by their desperate defenders but refused to go down. The final whistle blew, and our boys, bloodied but victorious, departed the field with a 6-4 win.

A week later the Gamecocks stumbled in a rematch against lowly Bingham and were lucky to escape with a 5-5 tie. We may have been guilty of looking ahead, for the next week we had to travel to Roanoke, Virginia to take on the most powerful team in the South, the Gobblers of Virginia Tech, and possibly America's finest halfback, the stocky Jim Carpenter.

Indeed, for a week prior to the game signs were posted throughout Virginia reading "See Carpenter Play," prompting a huge turnout for the game. Coach Benet had been eager to see how his young Gamecocks would perform against the number-one team in the South, and following the game, though we lost 34-0, he stated, "Considering their weight and experience, Carolina made a great showing and I am satisfied."

After twelve days of much needed rest, our boys again made a long trip to Charleston, this time to take on The Citadel for the first time in history, in a game played at Hampton Park. The Cadets were no match for the Gamecocks that day and went down to defeat by a score of 47-0. Homer Holmes was especially impressive at quarterback and scored our first two touchdowns that day on long dashes through the Citadel team.

So we finished the year at 4-2-1, and for Benet, his two year record now stood at 9-4-2.

1906 – 1907

Despite the game's gradual evolution toward safety and player protection, injuries and fatalities continued to mount on the gridiron. In 1905 alone, 159 injuries were reported, along with nineteen fatalities. President Theodore Roosevelt, himself an ardent fan of the game, called in representatives from fifteen colleges and demanded that changes be made. As a result came a new collegiate rules committee known as the Intercollegiate Athletic Association. The IAA made the following changes in football: the legalization of the forward pass; two halves of only thirty minutes each; increased first-down yardage from five to ten yards; and a neutral zone separating the two teams by the length of the football (line of scrimmage).

Nevertheless, there remained a growing fear among our faculty that the game and its players were simply getting out of hand. The faculty-dominated athletic committee issued a report in 1905 stating that conditions had reached the state where "high ideals are regarded as incongruous with the spirit of athletics and scruples are looked upon as

A 1907 Garnet and Black *sketch of an early Gamecock running back.*

mere prudishness." Finally, bowing to academic pressure, the board decreed on January 13, 1906, that football would no longer be played at the university. And that was it. As *The Carolinian* concluded: "Now the Board of Trustees have abolished football. And just in time for our centennial celebrations, too. A most clever idea."

A week prior to the State Fair of 1907, it was rumored that the trustees would be meeting. Students quickly circulated a petition requesting that football be reinstated at the University and presented it to the trustees. Then they stood and awaited an answer. The *Garnet and Black* reported that when President Sloan walked out of the old library to break the news, "The smile on his face was enough, and immediately yells for football and Carolina made the campus ring."

A team of sorts was hastily assembled, and two former Gamecock players, Reed Smith and Doug McKay, volunteered to replace the departed Christie Benet as coaches. Team manager A.M. Lumpkin was charged with the responsibility of arranging a schedule, no simple task at that late date. But he did manage to come up with three teams who would play us.

On November 16 we entertained the boys from the College of Charleston at our athletic field on Green Street. Tom Sligh, a 200-pound tackle, was called "the mainstay" of the team. George Cartwright and Heyward Gibbs also established themselves as new stars in the Gamecock firmament. And as the final whistle blew, Carolina walked off the field with a 14-4 victory.

Next, on a dreary Thursday, November 21, the boys from the Georgia Medical College in Augusta came to town. Toward the end of a scoreless first half, Carolina's Gibbs attempted a 20-yard field goal, and

Referee Ellison signaled it good, a 4-pointer for the Gamecocks. Immediately there was an outburst of protest from the young Medicals, who shouted that the ball clearly sailed outside the goalposts. When Ellison ignored this protest, the outraged GMC team then walked to the opposite end of the field for a hasty consultation. They then left the field and gathered in the gym across the street. When the Carolina team lined up for the second-half kickoff, the Medicals still did not appear. Ellison had no choice but to declare a victory for the Gamecocks by default.

Now with a 2-0 record for the year, our final game of the season came on Thanksgiving Day at College Park in Charleston against The Citadel, now coached by former Carolina star Ralph Foster. It was a hard-fought match, but Carolina finally won, 12-0, on the strength of three field goals dropped-kicked by Heyward Gibbs, one for forty-three yards.

The undefeated team of 1907, with captain L. W. Perrin seated in middle foreground.

Said Coach Foster following the game: "No team can beat a man who can kick a goal from the 45-yard line every time."

So it was, then, that the hastily-assembled 1907 Gamecocks enjoy the distinction of being the only undefeated team in the 100-year history of South Carolina football.

1908

In 1907, after a year's hiatus from the game, we sort of tiptoed our way back in. But 1908 saw us back in the swim. We scheduled nine games, and Christie Benet agreed to return as head coach. Some forty lads turned out as candidates for the team, giving us our biggest squad in history.

We lost only Gibbs, Sligh, Cartwright, Reeves, and Clarkson from the 1907 squad, while we had returning such first-stringers as the speedy Robert Gonzales at one end and Randolph Murdaugh at the other. James Hammond, who captained The Citadel team in 1907, was now enrolled at Carolina and had won the quarterback slot. Also on hand were Billy Perrin, Robert Cooper, and Joe Crouch, who, though a tackle, was called the best passer on the team and was reported to be able to throw the ball fifty yards as accurately as a baseball.

The tackles were "Big" Carter, who had been a star lineman with the Clemson Tigers in 1906, and John H. Brown, a former tackle with the College of Charleston. Two other Clemson men, Rastus Keel and Buddy Moore, were also playing for USC. And Sam Wilds, who had played well for Welsh Neck Academy, was also on hand.

After a practice game against the Ridgewood Athletic Club (which ended in a 0-0 tie), we played a little more aggressively the next week and downed the College of Charleston by a score of 17-0. This game was memorable in that we employed for the first time what is called the "forward pass." It was considered a dangerous play, but we made it work twice for short gains, Alex Dargan catching both of them. Dargan, in fact, scored twice for us that day, while Belser pushed over for the other score.

Then came Georgia, and we knew that this would be a major test to see just what sort of team we really had. The results were not encouraging. The Bulldogs outweighed us by fifteen pounds per man and bullied our line into submission all day. The final score, suffice it to say, was 29-6, our only score coming with Marion Mobley blocked a Bulldog punt and Holmes fell on the ball in the end zone.

Just how much the disruption of the team play in 1906 really hurt us was clear when we also lost the next game, a home game, to the Charleston Athletic Association, by a score of 15-4. And things looked no better when next came the powerful Davidson eleven.

In the absence of Clemson from our schedule, Davidson was to play us as a feature of State Fair. Our game was on Friday, and the day before, on Thursday, the Wildcats had met the Clemson Tigers on this same field and walked away victorious. Still hungry after that feast, the Cats scored four touchdowns in the first half, took a 22-0 lead to the sidelines, and never looked back. Thus, to Davidson's credit, she had traveled down to Columbia and, on two successive days, beaten Clemson 13-9, then USC 22-0. Quite an effort.

We split the remaining four games on our schedule to conclude the season with a subpar 3-5-1 record. We didn't know it right then, but in addition to the five games, we would also be losing our coach.

4

1909 – 1911

DISAPPOINTING YEARS

The 1909 season proved to be one of few victories, but it was not without its interesting highlights—chiefly the return of arch rival Clemson to our schedule.

Our hopes for a quick rebound from the 3-5-1 season of 1908 were considerably dampened when Christie Benet announced that the demands of his Columbia law practice would not permit him to continue as the Gamecock coach. In his place we hired Robert V. White, who had been captain of our 1908 eleven.

The season opened at Davis Field against the North Carolina Medical College, a team largely composed of former college players, many of them All-Southern. Consequently, our 5-0 loss was not as upsetting as it might have been, especially since only sterling defensive play on our part kept the score close. On the other hand, our next week's loss to John Heisman's Georgia Tech team, 59-0, was utterly discouraging.

But we had to put the bitter experience behind us as we prepared to meet Wake Forest for the first time ever at Davis Field the following Saturday. The interesting aspect of this game was that it was played in

a veritable hurricane that swept through the Columbia area on Saturday afternoon, with the rain coming down in sheets and a wind that threatened to blow the football off the field unless the referee held it down. The elements must have bothered us more than them. We lost, 8-0.

Five days later, in another game played at Davis Field, we finally earned our first win under Coach White, a 17-11 victory over the College of Charleston thanks to Irvine Belser's three touchdowns. We also had the pleasure of meeting Alfred Holmes VonKolnitz, then a fine halfback for Charleston, who would in a couple of years become one of the greatest Gamecock running backs in history.

Following the Charleston game, excitement on campus, indeed throughout the entire state, reached fever pitch as we prepared to meet the Clemson Tigers on Big Thursday of State Fair week—our first meeting since the confrontation of 1902. A memorably awkward episode occurred when our Athletic Advisory Committee, because of our poor showing to date, grew apprehensive about the approaching date

The Clemson game on Big Thursday, 1909 — one of the earliest known shots of the Gamecocks in action. (Clemson is in striped jerseys and stockings.)

with Clemson and persuaded Christie Benet to rejoin the team on the Monday preceding the game. Coach White said he could not tolerate such an insult and so resigned his position and departed Columbia for Boston. So we were once again with good old Christie Benet, just like in the old days before all the troubles began.

Just prior to kickoff, the "dope artists," or gamblers, in the crowd, were spotting Carolina as many as forty points, but our lighter, faster boys surprised everyone by holding the big Tigers to a single touchdown. That proved enough, since we were held scoreless, but Hammond, Ben Beverly, and Berte Carter shone on defense, and Francis Cain played an excellent game at quarterback.

This game marked the first time in history, by the way, that a football game in the Palmetto State would be "broadcast." The United Wireless Company installed instruments at the fair and had reports of the game sent by wireless to the city stations at the tall Barringer Building.

As we prepared to meet Davidson ten days later in Davidson, North Carolina, Christie Benet, unfortunately, was forced to return to his law practice. So we hired our third coach of the season, Eugene Oliver, a former Carolina player, to see us through our final three games of this dismal season. As it turned out, Davidson outclassed us in every department, and we lost again, 29-5.

The disastrous season continued the following week with a loss to Mercer's Fighting Baptists in Macon, Georgia. We could handle the Baptists, it seemed, and led 3-0 late in the game on the strength of Belser's field goal. But then darkness became the foe. Under a night sky so dark the stars could clearly be seen, their back Jacobs snuck over from three yards out and stole a win for Mercer.

THE CHRISTIE BENET ERA

However, in the final game of this long season, a come-from-behind win against The Citadel in Charleston gave us at least a spark of hope for 1910.

1910

Nineteen ten might be described as the year we went to the mountaintop—and then promptly fell off. Led by new coach John F. Neff, who had been a star player at the University of Virginia, the Gamecocks reeled off four shutout victories in a row. They wouldn't win again until 1911.

The new season kicked off at Davis field against the College of Charleston with a game in which we were for once aided, rather than hindered, by the elements. Our lone touchdown on this rainy afternoon occurred when Charleston dropped a punt and we recovered in their end zone.

A week later, Coach Neff's enthusiasm for the forward pass led to a victory over the Medical College of Georgia in Augusta. "Crip" Whitner threw two touchdown passes against the befuddled Cracker Sawbones, while our defense preserved the shutout.

Jack Crawford's three long touchdown runs sparked a 33-0 route of Lenoir the following week, and then it was time to face tough Wake Forest. Whitner's passes to McMaster Woodrow moved the ball into position, and Crawford connected on two field goals for the 6-0 win.

Then came November 3, Big Thursday of State Fair week. Our Gamecocks had suffered an unbelievable series of injuries during practice the preceding week, and now we were at about half-strength as we took the field against the big Clemson Tiger team. Clemson came into the game with a 3-2 record, not nearly as impressive as our 4-0 record, but it was no secret that Clemson's schedule to that point had been much tougher than Carolina's.

Coach, John H. Neff

John H. Neff, coach of the Gamecocks, 1910 – 11.

We held our own during the first quarter, but then Clemson began to demonstrate that they too knew how to work the forward pass, not to mention how to sweep our ends. The first half ended with the Gamecocks trailing 6-0, and we were still hopeful. But with most of our best players sitting on the sidelines, Clemson beat us soundly by a final score of 24-0. We still had not beaten Clemson since 1902.

The next two weeks provided no solace. First we suffered a sound thrashing, 53-0, at the hands of Davidson (our second-worse defeat in history), and then we were beaten 23-6 by North Carolina. A third straight shutout was only averted when, at the end of the game, Arthur Knight intercepted a North Carolina pass and returned it seventy yards for a touchdown.

Now 4-3 on the year, with not a victory under our belts in almost a month, we took on The Citadel at Hampton Park in Charleston on Thanksgiving Day. We were

4-0 against The Citadel at this point, and looked forward to an easy win here again today. But five minutes into the game, their quarterback, Legge, hit their tall, rangy end, Cullum, with a 25-yarder for a touchdown. Try as we might, we could never overcome this lead, and the game ended as a 5-0 shutout in their favor. It was our first loss in history to the Cadets, and it could not have come at a worse time.

And so ended the first decade of the twentieth century, a decade that had seen many changes in both football and the university. We had played under five head coaches during this period, whose combined won-loss record stood at 38-26-3. We had also seen the SCC become the USC. We could see nothing but sunlight ahead.

1911

Leading the Gamecocks in 1911 would be our quarterback and captain, W. C. "Crip" Whitner, who was chosen as one of the best football players in the nation by the New York *Times*. In the opening game of the season against the Georgia Bulldogs his flashy punt returns drew applause from even the Georgia stands. Still, the final score was 38-0, Georgia's favor.

A week later, on Octobr 14, we traveled to Charleston to take on the College of Charleston at Hampton Park. An interesting aside to the game is that our two new running backs, Dutch Passailaique and Fritz VonKolnitz, formerly starred for Charleston. We were happy to have them; Passailaique scored our first touchdown, VonKolnitz our second. Final score: USC 16, College of Charleston 0.

On October 21, we entertained a new guest at Davis Field, the powerful Gators of the University of Florida. Again, VonKolnitz electrified the crowd all day with his end sweeps for big yardage, while Whitner's forward passes to McMaster Woodrow kept us on Florida's end of the field throughout the second half. But Florida had a terrible weapon of its own, one Dummy Taylor, whom our boys found unstoppable. VonKolnitz managed to score for us, but Dummy came right back for the Gators. The game ended in a 6-6 tie (which seemed a relief for both teams).

Twelve days later, on November 2, came Big Thursday and the highly vaunted Clemson Tigrs. Some 3,500 fans packed the old race track grandstands as we took the field. Clemson had already lost three games, but these were to Auburn, Georgia, and Georgia Tech, while our lone victory had come at the expense of Charleston. The bettors in the crowd were giving Carolina and twenty points.

We had not scored on Clemson since 1902, a streak which unfortunately was not broken that day. Final score: Clemson 27, Carolina 0. The bettors, as usual, knew what they were doing.

The misery continued over the next two games. Despite the best efforts of Whitner, Passailaique, and VonKolnitz, the Gamecocks suffered two shutouts. North Carolina handled our boys 21-0, and Davidson prevailed in a fierce battle, 10-0. Then came our most memorable game of the season, at least from the standpoint of crowd frenzy. We were playing The Citadel in Charleston on Thanksgiving Day, and the excitement came in the fourth quarter with the game still scoreless. The Cadets thought they had finally pushed the ball over for a touchdown, but the line judge, Mr. James Driver, called a motion penalty, nullified the score, and penalized The Citadel five yards. As *The State* reported:

It is charged by the Carolina boys that one officer of the cadet corps led the attack upon Mr. Driver with the remark, "You have been giving us a dirty

Coach Neff's 1911 squad.

deal the whole afternoon." The officer is said to have seized Mr. Driver around the neck and struck him in the face. Several cadets rushed in, it is said, and began to strike at the field official. Carolina's boys went to the assistance of Mr. Driver and the police officers rushed into the field and separated the students. In the meantime, there were several bleeding noses and battered faces, but Mr. Driver shows tonight no evidence of any injury. The cadets who made the attack were not players, but spectators along the lines.

The coed sponsors for both teams grew faint with horror during the riot, it was said, and had to be attended by physicians in the crowd.

The game ended in a 0-0 tie, our second of the season. In fact, we had not scored over the past five weeks, and some disgruntled fans were heard to mutter that they were happy the season was finally at an end.

5

1912 – 1915

BACK ON TRACK

Coach Neff had gone 5-8-2 over the past two seasons, but we were hoping for better days under new coach N. B. "Red" Edgerton, a former Davidson star. Incidentally, Coach Edgerton remains noteworthy as the first Carolina coach ever to be signed to a multiyear contract.

Supporting the new coach were returning stalwarts Fritz VonKolnitz, now a junior and the team captain, and big fullback Dutch Passailaique. Then there were "the Blond Viking," Dan Heyward, who was VonKolnitz's partner at halfback, and the redoubtable Billy Harth at quarterback. The line featured John "Big" Mills and W. B. "Wop" McGowan at tackle, along with Deck Sligh and the great Luther Hill on the ends. The first game of the season came against Wake Forest at Davis Field. In the second quarter Dutch Passailaique thrilled the home crowd when he made a sensational leap over the Wake Forest line for our only touchdown of the day. VonKolnitz added a field goal in the final quarter, and the game ended 10-3 in our favor.

The next two weeks brought tough losses, though. First we traveled to Charlottesville and suffered a 19-0 shutout to a Virginia team rated as one of the best in the nation. A week later we fumbled away a great chance to beat Florida in Gainesville. We led 3-0 by virtue of a VonKolnitz field goal, but Florida

Coach Red Edgerton (1912 – 15), the first coach in USC history to receive a multiyear contract.

picked up a Carolina fumble in the fourth quarter and rambled across the goal line for the decisive score.

Then we had a chance to show what we could do against an average team, and we took advantage of it, walloping the College of Charleston 68-0. Dutch Passailaique scored five touchdowns that day, which tied Guy Gunter's record for touchdowns in a single game.

Then came Big Thursday and the Clemson Tigers. It was a matter of record that not only had we not beaten the Tigers in recent memory, we had not even scored on them since 1902. The Tigers of 1912 were not quite on a par with their usual powerful eleven, but they were still considered good enough to overpower the smaller Gamecocks. Little did they suspect....

Throughout the first quarter the game seesawed back and forth, neither team able to gain an advantage, but just moments into the second quarter, Captain Johnny Kangeter of Charleston went over for the Tigers, and they took the lead at 7-0. Before our hearts could sink, though, our linebacker Billy Harth grabbed a Clemson fumble and rushed thirty-five yards through a broken field for a Carolina touchdown. Later in that quarter, VonKolnitz again put the crowd on their feet when he very calmly booted a field goal from the Clemson ten to give us a 10-7 lead at halftime.

Clemson kicked off to open the second half, and Carolina returned the ball to our 45-yard line. From there VonKolnitz ripped off thirty-five yards on an end sweep. Then, on the next play, Passailaique circled end for twenty yards and another touchdown. Score now: USC 16, Clemson 7. On the next series Clemson fumbled the ball at their thirty, we recovered, and Dan Harth made one of the finest runs of the day on the next play, taking the ball to the Clemson ten. Then it was Heyward, "the Blond Viking," taking it in on the next play to give

Fritzie VonKolnitz, captain of the great Gamecock team of 1912.

Carolina a 22-7 lead. There was delirium in the stands as the Gamecocks held on for the win.

A gratifying 6-6 tie against potent North Carolina (which outweighed us by twenty pounds per man) kept our record respectable at 3-2-1. Then we improved upon it with a 65-0 walloping of Porter Military Academy, a game in which VonKolnitz tied the record of five touchdowns in a single contest.

Then came a convincing win over The Citadel on Thanksgiving Day, which brought us not only a good 5-2-1 season, but the undisputed state championship of South Carolina as well. What was more, John "Big" Mills, Fritz VonKolnitz, and Luther Hill were named to the first All-State team following the season.

1913

Gone from the great team of 1912 were such stars as Dutch Passailaique, Ted Girardeau, Billy Harth, and Jerry Porter. Returning, however, were Burnet Stoney, W. B. "Wop" McGowan, John "Big" Mills, Deck Sligh, Luther Hill, Dan "the Blond Viking" Heyward, and Bob Langston.

One of the great mysteries of the 1913 season was the playing status of Fritz VonKolnitz. It was reported that he was not permitted to compete in games against SIAA schools, such as The Citadel, in 1912. In 1913 he played in three games, versus North Carolina, Wake Forest, and Davidson, and was sensational when he did play. But he was not allowed to play against Virginia, Clemson, Florida, or The Citadel. What infraction he was guilty of simply isn't known.

Despite our high hopes, the season got off to a rocky start. With Passailaique departed, VonKolnitz ineligible, and team captain "Big" Mills in California on unspecified business, we were humiliated by Virginia, 54-0. VonKolnitz returned from the bench the following week and scored three touchdowns in a key win against Wake Forest, but this game was followed by a tough loss to the always huge Tarheels of North Carolina, 13-3.

Then came Big Thursday, which, unfortunately, brought no relief.

Clemson was now under the direction of Coach Bob Williams, who had guided USC to two of its finest seasons in 1902-03. Williams had installed a new offensive set at Clemson much like the T-formation that would become popular throughout the nation some forty years later. To say that this new formation gave us fits would be an

VARSITY TEAM

Coach Red Edgerton and his first-stringers of 1913. Team captain John "Big" Mills is seated, center; inserts are Fritzie VonKolnitz, left, and Luther Hill.

understatement. We wound up on the short end of a 32-0 score, and even Clemson's big tackle, W. A. "Tubby" Schilletter, scored two touchdowns for the Tigers.

We were now 1-3 on the season, with three tough games to go, but fortunately things begun to jell at this point.

The Florida Gators, another Southern power, arrived in Columbia on Friday afternoon. They were one of the two teams that had beaten us in 1912, and now we hungered for revenge. With VonKolnitz on the bench, his substitute, Dan Heyward, was the star of the game, constantly churning through ankle-deep mud for big gains, or getting off booming punts, or making timely tackles. John Mills was a stone wall on defense. In the end, we surprised both the Gators and the experts by taking a 13-0 upset win.

Then came our old adversaries, the Davidson Wildcats, on their home field where they had not lost a game since 1901. But VonKolnitz, the game's leading ground gainer, kicked a 30-yard field goal in the second quarter to give us a 3-0 lead. Then in the fourth, Felix Langston, who had intercepted two Davidson forward passes earlier in the game, picked off a third and rambled thirty-five yards for a score.

For the second time in two weeks, we had pulled off a major upset, and our record now stood at 3 and 3. Then in the finale, even with VonKolnitz ineligible, the Gamecocks breezed to a 42-13 victory over The Citadel and thereby salvaged a successful season. Luther Hill, by the way, was named to the All-State team for the second year in a row.

1914

In Europe Archduke Ferdinand had been assassinated, and the world plunged into war. On the campus of the university, our young men heard the news and worried that it would all be over before we Americans had a chance to show what we could do. There was much talk of running away to Canada to join the Royal Canadian Expeditionary Force, to do something, anything, to experience the "thrill and glory" of combat. Many, in fact, would get their chance, but at least in the early days of the war, the closest our young men would get to combat would be the gridiron battles at Davis Field.

Coach Edgerton was back for his third year, a record for USC coaches, but 1914 turned out to be not a great year for the Gamecocks. We played our first eleven-game schedule, but won only five, lost five, and tied one.

After an easy opening win over the Charleston Navy Yard, we lost to Georgia Tech on a muddy field in Atlanta by a score of 20-0. A week later the Tarheels of North Carolina spanked us by a score of 48-0, a game in which Luther Hill was lost with a sprained ankle. Then, to add to our woes, Virginia laid on a 49-7 drubbing.

Next, thank God, came the Indians of Newberry College, a small institution of the Lutheran persuasion in the midlands of South Carolina, who were only in their second year of football. We saw them as an opportunity to vent a little frustration, but they refused to cooperate. Final score: 13-13.

Big Thursday brought Clemson to Columbia, and with the Tigers heavily favored, we were hopeful when the half ended with the score only 6-0. We had denied them all but two Dopey Major field goals. On the first play of the final quarter, however, Clemson exploded our dream of an upset when their big fullback, Webb, dashed sixty-five yards for a touchdown and a 12-0 lead. Webb would score twice more before the day was done, and the Tigers took the game 29-6.

First-stringers of 1914 ready to play: (linemen) Fant, Otis Going, Burnet Stoney, Ted Girardeau, Harry Hampton, Mack McMillan, Luther Hill; (backs) Dan Heyward, Felix Langston, Jerry Porter, Dick Kerr.

The following week Runt Coggerhall, our 110-pound quarterback, passed us to a 25-0 victory over the Wofford Terriers, and Wake Forest extended our winning streak by falling 26-0, largely due to Burnett Stoney's passing for an incredible 218 yards. But then we returned to the other side of the ledger in a tough 13-7 loss to Davidson.

In a rematch against Newberry the following week, however, we unleashed a season's worth of fury and poured it on for a 46-7 win. Our captain Luther Hill played brilliant defense, spending most of the afternoon in the Indians' backfield and keeping them thoroughly stymied.

We finished the season by edging The Citadel, 7-6, thanks to the slashing runs of H. R. "Cotton" Going. Our fifth win made our season respectable, if not spectacular, and our spirits were further lifted when Luther Hill, Burnett Stoney, M. K. McMillan, and Ed Girardeau made the All-State team.

1915

If 1914 was a disappointment to the Carolina faithful, they had only to wait a few months. The year of "the ringer" was at hand.

The 1915 season started with a bang, as in quick order the Gamecocks, led by the incredible arms of Jimmy Detling and Big Bill Folger, smashed Newberry 29-0, Presbyterian College 41-0, and North Carolina A & M 19-10. Then, with Big Thursday and Clemson College next on the agenda, rumors of irregularities in our athletic program begun to emerge.

The background was this: Coach Edgerton, not deaf to the criticism following the disappointing seasons of '13 and '14, made an impassioned plea before an assembly of students, faculty, and administrators to be given one more year on his contract. If such an extension were forthcoming, he promised, Carolina would beat Clemson and at least tie Virginia in 1915.

The action is fast and furious, if somewhat hard to distinguish, in the 1915 Clemson game.

Edgerton's contract was indeed extended, and at that point certain influential USC alumni, smarting from all the indignities suffered at the paws of Clemson over the years, decided to come to the coach's assistance. Their plan was simple: to comb the nation and recruit the best football players money could buy.

Indeed, after the first three games of the 1915 season, it seemed that the mediocre Gamecocks had become an overnight powerhouse. Clemson, the next team on our schedule, was curious as to how the Gamecocks could have undergone such an amazing metamorphosis in the short space of a year. And who were all those new Gamecock faces walking around with the Yankee accents?

So Clemson began meddling, and it wasn't long before its student newspaper, *The Tiger*, cited *Spaulding's Official Football Guide* for 1912 to the effect that several members of the Carolina squad had been playing on other college teams. Some members, wanting free tuition, had stated they were residents of small South Carolina towns: "Can anyone be found," asked *The Tiger*, "who ever heard of a town called New Brooklyn in Lexington County, South Carolina?"

Proud of their investigation, Clemson even trotted a telephone operator (called "a ringer") out before the press, whose story created a storm of controversy. While *The Tiger* representatives stood by smirking, this gum-smacking ringer testified that she had overheard a telephone call from a USC alumnus to an athletic broker in Pennsylvania who sold football players to the highest bidder.

Of course, the university formally denied that any such plot existed. It does seem strange, however, that coincidental with the Clemson probe, four prominent football freshmen suddenly vanished from both the USC lineup and the USC campus, never to be heard from again. And then, as though to confirm the charges, two weeks after the game the president of the university sent a wire to Clemson informing the school that he had become aware of certain irregularities in the Carolina program and offering to forfeit the game by any score Clemson might suggest. Clemson very graciously declined his offer. The game had ended, by the way, in a 0-0 tie.

Following the Clemson game, and despite our embarrassment, we resumed our winning ways for a couple of weeks against inferior opposition, defeating Wofford 33-6 and Cumberland 68-0. But in our last three games, again burdened by prosperity, we lost to Virginia, 13-0, Georgetown, 61-0, and finally (indignity of indignities!) to The Citadel, 3-0.

We finished the year with a 5-3-1 record, which was at least respectable. As for Coach Edgerton, who was totally innocent of any wrongdoing in the "ringer" matter, he resigned following the 1915 season to devote his energies to his budding Columbia medical practice.

6

1916 – 1919

THE WAR YEARS

The president of the university in 1915 was Professor William S. Currell, a man of high principles, who had been disconcerted to learn that there were people in the world who might not eagerly adhere to the university's honor system. Reforms were obviously necessary, and Dr. Currell, in his zeal, abolished the alumni-controlled Athletic Committee and placed athletics directly under the control of the administration and board of trustees.

So, suddenly, we had gone from almost no control over athletics to total control. And that total control was now in the hands of an academic who once boasted that he had never wasted a moment of his life at a football game and could not understand why anyone else would.

Such was the unfortunate situation that greeted Dr. Rice Warren, our twelfth head coach since 1892, when he strode on campus in September of 1916, a young idealist full of hope for our athletic future. Foremost among the new rules was one which stated that henceforth freshmen would not be eligible for varsity competition. Thus, one of Coach Warren's first responsibilities was to organize

M. K. McMILLAN
FOOTBALL CAPTAIN

Mack McMillan, captain of the 1916 Gamecock squad.

The Gamecocks take on Wofford at Davis Field, 1916.

a freshman team and hire former Carolina star Dixon Foster to coach them. Their mediocre record against state high school teams was considerably better than the one compiled by our "reformed" varsity of 1916. A foreshadowing of what great disasters lay ahead became apparent when we were clobbered on October 7 by a squad of gangly youth from Newberry College, 10-0. The next week we surprised Wofford, in Spartanburg, 23-3, but then came four decisive losses. Tennessee beat us, 26-0, despite Dick Kerr's strong running; Clemson weighed in with a 27-0 drubbing; an inferior Wake Forest squad whipped us, 33-7; and then always tough Virginia landed its blows, 35-6. Our alumni were not happy.

The next week we found a modicum of respectability when we downed the Baptists of Mercer by a score of 47-0. Frank Simrill, Dick Kerr, Frank Hampton, and Coley Seaborn ran wild in this contest and proved too much for the Baptists to handle. But the next week brought revenge for the Baptists, as the Mountaineers of Furman University,

led by Speedy Speer's touchdown runs of fifty and eighty yards, routed the Gamecocks 14-0.

Then came our annual Thanksgiving day prom with The Citadel. As usual, we were expected to waltz them around the field once or twice before administering a good thrashing, but such was not to be. The Cadets lost only to Georgia that year, and they commenced to beat us like they owned us, winning 20-2.

So we finished the season with a 2-7 record, our only wins coming at the expense of Wofford and Mercer. Our students and alumni were disconsolate, but President Currell must have been well satisfied.

1917

Coach Warren departed Carolina following the 1916 season for the greener pastures of VMI, and our former coach, Dixon Foster (the "Little Napoleon"), was promoted to the head job. He was looking

Carolina defenders ready to pounce, 1917.

forward to working with a virtually all-veteran team, but 1917 marked America's entry into World War I. Of the 1916 returnees upon whom we'd counted so heavily, twenty-five wound up in service before we reported for drills in September of 1917.

On the first day of practice, only four lettermen from 1916 were on hand: Sumpter "Babe" Clarke, Coley Seaborn, Harry Hampton, and J. H. "Dummy" Moore. A few days later Rut L. "Dago" Osborne showed up; he was a veteran of the 1915 campaign who'd dropped out of school for a year, and now he would prove invaluable at quarterback.

Young and inexperienced as it was, Carolina was enough of a team to rout Newberry, 38-0, in the opener. And almost enough to upset a heavily favored Florida team in Gainesville. But three second-half touchdowns against our smaller, exhausted squad enabled Florida to escape with a 21-13 victory.

On Big Thursday the oddsmakers again made Clemson a prohibitive favorite, but Osborne's booming punts, fullback George Brown's running, and Seaborn's 75-yard interception return for a touchdown kept the Gamecocks alive in what spectators called the most exciting game ever played in Columbia. It was exciting especially for Tiger fans, as Clemson prevailed, 21-13.

The rest of the season included disappointing losses to Erskine College, 14-13; Wofford, 20-0; and Presbyterian, 20-14, thus establishing a record no one could be proud of. It was the only year in history that we would lose to three of the Little Four (Newberry being the fourth).

In the meantime, however, we had played our best game of the year to beat a good Furman team, 26-0, a game in which Ed Smith starred with three interceptions. And we closed out the year with a big win over the reigning state champions, The Citadel, shutting them out, 20-0.

1918

Nineteen eighteen was not a year to be much concerned about football. The war in Europe raged on, and we learned that 531 USC alumni were now serving in the Armed Forces. As though that were not enough, by mid-September the entire city of Columbia, including the University, was firmly in the grip of the great flu epidemic that swept the nation that year. University classes were cancelled from October 15 until November 6.

Given these conditions, we played an abbreviated schedule of four games. With Coach Dixon Foster wearing the gold bar of a Navy ensign, Camp Jackson athletic director Frank Dobson directed the team for the first two games, and last year's quarterback Rut Osborne took over for the final two.

The State Fair had been cancelled because of the war, but the traditional USC-Clemson game would proceed as usual. Both teams were decimated, but we did have four returning regulars from 1917: Captain J. H. Moore and Ted Beall at tackle, Heyward Brockington at end, and George Brown in the backfield.

Luck turned her back on us, though, when Beall, our anchor on the line, was injured on the first play of the game and had to be carried from the field. Still, we held the Tigers to only two scores throughout the first three quarters; then gallantry gave way to exhaustion. Our smaller team collapsed in the final period, and Clemson routed us, 39-0.

That would prove to be our only loss of the year, however. Two weeks later we met and destroyed our old enemies, the Furman Mountaineers, 20-12, then followed that win with a 13-0 whitewash of Wofford. The brief season ended with a rain-soaked, 0-0 tie against The Citadel on Thanksgiving

J. H. Moore, team captain in 1918.

Day.

We finished with a 2-1-1 record for the year. Not bad, but what was infinitely better was the news a few weeks earlier that the armistice had been signed, bringing an end to World War I.

1919

With the war over, the fall of 1919 saw a return of both Coach Dixon Foster and a welcome sense of normalcy to the university. We were playing a nine-game schedule and thought we had the players to back it up: there was the fearless Heyward Brockington at end, then the two Smith brothers, Ed at center and Burney at end, Max McMillan and Martin Goodman at tackles, Harry Lightsey at guard, and in the backfield Rube

Starting eleven of 1919: (linemen) captain Heyward Brockington, Simmons, H. M. Lightsey, Ed Smith, Alex Waite, Martin Goodman, Burney Smith; (backs) Herbert Timmons, Coley Seaborn, Gus Allen, Rube Skinner. Coach Foster stands in background.

Skinner, Michael Blount, Gus Allen, and Herbert Timmons.

Little did we know! We disappointed ourselves by losing our opener to Presbyterian College, 6-0, but we made up for it the next week, blanking Erskine, 6-0. Then came Georgia and another defeat, 14-0, when the Georgia timekeeper allowed the first quarter to last fifty-seven minutes. Then Davidson likewise blanked us, 7-0.

At that point we were 1-3, having scored only one touchdown all season, and quite puzzled as to the answer to our problem. The State Fair brought Clemson to town, whom we had beaten only once since 1902. Over five thousand fans flooded the race course area where we played, far too many to be adequately accommodated, so they filled the stands and stood five deep around the playing field. As the game got underway, hundreds spilled over onto the field, despite the futile attempts of the police to move them back behind the sidelines. Most of the fans were pro-Carolina, and on several occasions they impeded the progress of the Clemson team. But not sufficiently, as we again fell to the Tigers, 19-6.

As for the rest of the season, we somehow managed an incredible 6-6 tie with the big

1919 team captain Heyward Brockington.

Vols of Tennessee (they averaged 164 pounds per man). But that miracle aside, we went down to Washington & Lee, 26-0, to Florida, 13-0, and to The Citadel, 14-7, finishing the year with a 1-7-1 record. Forty-seven years would elapse before we would have a more disastrous season.

7

1920 – 1924

THE SOL METZGER ERA

Dixon Foster resigned at the end of the 1919 season, and Sol Metzger became the university's new head football coach. Metzger had been an all-America end at the University of Pennsylvania in 1903, and as coach at the same institution, he won the 1908 national championship. His arrival on our campus, culminating the efforts of some hard-working alumni, was regarded as quite a coup for USC.

Metzger was signed to an unheard-of five-year contract, and his record during those years was 26-18-2. His winning percentage of .548 is one of the best in school history. Metzger also defeated Clemson three out of his five years here, making him the darling of USC alumni everywhere.

It should be pointed out, however, that during his first two years, Metzger had some help. Indeed, behind our successes of 1920 and 1921 lies the story of "the transfer."

1920 – 1921

Tatum Wannamaker Gressette enjoys the distinction of being the oldest man on the face of this earth to have once served as captain of a Carolina football team. He was born in St. Matthews in 1899 and distinguished himself early for his athletic prowess.

In 1918, while World War I raged in Europe, he entered Furman University, and for only one reason—to play football for the Purple Hurricanes. He was billed as a triple-threat running back who could run, pass, and kick with the best of them. He had also developed the rare knack of drop-kicking a football some sixty yards, and easily made Furman's starting lineup as a freshman.

He did so well that in 1919 Richmond persuaded him to depart Furman and try his hand—or foot—with the Spiders. He

Sol Metzger, head coach of the Gamecocks, 1920 – 24.

Tatum Gressette

enrolled at Richmond, but two days later a letter arrived from The Citadel offering him a better deal, so he caught the next train headed south and enrolled there. He'd hardly had time to have his head shaved, he says, when he received a surprise visit from the mayor of Charleston, Tom Stoney, and a contingent of USC alumni. They said they were tired of watching USC being trampled by Clemson College and were visiting colleges all over the state in hopes of recruiting a team that could put a stop to it. Gressette was impressed. The next day he arrived in Columbia, bag and baggage, ready to don the garnet and black of USC. Asked if he was paid to transfer, Gressette says simply, "I would never say anything detrimental to the university."

Since he'd enrolled in four different colleges over the past two weeks, the University had little choice but to list Gressette as a transfer student, and he had to sit out the 1919 season. It was then that

Carolina, aware of its secret weapon recruited by Mayor Stoney, coined the slogan "Just wait till next year."

Yet, despite our high hopes for 1920, the Gamecocks were 2-2 going into the Clemson game on Big Thursday, with wins over Presbyterian and Wofford, and losses to UNC and Georgia. The game was played on October 28, an unseasonably hot day, with a record crowd of some 7,000 perspiring fans crammed into the old wooden grandstands at the Fairgrounds.

Gressette remembers: "Clemson had beat us seven years in a row, and people were having a fit. Of course Mr. Stoney and those fellows had recruited me for only one reason — to beat Clemson. And I was determined to give it everything I had.

"I'd spent the past year getting right. I don't mean to sound like I'm bragging, but I tried to put a spirit into that 1920 team. I told 'em that we could win if we thought we could win. We had to get right mentally.

"We weren't an outstanding team, but we finally got that old Gamecock spirit. For two weeks prior to that game, we met every night, and we kept talking it, talking it, beat Clemson, so that by the time Big Thursday rolled around, we were convinced. I'd never heard of brainwashing at that time, but that's what it was."

On the second play from scrimmage that day, Gressette caught Clemson sleeping and completed a 40-yard pass to end Dave Robinson down to the Tigers' 30. But then the Tigers held. Facing fourth and ten, the Gamecocks huddled.

"I told the boys on the line to hold 'em out for just two seconds and I'd get us a field goal. Just give me two seconds."

And that's how it went. Gressette took the snap from center, dropped back two steps, then calmly unleashed a booming drop-kick that split the uprights some fifty yards away, and the Gamecocks took a 3-0 lead.

It was the only score of the game, and fifty-nine minutes later, jubilant Carolina fans and players walked away with their first victory over Clemson since 1912.

In 1921 Gressette was elected team captain, and under his leadership the Gamecocks enjoyed one of their finest seasons ever, defeating Erskine, Newberry, Presbyterian College, and The Citadel, tying Florida and UNC, while losing only to Furman. Most importantly, they again defeated Clemson, blanking the Tigers 21-0, the first time in history that USC had beaten Clemson two years in a row.

Following his graduation, Gressette coached and refereed for a good many years before being appointed Director of the South Carolina State Retirement System in 1940, a position he would hold until his retirement in 1972. He is a former president of the South Carolina Golf Association and a member of the South Carolina Golf Hall of Fame. He is also a member of the South Carolina Athletic Hall of Fame. He and his

1921's assistant managers reflect the fashions of the Roaring Twenties.

wife continue to make their home in Columbia.

1922

With a lineup studded with veterans from the previous campaign, it was assumed that the 1922 Gamecocks could only improve on 1921's 5-1-2 record. In fact, experts at the time considered the 1922 Gamecocks to be one of the best teams ever assembled at the University. It turned out to be a year of near misses.

The season opened as brightly as predicted, with an easy 13-0 win over the Seceders of Erskine College. Captain Alex Waite scored both Carolina touchdowns. Then came a 7-0 shutout over Presbyterian —a hair-raiser, but a second win nevertheless.

At Chapel Hill the next week, however, we ran out of steam, fumbled twice in the first five minutes, and virtually handed the Tarheels a 10-point lead. In the third period our fullback Rock Snipes took a hand-off at his own 33 and rambled sixty-seven yards for a touchdown to cut the lead to 10-7, but that's the way it ended.

A 20-0 shutout over Wofford gave us a respectable 3-1 record heading into Big Thursday on October 26 at the Fairgrounds. Would Sol Metzger's boys make it three in a row over the Tigers? Another almost.

Twice in the first half Clemson had first and goal inside the ten, and twice we held, as the half ended in a scoreless tie. The tables were turned in the second half. Behind the hard running of W. T. Holland, Al Ambs, and Snipes, we twice drove the length of the field to within feet of the goal line, and twice they held.

In the fourth quarter, Clemson drove to the Gamecock ten, where we held and forced a field goal attempt. Frankie Meyer blocked it but the Tigers recovered and maintained possession. Three players later, Clemson's Robinson tried again, this time connecting from the 20-yard line and giving the Tigers a 3-0 victory.

Nine days later we played host for the first time ever to the powerful Tigers of the University of the South. For three quarters they pushed us up and down the field— denying us even a single first down—but somehow they led only 7-0. Then in the fourth quarter Fulton went to work, hitting Waite, Meyer, and Snipes, and finally finding Meyer in the end zone for a touchdown strike. Unhappily, Ambs missed the extra point, and we barely lost once again.

We took out our frustrations against Furman the next week, intercepting an all-time record ten passes in the process. Fullback Bill Holland bulled over for three touchdowns as we took an easy 27-7 win. A routine win over The Citadel a week later, highlighted by Alex Waite's 30-yard run on a fumble recovery, pushed our record to 5-3. Our season ended against Centre College of Kentucky, one of the strongest teams in the nation—and they proved it. Making twenty-five first downs to our four, they routed us 42-0.

If our 5-4 record was disappointing, it was also deceptive. Only one team had clearly outclassed us. Also, it was a mark of the '22 team's strength that five players made the All-State team: Harry Lightsey, Joe Wheeler, Johnny MacMillan, Frankie Meyer, and Bill Holland.

1923

If our performance in 1922 was almost great, the record for 1923, Coach metzger's only losing campaign, was truly disappointing.

After a routine 35-0 opening win over outmanned Erskine, we set the tone for the season with two straight losses on turnovers.

Against the Blue Hose, a high punt bounced off of halfback Bill Jeffords' chest and right into the hands of Presbyterian's Bomar, who raced sixty-five yards for a touchdown and a 7-3 win. A week later against the Wolfpack of North Carolina State (formerly the Cadets of North Carolina A&M), a Wolfpack defender picked off a Bill Holland pass and took it in from fifty-five yards out. The final: State 7, USC 0.

Newberry put us back in the win column the next week, but at the heavy price of our captain Joe Wheeler, who was out for the next two weeks with a severe concussion.

Ten thousand fans turned out on Big Thursday, by far the largest crowd ever to witness a football game in the Palmetto State. The spectators got their money's worth. The two teams punished each other to no avail in the first half, then, in the third period, Clemson drew first blood on a 20-yard touchdown pass from Detterer to Garrison. The Gamecocks struck right back when Frankie Meyer scooped up a blocked Tiger punt and took it in from the fifteen. The difference in the game? Sic Sizemore's

extra point attempt was blocked, and Clemson held on for a 7-6 victory.

Still reeling from this setback, we suffered two more losses — to UNC and Furman— before finally righting ourselves against The Citadel. A touchdown pass from Jack Wright to Frankie Meyer and a 50-yard ramble by Bill Holland accounted for the scoring in this 12-0 shutout.

We came closer than expected the next week against powerful Washington & Lee, but still lost, 13-7, and took a dismal 3-6 record into our final game of the season. Badly needing a springboard to launch us into next season, we parlayed two T. H. Brice touchdowns into a 14-7 win over a good Wake Forest team.

It was a victory to ease the pain of a most unhappy season.

1924

The 1924 season would be Coach Metzger's last, and he made sure to go out a winner. It proved to be a fine campaign overall,

The Gamecocks of 1923: (linemen) Frankie Myer, J. C. Long, Bob Gunter, captain Joe Wheeler, Henry Bartell, T. B. Simmons, W. W. "Red" Swink; (backs) W. H. Jeffords, Alex Jascewicz, H. B. Rhame, and W. C. "Sic" Sizemore.

punctuated by two huge victories.

We opened by clobbering a solid Erskine team, 47-0, in a game played in ankle-deep mud at Davis Field. A tough loss against Georgia in Athens the following week failed to dampen our spirits, and we bounced back with two revenge-sweetened, shutout victories—over North Carolina Sate, 10-0, and Presbyterian (who had spoiled our opener the previous season), 29-0.

Now it was Big Thursday, and again 10,000 fans poured into the Fairgrounds. The biggest game on our schedule was made even bigger by the fact that Coach Metzger was 2-2 against the Tigers, so the outcome of this game would largely determine his USC epitaph.

In the third quarter, after the teams had once again battled to a scoreless first half, we finally got the break we needed. A long Clemson pass fell squarely into the arms of our Blake Edmunds, who dashed back down the sidelines with nary a Tiger within reach. Crossing the Clemson ten, however, Edmunds blundered by glancing back over his shoulder at any would-be pursuers; he stumbled and went down on the five. Three running plays gained nothing, but then P. J. Boatwright put his toe into the field goal that proved the only points of the game. For the third straight year in this vaunted series, the margin of victory was three points or fewer.

After a hard-won, 14-3 victory over The Citadel, our record stood at 5-1 as we prepared to face the Tarheels of North Carolina. Our overall record against UNC was 0-10-2, so a victory here would rival a Clemson win in significance.

Boatwright opened the scoring with a 20-yard field goal in the first quarter, and Bill Jeffords closed it with a TD pass to Bill Swink in the third. But it was enough, as USC held on for a monumental 10-7 win. Jeffords also boomed a 90-yard punt on this historic afternoon, a Gamecock record that still stands.

We suffered a predictable letdown the next week against Furman and were shut out, 10-0; then, before we could recover, powerful Sewanee pounced on us for a 10-0 win.

However, on Thanksgiving Day, led by our four seniors — Frankie Meyer, Tom Brice, J. C. Long, and Blake Edmunds — we took a close win over tough Wake Forest, concluding our season with an enviable 7-3 record.

With his successful five-year tenure at an end, Coach Metzger returned to his New Jersey home to devote all his energy to his syndicated sports column.

8

1925 – 1927

BRANCH BOCOCK AND HARRY LIGHTSEY

Behind our new coach, Branch Bocock, an assistant at Georgia before coming to Columbia, we began the 1925 season with a strong team and high expectations. At least in one respect, those expectations would be fulfilled— and then some.

After an opening-day romp against Erskine (marked by the emergence of sophomore halfback Bob Wimberly), we reverted to tradition and lost to UNC. It was a tough game — their only score coming on a blocked punt — but the final score read 7-0.

The close games went our way the next two weeks, however, as we slipped by NC State, 7-6, and then, in a nice turnabout, blocked a punt to beat Wofford, 6-0. We were now 3-1 on the season, and Big Thursday was at hand.

Somehow, 13,000 thousand fans — the largest crowd ever to witness a sporting event in South Carolina — poured into the Fairgrounds. Those who hoped Clemson

would win its first game of the season would leave bitterly disappointed.

A Jazz Jascewicz field goal put the Gamecocks up early, but it was our next score that set the tone for this game. Our quarterback Bill Rogers punted high and deep to Clemson, and as the ball came down, it barely grazed the befuddled Tiger safety; it then bounced twenty yards in the air and landed in the arms of punter Rogers, who, without breaking stride, streaked on into the end zone.

Could a rout be underway? Yes. Before the day was done, Jascewicz kicked three field goals (a record at that time), Rogers scored his second touchdown, and W. R. Jeffords also added a TD. Meanwhile the Tigers managed but two first downs all day. Final score: Gamecocks 33, Tigers 0.

Still high from that experience, we trounced The Citadel, 30-6, before being brought back to earth by tough Virginia Tech. The Gobblers recovered a fumble in

Halfback Bob Wimberly (#7) rambles around end for a first down in Carolina's 33 – 0 win over the Tigers.

our end zone to beat us, 6-0. As though that weren't misfortune enough, we lost to Furman two weeks later by virtue of an errant snap. W. M. Boyd hiked the ball over our punter's head and into the end zone, and when Bill Rogers tried to scoop it up and run it out, he was tackled just inches behind the goal line. The two-point safety was the only score of the game.

We concluded the season in fine fashion, though. Against Presbyterian, Bill Rogers threw three TD passes to Jeffords for the victory, and a week later we shut out highly regarded Centre College, 20-0.

With a 7-3 record, Coach Bocock was off to an impressive start.

1926

Two impressive shutouts—a 41-0 rout of outmanned Erskine and a hard-fought, 12-0 win over new foe Maryland—fired our hopes of another outstanding season under second-year coach Branch Bocock. Bill Rogers' pinpoint passing, Bob Wimberly's beautiful running, and the hard-nosed defense of team captain W. M. Boyd looked to be a potent combination. The opening of our new stadium, Melton Field, named in honor of our late president Dr. William Davis Melton, also augured well for the new year.

As usual, however, UNC tried to spoil our dreams with a 7-0 defeat, but we bounced back with a 27-13 win over Wofford. Again were were 3-1 as Big Thursday and the Clemson Tigers loomed ahead.

Like last year, we opened the scoring with a field goal, this time a then-record 47-yarder from the toe of Bill Boyd. That was the extent of the first-half scoring, but in the second half Bill Rogers, fullback Power Rogers, and Red Swink put on a show, and the final score read USC 24, Clemson 0. Not only was this the first time in history that we had beaten Clemson three times in a row; we had also shut them out all three years.

Our euphoria was short-lived. The Citadel whipped us, 14-9, on October 28, and, just two days later, the powerful eleven from the University of Virginia overcame a valiant defensive effort on our part and went home with a 6-0 victory.

The following week we traveled to Richmond and played one of our greatest games ever against the highly rated, undefeated Gobblers of Virginia Tech. Bill Rogers passed for 282 yards, a single-game record that would stand at USC for some 40 years, and his three touchdown strikes were more than enough to take the Turkeys, 19-0.

We split our final two games. The Furman jinx dogged us again as we dropped a 10-7 decision, and then we rebounded for our third straight win over NC State, 20-13.

Our season record of 6-4 was not all we had hoped for, but it was certainly respectable. Also three of our boys—W. R. Price, Bill Boyd, and Bill Rogers—were named to the All-State team.

Coach Bocock, citing "personal reasons," retired after the '26 campaign and returned to his home in Virginia.

1927

Upon the abrupt departure of Branch Bocock, former Gamecock lineman Harry Lightsey, now a young Columbia lawyer, agreed to coach the team on a temporary basis. He had a veteran team to work with, not to mention sophomore halfback Ed Zobel, who would become the toast of Southern football over the next three years. On the other hand, brilliant Bob Wimberly broke his leg during preseason practice and was lost for the year.

The '27 season got off on the right foot with a 13-6 win over perennial whipping-boy Erskine, a game in which Zobel announced his arrival on the varsity by scoring both touchdowns. But in game two, Maryland gained revenge for the year before; they ran a double-screen pass all afternoon, totally bamboozling the Gamecocks and scoring a 26-0 victory.

Despite his short tenure, Harry Lightsey enjoys the distinction of being the first coach in USC history to notch a victory over Virginia. Trailing 12-0 in the fourth quarter, Tom Magill shuffled a lateral pass

Left end Sam Burake scoring on a pass from Bob Wimberly in USC's upset win over VPI.

to Bill Rogers, who took it in from the eight. Then, with two minutes to play, Ed Zobel snagged a tipped pass and raced fifty yards for the game-winner.

Coach Lightsey added to his laurels the following week. He became the first Gamecock coach ever to beat Virginia and UNC in the same year. It was Carolina's first-ever Homecoming Game, and, inexperienced in these matters, we had failed to schedule a patsy. But with Magill crashing through three defenders for one score, and Red Swink turning an interception into a 45-yard TD scamper, we held off the Tarheels for the second time ever.

Then came Clemson, now under the direction of Josh Cody, who would prove one of their winningest coaches ever. For three nerve-wracking quarters the game remained scoreless, but then Cody showed his savvy. Knowing we were injury-riddled and exhausted, he had saved his reserve backs for this final period, and these fresh troops ran their way to a 20-0 win.

After only three days rest, it was time for our traditional battle against the Citadel at the Orangeburg County Fair, and it proved a classic. A perfect, 40-yard strike from Zobel to Emmett Wingfield proved to be the difference, as the Gamecocks prevailed, 6-0.

That, however, was our last gasp. With Zobel out of the game with a concussion, VPI routed us, 35-0. Then the Purple Hurricanes of Furman took advantage of the battered Gamecocks, 33-0. And in the season finale, All-Southern halfback Jack McDowall and NC State whipped the poor Gamecocks into submission, 34-0.

Harry Lightsey had done his best, but a 4-5 season was a disappointment. It was time to start again.

9

1928 – 1934

THE BILLY LAVAL ERA

Following Harry Lightsey's resignation, the Carolina trustees knew just whom to turn to—the man who had beaten us five straight years: Billy Laval, head coach at Furman University.

Laval was a man of grim visage and wry humor, who took football seriously and demanded that his players do likewise. He once made the comment that leisure time was not for athletes, and he insisted that his players adhere to a Spartan regimen.

Prospects were bright. Eleven seniors were returning, including Bob Wimberly, whose broken leg had now healed. Also, Ed Zobel was back as a junior, and outstanding back Bru Boineau had moved up from the freshman squad.

We didn't have to wait long to be tested. After the routine opening-day win over Erskine, it was time for what everyone agreed was USC's biggest game in history. We were traveling all the way to Illinois to face no less than the fearsome University of Chicago and the legendary Amos Alonzo Stagg. Indeed, of such stature were the Big Maroons (and of such slight stature were the lowly Gamecocks) that Chicago announced they

Billy Laval, Gamecock head coach, 1928 – 34.

Ed Zobel circles end for a touchdown in USC's 6–0 upset of Amos Alonzo Stagg's top-rated Chicago team.

would play two games that Saturday, the first against USC and the second against Ripon College.

When our boys, accustomed to playing before a few thousand fans at Melton Field, were greeted by the 35,000 spectators at Stagg Stadium, they must have been overawed. But they didn't play like it. After a scoreless first quarter, Ed Zobel drew blood with a 3-yard TD dash around end. From that point, the defense prevailed, and by that 6-0 margin USC had scored one of the greatest victories in Gamecock history.

Before we had time to properly celebrate, however, we had to travel to Charlottesville and take on another powerhouse, the University of Virginia. But this game became the Ed Zobel show; he intercepted a pass for a touchdown and scored twice in the fourth quarter to lead USC to a huge 24-13 victory. Consecutive wins over Maryland, 21-7, and Presbyterian, 13-0, pushed our season record to 5-0, and people

were saying that it was time for Billy Laval to run for governor. But then came Big Thursday.

For the only time in history, both Clemson and USC were undefeated going into their game (and Carolina would never again enter the game with a perfect record). But with Zobel out of the game early with an injury, what was touted as a toss-up turned into a rout: Clemson 32, USC 0.

Oddly, the next two weeks provided eight quarters of scoreless football, and 0-0 ties against both The Citadel and UNC. We broke the drought the following week when Carlisle Beall hit Bru Boineau with a 72-yard TD strike, and we held on to beat Furman, 6-0. But we lost the final game of the season when NC State played what some considered its finest game ever, whipping our Gamecocks 18-7.

Still, our 6-2-2 record was nothing to sneer at, and the Billy Laval era was off to a promising start.

1929

In 1929 one of our youngest teams confronted one of our toughest schedules. Still, only a tough, 6-0 loss to revenge-minded Virginia scarred our record before Big Thursday.

We handled Erskine in the opener, and then, after the Virginia loss, we played two fine games. Bru Boineau's 85-yard kickoff return to open the second half, along with Ed Zobel's 70-yard interception return sparked a 26-6 win over Maryland. The next week, Crip Rhame ran the opening kickoff back for a touchdown, and we proceeded to rout Presbyterian, 41-0.

The question now was, could we break Clemson's two game winning streak over our Gamecocks? When the Tigers clawed their way to a 14-0 lead in the second period, it looked like the answer was no. But just before halftime, Crip Rhame leapt high in the air to intercept a Goat McMillan pass and returned it eighty yards for a touchdown. At least we were in the ballgame.

The third period was scoreless, and when Bru Boineau returned an interception seventy-five yards for the tying touchdown, the newly created Carolina "cheering section" sent up an insane chorus. Unfortunately, Goat McMillan redeemed himself, taking the ball over from fifteen yards out for the winning score. Clemson had made it three in a row after all.

The following Thursday in what had come to be called the Little Classic, Bru Boineau scored twice—once on a 70-yard punt return—to spark a 27-14 win over The Citadel. Then came Homecoming and another match against UNC. We still had not learned how to schedule an appropriate opponent for Homecoming, and this year we paid for it: North Carolina 40, USC 0.

The rest of the season adhered to this win-and-lose pattern. A gratifying 2-0 win

Julian Beall, captain of the '29 squad.

over Furman was followed by a 20-7 loss to a superior Florida Gator team. Back up the next week, we played a great game to beat NC State, 20-6. Hap Edens scored first on a sensational 85-yard run from scrimmage, and Crip Rhame threw two beautiful TD passes, one to Boineau and the other to Hugh Stoddard.

For the finale, we traveled to Knoxville to take on legendary Bob Neyland's Tennessee Volunteers, a team currently enjoying a 28-game winning streak. This was the team of the two great halfbacks "Hack and Mack," Buddy Hackman and Gene McEver, and these two greats had a field day against the smaller, bewildered Gamecocks. In fact, McEver scored thirty-three points on the day to wind up as the national scoring leader that year. The final score, if it must be mentioned, was Tennessee 54, Carolina 0.

So we ended the year with a mediocre 6-5 record, but three of our boys—Monk Shand, Bru Boineau, and team captain Julian Beall—were named to the All-State team.

Ed Zobel, All-State halfback in 1929.

In fact, Beall was All-State, All-Southern, and Honorable Mention for the All-America team, the first Gamecock ever to be so recognized. Also, halfback Hugh Stoddard became our first recipient of the coveted Jacobs Blocking Trophy, given annually to the finest blocker in the 23-team Southern Conference.

1930

In 1930 Carolina played perhaps its toughest schedule in history, including such Southern powers as Duke, Georgia Tech, LSU, Clemson, and Auburn. It proved to be a season of huge wins—and bitter losses.

After tuning up against Erskine, we traveled to Durham to take on Wallace Wade's highly favored Duke Blue Devils. Perhaps they took us too lightly. At any rate, with the defense scoring twice (Frank Bostick on a blocked punt and Tom Brantley on an interception), and Hap Edens scoring ten points on the offense, USC chalked up a tremendous upset, 22-0 (Duke's only loss of the year).

At Grant Field in Atlanta the next week, we were not so fortunate; the Golden Tornados (as they were then called) blew us away, 45-0. And that was nothing, said the oddsmakers, because arriving at Melton Field the following Saturday were the Bengal Tigers of LSU, led by Joe Almokary, the leading scorer in the conference. This team was averaging eighty-one points a game thus far into the season.

Once again we rose to the occasion. The big break came when their punter, standing on the goal line, shanked his kick and put the ball out of bounds on the 23-yard line. Miles Blount immediately burst off right tackle, shook loose from two defenders, and raced in for the TD. LSU scored later in the half, but the great Almokary delighted Gamecock fans by missing the extra point. The defense, anchored by captain Bob Gressette, came through brilliantly in the second half, and the game ended with USC on top, 7-6.

Never a team to handle prosperity, we again fell to Clemson on Big Thursday. Bru Boineau's 66-yard touchdown dash was the only highlight for the Gamecocks, while the Tigers' Maxcey Welch riddled us with a superb passing attack. The final: Clemson 20, USC 7.

Consistently inconsistent, we handled The Citadel, 13-0, the following Thursday, but nine days later were shut out by Furman,

14-0. Those pesky Baptists not only beat us, but had the effrontery to break Bru Boineau's collarbone as well.

Now it was time for a winning streak. We beat powerful Sewanee at Melton field, 14-13, when the Purple Tigers missed an extra point that would have tied the game. Then, led by sophomores Tommy Reynolds and Miles Blount, we shut down NC State, 19-0.

Our season would end against Auburn, a team that hadn't won a conference game in four years. Unfortunately, that streak ended with this game, and so did ours. Our only score came when Coach Laval sent in Bru Boineau, shoulder cast and all, and he swept the end for a 35-yard touchdown run. That would be the great Boineau's last heroics in a Gamecock uniform, and Auburn took the win, 25-7.

From this respectable 6-4 team, Monk Shand, Bru Boineau, and Bob Gressette were named to the All-State team.

Considering the talent we had lost to graduation, as well as the killer schedule we faced in '31, Coach Laval would need a miracle to survive. He got one.

Earl Clary, a superstar halfback at Gaffney High, shunned suitors from such national powers as Michigan, Harvard, and Princeton, and decided to cast his lot with Coach Laval and the Gamecocks. Many old-timers insist that Clary became the finest running back ever to don cleats for the Carolina eleven.

He wasted no time proving himself. The Blue Devils of Duke came to Columbia for our opening game of the season, and Clary rushed for 103 yards and scored the game's only touchdown. His elusive lateral moves left one befuddled Duke defender muttering, "It was like trying to tackle a ghost," and from that day on Clary was known as "the Gaffney Ghost."

Other stars of the great win over Duke

Halfback Miles Blount goes off-tackle for the score in Carolina's huge 6 – 0 upset of nationally ranked LSU.

Earl Clary's touchdown dash in USC's 7 – 0 upset of Wallace Wade's Duke team in 1931.

included Fred Hambright and Dick Shinn on offense and captain Miles Blount on defense, while Grayson Wolfe's booming punts kept the Devils on their heels all day. Despite two TD passes from Wolfe, one to Clary and the other to Hambright, USC fell to Georgia Tech in Atlanta the next week, then followed that disappointment with a tough loss to LSU in Baton Rouge, 19-12.

On Big Thursday, first-year coach Jess Neely brought his Tigers to town riding a four-game win streak over the Gamecocks. It was time to put a stop to such nonsense, but our team was listless throughout the scoreless first half. Was it because Coach Laval made them change from their black jerseys into bright red ones during halftime? For whatever reason, Clary, Shinn, and Blount all scored in the second half for a 21-0 victory. The Gaffney Ghost rushed for 147 yard on the afternoon, more than the entire Clemson team.

We pushed the winning streak to three with wins over The Citadel and Furman during the next two weeks. Clary scored three TDs against The Citadel, while the Furman win was sparked by six interceptions on the part of the defense. The Furman game, by the way, clinched our first state championship since 1912.

A 6-6 tie against Florida in Tampa hurt less that the knee injury Clary suffered during the game. We didn't need him in our 21-0 win over NC State the following week, but his absence during the first three quarters of the Auburn game, a 13-6 loss, probably made the difference.

A season-ending loss to Centre College gave us a record of 5-4-1, which wasn't bad considering the tough schedule. Also, Fred Hambright won the Jacobs Blocking Trophy, while Earl Clary and Bryant Adair were both named to the All-South Atlantic All-Star team, a squad chosen from teams in Maryland, Virginia, and the Carolinas.

Even more encouraging, the Gaffney Ghost still had two years to play.

1932

The '32 Gamecocks were being touted as perhaps the finest football team ever to represent the university, and we started with wins over Sewanee and Villanova. But they weren't easy.

The 7-3, comeback win over Sewanee made one thing clear: opposing defenses would forever more be keying on the Gaffney Ghost, whether he had the ball or not. The Villanova game was equally tough. Our lone score came on a long pass from Grayson Wolfe to Tom Craig, and the defense held on for a 7-6 upset victory.

An unforgivable letdown resulted in a 6-0 loss to lightly regarded Wake Forest, but we rebounded with a 19-0 shutout of Wofford—a tune-up for Big Thursday.

Clemson surprised everyone by holding USC scoreless in the first half, perhaps because Coach Laval started Dick Shinn in place of Clary. In the second half, Clary resumed his rightful place, running brilliantly and tossing a TD pass to Allie McDougal. The result was a 14-0 win, our second straight over the despised Tigers.

Then came two bitterly tough losses. First we ventured to New Orleans to take on defending national champion Tulane. Their great All-American halfback Don Zimmerman ripped us for a 37-yard touchdown in the second minute of play, but that was all we gave up. Unfortunately, they gave up nothing, and we were on the short end of a 6-0 score. Then, back at the Fairgrounds for Homecoming, we lost by an indentical score to mighty LSU. The Bengals, by the way, would remain undefeated for the year, claim the Southern Conference championship, and take a trip to the Rose Bowl.

Our losing streak hit three when we lost, 14-0, to nettlesome Furman, but we finally bounced back with a 19-0 shutout of The

"The Gaffney Ghost," Earl Clary

Citadel. Clary scored twice to ice the win. The Ghost also scored our lone touchdown the next week against NC State, but we could have used two. Final score: USC 7, NC State 7.

Next came the biggest game of the season, bigger even than Clemson or LSU. We were traveling to Birmingham to take on the number-one team in the nation, the mighty Plainsmen of Auburn. Auburn was 9-0 on the year and, with a 13-0 lead at

Fred Hambright ready to gather in a pass from Harold Mauney against NC State.

halftime, looked to make us victim number ten.

But in the second half, led by Clary and Harold Mauney, we made a spectacular comeback to earn a 20-20 tie. Clary had 110 yards and two touchdowns on the day, and until then no team had scored more than seven points against Auburn all year. Though a tie, this game would go down as our greatest "moral victory" of all time.

The tie also, by the way, bumped Auburn from the Southern Conference championship. Both Auburn and LSU ended the season with 9-0-1 records, but thanks to the intercession of Huey Long, who pointed out that LSU had beaten us in Columbia while we had tied Auburn in Birmingham, LSU claimed the crown.

1933

Billy Laval returned for his sixth season in 1933 and brought with him a talented, veteran team that included Earl Clary, the great blocking back Fred Hambright, quarterback Grayson Wolfe, Nelson Fortson, Henry McManus, Buddy Morehead, Joe Shinn, and Joe Johnson. He would need them all, for again we faced a deadly schedule. This year, by the way, marked a new conference alignment. Thirteen teams from the original Southern Conference withdrew to form the new Southeastern Conference, so that now the Southern Conference consisted of USC, Clemson, UNC, NC State, Duke, Virginia, VMI, VPI, Washington & Lee, and Maryland, with Furman, Davidson, Wake Forest, Georgetown, The Citadel, and Richmond to be considered for future membership.

After an easy opener against Wofford (in which Earl Clary scored twice, then gave way to his younger cousin Wilburn Clary, who also scored twice), the Gamecocks started to backpedal. First we lost to Pop Warner's Temple Owls, 26-6, then we were beaten by Villanova, 15-6.

It was again Big Thursday, and Clary, injured during practice that week, sat on the sidelines. But early in the first period Harold Mauney tossed a short pass to Hambright, who danced his way twenty-five yards for a touchdown. That was it: USC 7, Clemson 0—our third straight shutout over our archrivals.

A short forty-eight hours later, we beat favored VPI on the strength of two Clary TDs, only the third time in eight years that the Gobblers had been beaten at home. Now we were were 4-2 as we boarded the train for Baton Rouge and the potent Bengal Tigers. The oddsmakers were nervous at the half, as we led 7-3, but the Tigers roared back in the second half to take the victory, 30-7.

A win over NC State and a frustrating tie against always troublesome Furman gave us a 5-3-1 record as we headed into our finale, another confrontation with national power Auburn. Could we manage another tie, another "moral victory"? Coach Laval was having none of it. He told the team he was looking for a win, nothing less. But would they provide it?

In the first quarter, Clary tacked an Auburn runner in the end zone for a safety and a 2-0 lead; then he raced fifty-six yards for a second-period score to make it 9-0 at the half. But the Plainsmen came back in the second half for two TDs and a 14-9 lead. Clary, however, wasn't through. He scampered for a 29-yard, fourth-quarter touchdown that won the game for us, 16-14. It was one of our greatest victories ever, and quite a final curtain for the Gaffney Ghost. Our offense scored eighty points that year, with Clary supplying seventy-three of them. It was a satisfying 6-3-1 season, and we tied with Duke for the Southern Conference championship.

Freeman Huskey, Tom Craig, and Arthur Morehead made the All-State team. The Gaffney Ghost was All-State for the third straight year, All-Southern, and Honorable Mention All-American.

1934

The big news of the '34 season was the completion of our new facility, Municipal Stadium. It was built with WPA money and had a seating capacity of 18,000.

In the final game ever played at Melton Field, we defeated Erskine 25-0. The next week, on October 6, we dedicated Municipal Stadium in a game played against VMI in a torrential downpour. Only moments into the first quarter, our John Rowland scooped up a blocked punt and scooted fourteen yards for our first touchdown in the new stadium. We went on to win, 22-6, and so had a 2-0 start on the new year.

After a tough 6-0 loss to NC State, we got back on the right track with a 20-6 win over The Citadel. Our great quarterback Harold Mauney was superb, running and passing for all of our scores.

The win gave us a solid 3-1 record heading into Big Thursday, and a record crowd of 17,000 turned out to see if USC would make it four in a row over the Tigers. We couldn't; Clemson ended their Big Thursday drought with a 19-0 shutout.

It was win one, lose one for the remainder of the season. Mauney's two touchdown passes led us to a fine upset win over VPI, but then we traveled to Philadelphia for a 20-0 whipping at the hands of Villanova.

The next week we managed to squeeze by our *bête noire*, Furman, 2-0, but then lost to Washington & Lee in the finale, 14-7. Thus ended a less than spectacular 5-4 season, and on that note Billy Laval decided to bow out. We regretfully bid farewell to one of the most successful of all Gamecock coaches.

Municipal Stadium (later called Carolina Stadium) was a WPA project completed in 1934.

1935 – 1937

THE DON McCALLISTER YEARS

Considering all the players we lost to graduation in '34, Laval no doubt picked the right moment to move on. In his place we hired Don McCallister, who had coached the Waite High School team in Toledo, Ohio, for the past nine years. He had compiled an outstanding record of 81-9, but his resumé did him little good at USC.

We opened the 1935 season with the usual whipping of Erskine, but the season slid downhill from that point. We dropped three games in a row—to Duke, NC State, and Davidson—before righting ourselves against The Citadel, 25-0.

So we carried a 2-3 record into the Clemson game at Municipal Stadium. More than 16,000 fans showed up despite the threat of rain, though USC fans, perhaps sensing the outcome, were somewhat more subdued than usual. Their intuition was well placed.

Coach Don McCallister, 1935 – 37.

The Tigers scored eleven points in the first half, but than added another thirty-three in the second frame to take a 44-0 victory. It was our worst loss to the Tigers since the 51-0 humiliation of 1900.

After two more losses—to VPI and detested Furman—we eked out a 2-0 win over Washington & Lee. Then, in the season finale, we reverted to form and dropped a 22-0 decision to the Florida Gators.

It was not a good year. We scored a total of seventy-three points in 1935, forty-eight of those coming at the expense of Erskine and the Citadel. Our opponents racked up 187 against us, and the record for the year wound up at 3-7.

On the positive side, both Wilburn Clary and guard Paul Gaffney made the All-State team. And team captain Clay "Bud" Alexander was outstanding on defense all year.

1936

The 1936 season found the Gamecocks preparing, for the first time in history, for a 12-game season. Furthermore, new athletic director William H. Harth, a man of vision, recognized the value of good public relations. He immediately set about organizing radio broadcasts of Gamecock football games throughout the state, dotting the landscape with billboards, inviting high school students to games, and planning lively halftime activities. He also installed a PA system in the new stadium and placed large scoreboards at each end.

More excitement about the new season was generated with the addition of Bru Boineau and Earl Clary to the coaching staff. Also, fans were anxious to witness the skills of the third Clary—Earl and Wilburn's cousin Ed—to don the garnet and black.

In fact, led by captain Bob Johnson, the '36 team was built around a nucleus of

outstanding running backs and fifteen returning linemen. Unfortunately, however, despite the expectations, the season turned out to be much like the preceding one.

After disposing of Erskine in the opener, we suffered two quick losses, to VMI, 24-7, and Duke, 21-0. Over the next two weeks, however, we looked as though we meant to turn our season around. Behind the outstanding play of quarterback Ralph Dearth, end Bob Johnson, and halfback Art Urbanyi, we upset Florida, 7-0, and did the same to VPI, 14-0.

So when a record crowd of 19,000 crammed themselves into the 18,000 seats in Municipal Stadium, we hoped to give the Carolina contingent something to cheer about. Instead, however, the spectators watched the Tigers dismantle our Gamecocks, 19-0. Ed Clary's fine passing and deep punts were for nought, as we failed to score against Clemson for the third year in a row.

Led by high-stepping Jack "Gashouse" Lyons, we rebounded against The Citadel, 9-0, but then we were knocked reeling by four losses in a row—to Villanova, Furman, UNC, and Xavier of Ohio. We did manage to wrap up the season on a happy note, upsetting Miami (of Florida) 6-3 on Jack Lyons' 60-yard scamper in the third quarter.

Despite our 5-7 record and Coach McCallister's overall mark of 8-14, the athletic advisory committee voted to extend McCallister's contract through 1938 at an annual salary of $4,000. But deep rumblings of discontent from disgruntled USC alumni were being heard around the state. McCallister would be well advised to come up with a winner in '37.

1937

Again, for reasons known only to himself, Coach McCallister came up with a 12-game

Tommy Lonchar (#71) about to put the crunch on a Bulldog running back.

schedule for 1937. But our prospects looked bright when we started by defeating Billy Laval's Emory and Henry team, 45-7, and then tying a strong UNC eleven, 13-13. However, then came losses to Southeastern powers Georgia and Alabama, and again we found ourselves mired in the Dismal Swamp of a likely losing season.

The next week, though, we took Davidson by a 12-7 score and so carried a 2-2-1 record into Big Thursday. Again, 19,000 faithful squeezed into the stadium for the match-up, and for a brief moment it looked like we might make a game of it. Ed Clary tossed a 28-yard scoring strike to Bill Simpson for an early 6-0 lead. But the game soon devolved into what the *Garnet and Black* called "another State Fair nightmare," and

Clemson walked away with a 34-6 victory. McCallister was now 0-3 against Clemson, which did nothing to endear him to our increasingly unhappy alumni.

Our 21-6 victory over The Citadel the next week did little to assuage our hurt feelings. Nor did the two losses we then suffered to Kentucky and—once again!—to bothersome Furman.

We took out three years' worth of frustration against hapless Presbyterian the next Saturday, jumping all over the smaller team 64-0. But no sooner had we finished gloating than Catholic University knocked us off, 27-14. Like we did a year earlier, though, we finished the season with a gratifying win over Miami, the only score coming via a Tommy Lonchar field goal.

In 1937's Sports Picture of the Year in South Carolina, a photographer catches Gamecock captain Jack Lyons just before he was tackled by a Citadel fan.

As for McCallister, a man of genial disposition, the athletic advisory board could not decide which way to turn. At the end of the season and, after considerable debate, they proposed that he be retained for another season (they had already extended his contract through '38, remember), but that his assistant coaches be terminated.

But the controversy was too much for the shy McCallister, and he resigned during the Christmas holidays. His successor at Carolina would become the granddaddy of all Gamecock coaches, the personable Rex Enright.

11

1938 – 1942

REX ENRIGHT AND THE PREWAR ERA

Born in Rockford, Illinois, in 1903, Rex Enright had played fullback under the fabled Knute Rockne at Notre Dame as an understudy to Elmer Layden of the famous Four Horsemen. His senior year, in 1926, he became the starting fullback.

After coaching stints (in both football and basketball) at UNC and the University of Georgia, Enright accepted a four-year contract from USC at a salary of $5,500, making him the highest paid coach in the history of Carolina football.

Enright used his connections to schedule some of the biggest names in college football for the Gamecocks over the next five years. His philosophy, as he explained to sometimes puzzled fans, was, "Regardless of the strength or weakness of the opposition, you can't win them all. So if you're going to lose, lose to somebody big. It's less embarrassing."

Enright was welcomed to USC football by a veteran team. Our co-captains were W.

Coach Rex Enright, 1938 – 42, 1946 – 55.

Ed Clary lands for the tying touchdown against Villanova in '38.

R. "Pop" Howell and Larry Craig. Back for another season were such stalwarts as Ralph Dearth, Earl "Big" Durham, Gene Robinson, J. B. "Pinhead" Henson, Herbert Stroud, Alex "Jeep" Urban, Al Grygo, Stan Nowak, and Joe Patrone. Also Ed Clary, team MVP in '37, would be back for another year.

As usual, we opened with a pounding of the Erskine Seceders, then surprised everyone the next week by beating a strong Xavier of Ohio team, 6-0, in Cincinnati. This promising start, however, was tarnished by two single-point losses—to Georgia, 7-6, and Wake Forest, 20-19. It looked like we needed an extra-point kicker.

So, at 2-2 on the young season, and led by Grygo, Urban, and Clary, we headed to the Sumter County Fair for what proved to be a great game against Davidson. On the very first series of downs, our DeWitt Arrowsmith intercepted a Davidson pass on

our five and raced back upfield ninety yards, finally being pulled down on the five. Pinhead Henson took it over on the next play. In the second half, Grygo, Clary, and Gene Robinson (on a pass from J. B. Williams) all scored to make the final 25-0.

Clemson, having beaten tough Tulane, came to the State Fair classic an odds-on favorite, and the oddsmakers were right. The Tigers scored on the first series of the game and held a 20-0 lead at the end of the first quarter. It was 34-0 and late in the third quarter when we finally woke up, so our two touchdowns didn't make much difference. This was our fourth loss to Clemson in a row.

But we bounced back from the Clemson debacle with three straight weeks of impressive football. First, at the Orangeburg County Fair, we met the Villanova Wildcats, who were riding a win streak of thirteen games and were highly favored to zap our gang of Southern hicks. But such was not the case. Led by Wallace Craig, Ed Clary, and Jerry Hughes, we upset the Wildcats and the bettors in the crowd with a surprising 6-6 tie.

Inspired by that performance, we went on to score two big wins. By virtue of a 60-yard pass from Clary to Alex Urban, we shut out the Duquesne Nightriders, 7-0; then, the following week, Clary and Rick Stoud led the way to an extremely gratifying slaughter of Furman, 27-6.

The next week, however, we lost to the Fordham Rams, one of the top-ranked teams in the nation, in a game played in New York City in a sea of mud. We scored twice in the second half, but both our TDs were nullified on penalties, and we lost a tough one, 13-0. In the season finale, though, we scored a fine win over a strong Catholic University squad at Griffith Stadium. Oddly enough, we scored on the first play of the game when Ed Clary threw a short pass to Ben Joe Williams, who then raced eighty-two yards for the touchdown. That was it; we had notched another big intersectional win, 7-0.

Enright, in his first year as head coach, had completed the season with a respectable 6-4-1 record against some outstanding opposition. Larry Craig, our team captain for '38, was named All-Southern, then won a starting berth at end with the Green Bay Packers, thus becoming the first USC man ever to play pro football.

1939

The 1939 Gamecocks would prove only

Heber "Rock" Stroud carries both the ball and a Clemson defender against the Tigers in '39.

Halfback Al Grygo on a sweep against Wake Forest.

half as successful as their '38 predecessors, but our losses from that squad were heavy. Gone now were Ed Clary, Jack Dorflinger, Pop Howell, and Big Durham, while the great Al Grygo and Alex Urban were declared ineligible because of academic problems. DeWitt Arrowsmith broke his ankle in preseason drills, and injuries sidelined several others.

Consequently, we lost the first three games of the season (to Wake Forest, Catholic University, and Villanova) before finally edging Davidson, 7-0, on the fine running of halfback Harvey Blouin.

Then, on Big Thursday, Clemson arrived in Columbia with one of the best teams in America. Their great tailback that year, Banks McFadden, was named All-America in both football and basketball, the only South Carolina collegiate athlete ever to earn that distinction in two sports. So we suspected what we were in for, and we were.

Final score: Clemson 27, USC 0.

The next week we surprised everyone by tying the Mountaineers of West Virginia, 6-6, at the Orangeburg County Fair, but we then lost to both Furman (20-0) and Georgia (33-7). On the other hand, we concluded the campaign with wins over both Florida (7-0) and Miami (7-2), thus claiming the championship of the Sunshine State.

So it was a 3-6-1 year, and naturally disappointing, despite all our valid reasons for not fielding the kind of team we'd hoped for.

1940

With 1939 behind us, however, prospects for 1940 were encouraging. The great Al Grygo had overcome his academic problems and was again a threat at left half. Then there were Alex Urban, Harvey Blouin,

Big Harvey Blouin pounds The Citadel's line in 1940.

Bobo Carter, Joe Patrone, Dutch Elston, and team captain Kirt Norton, quite a nucleus of veterans around which to build a winning club. This year also saw the varsity appearance of Lou Sossamon, who would star at center for the next three seasons.

Unfortunately, those bright prospects were soon dimmed; playing one national power after another, USC dropped its first four games. Georgia, led by their great All-America halfback Frankie Sinkwich, began our downhill slide with an October 5 game in Columbia. Sinkwich ran for two TDs and threw for another as the Bulldogs prevailed, 33-2.

The next week, against Duquesne in Pittsburgh, we looked better. Grygo hit Urban for two TDs; then, following Duquesne's second score, he returned the kickoff for a 94-yard touchdown to give us a 21-13 lead. But the Dons, demonstrating why they were the fifth-ranked team in the nation, roared back with two touchdowns to take a 27-21 win.

We had not beaten Clemson now since 1933, a drought of some six years. That fact, combined with our strong showing against Duquesne, served to draw a record crowd of 21,000 fans for 1940's Big Thursday game. All the same, the odds had Clemson favored by twenty-five points.

The Tigers jumped off to a 14-0 halftime lead, but in the third quarter DeWitt Arrowsmth took a Tiger punt at his own 25-yard line and dashed for the right sideline. The pursuing Tigers failed to notice Al Grygo circling from the opposite direction and were totally fooled when he took the lateral from Arrowsmith and streaked seventy-five yards for the score. (Before long this punt reverse, designed by Enright especially for this game, would be adopted by every team in the nation.)

In the final quarter, Urban intercepted a

Clemson pass and returned it for another USC touchdown, but again it wasn't enough, and the final score read Clemson 21, USC 13.

Loss number four came against a great Penn State team by a score of 12-0 at University Park, but we surprised Kansas State the next week, 20-13. Before we had fully savored our first win of the year, however, those damnable Furman Hurricanes ruined our party with a 25-7 thrashing.

In a night game in Miami, another Gaffney Clary, this one named Buford, made his debut for the Gamecocks and played a sensational game in our surprising 7-2 victory. We stepped backward the next week in a 7-6 loss to Wake Forest, but in our final game of the season The Citadel made the mistake of inviting us to their Homecoming. Our 31-6 victory gave them little to cheer about.

The win against The Citadel gave us a 3-6 record for the year—hardly inspiring, but at least Gaffney, South Carolina had supplied us with two more potential Gamecock stars: Lou Sossamon and Buford Clary.

1941

Improvement was the keynote for '41, and looking at the season game by game, we gave a pretty good account of ourselves that year.

Again led by Lou Sossamon and Al Grygo, plus a new halfback sensation out of Rockford, Illinois (Enright's hometown), named Stan Stasica, we opened the season with a big victory over UNC, 13-7. Buford Clary went fifteen yards for a score in the first quarter, but UNC came back to take a 7-6 lead. Then, late in the game, Stasica gave the fans a taste of the future when he breezed through the entire Tar Heel team for sixty-six yards and the win-

ning score.

After a predictable loss to Georgia and Frankie Sinkwich, 34-6, and a 6-6 tie with Wake Forest, we were eagerly looking forward to Big Thursday. Again, though, the experts gave us little chance against the undefeated Tigers, and all the more so with Al Grygo on the sidelines with an injury.

Yet another record crowd—23,000—turned out for the game, many of them Clemson alumni who hoped to see the Tigers continue their march to another big bowl game. But only minutes into the first quarter, Stasica started to his right on what seemed an end sweep, then looked downfield and zinged a perfect 46-yard strike to Harvey Blouin at the Tigers' 13-yard line. On the next play Ken Roskie flipped a pass to Dutch Elston for the score, and, cliché or not, pandemonium reigned in the Carolina stands.

We increased our lead to 12-0 in the second quarter when Stasica hit Roskie in the end zone. Minutes later, following a Butch Butler fumble, Al Grygo bulled over for another Carolina score, and we found ourselves with an 18-0 halftime lead. Clemson closed to a breath-quickening 18-14 in the second half, but we held on to take our first victory from the Tigers since 1933. Three weeks later, during halftime of the Furman game, Enright was presented with a brand new Cadillac by adoring fans in appreciation of his finally bagging the big Clemson cat. This gesture prompted Clemson coach Frank Howard, recalling that the Tigers had missed a winning score by mere inches, to comment: "The only difference between a Cadillac and a coffin is a few feet of dirt."

After a too-close 13-6 win the next week over The Citadel, we suffered a narrow 3-0 loss to Kansas State. The game followed a two-day train ride to Manhattan, Kansas, and was played in a near-blizzard.

But we won the state championship the

next week when we defeated our ancient enemy Furman University. Stasica again led our attack, dashing eighty-five yards on a punt return in the first quarter, then going fifteen yards for a second score in the same quarter. Steve Nowak scored moments later on a 30-yard pass interception. It had been a long time since we had beaten Furman and Clemson in the same year.

We lost the season's penultimate game to Miami, 7-6, on Patrone's missed extra point, then in the finale had to face highly rated Penn State. Despite a 31-yard dash for a score by Stasica and a 35-yard TD pass from Stasica to Blouin, the Nittany Lions proved too deep for us, winning 19-12.

Once again, our 4-4-1 record was not that impressive at first glance, but considering that our losses were close games against some truly outstanding teams, our record looks more respectable.

It was also heartening that Dutch Elston won the Jacobs Blocking Trophy for the state of South Carolina. And as for the All-State team, Sossamon and Stasica were unanimous selections. Dutch Elston was chosen at quarterback, while Bill Applegate, Bobo Carter, and Steve Nowak were also named to the team. Sossamon and Stasica, by the way, were also named All-Southern.

1942

By the fall of 1942, with the war now raging in both Europe and the Pacific, the University of South Carolina men mobilized for what we knew was to come: service in the military and very likely combat.

In fact, the first bad news of the upcoming season was that "Manly Stanley" Stasica, our junior halfback sensation and the man we'd depended on to carry the mail in '41, had been drafted and was now wearing the uniform of an Army private. Actually, between graduation and Uncle Sam, our '42

Sossamon A. P. second All-American and mighty center for U. S. C.

Lou Sossamon

squad had been decimated.

And our record proved it. A surprising tie against Tennessee (which would win the Sugar Bowl at the end of the season) and a victory against The Citadel were the only bright spots in an otherwise dark year. We finished at 1-7-1, our worst season since 1919.

But one great story did unfold during 1942—that of Lou Sossamon, USC's first bonafide All-American.

Sossamon remembers his very first football game. At 130 pounds, he was a scrawny B-team center for Gaffney High in a game against Boiling Springs (North Carolina). With the ball on Boiling Springs' 10-yard line, Gaffney's quarterback huddled his team and said, "Okay, men, let's show 'em a thing or two. We're gonna ram it right up the middle. Sossamon, you be sure to move that guard to the right."

But Sossamon, in words that have become immortal in the Gaffney area, replied, "I ain't moved nobody all day. Maybe we better show 'em a thing or two around end."

Sossamon soon graduated from the B-team, and when the Gaffney Indians went undefeated in both '37 and '38, Lou was named to the All-State and All-Southern teams and chosen to play in the annual Shrine Bowl Game.

In 1939, while his parents (owners of the Gaffney *Ledger*) were attending a press conference in Columbia, Lou decided to stroll over to the USC athletic department to visit with his old friends from Gaffney, the Clary boys. He ran into Rex Enright, who offered him a scholarship on the spot. Lou readily accepted the offer, and the next four years, as they say, are history. He made the All-State and All-Southern teams for three consecutive years, then made the Associated Press All-America team his senior year, despite USC's terrible 1-7-1 record.

After his discharge from the service in 1945, Lou was recruited to join the New York Yankees football team of the newly forming All-America Conference. He would be playing alongside such stars as Georgia's Frankie Sinkwich, Illinois' Buddy Young, Notre Dame immortal Angelo Bertelli, and Furman great Dewey Proctor.

The Yankees proved to be an excellent team, consistently outdrawing their NFL counterparts, the New York Giants. For four years Lou anchored the Yankee line at center, compensating for his smallish, 210-pound frame with speed, aggression, and hard-nosed play.

Upon his retirement from pro ball, Lou joined his parents on the Gaffney *Ledger*,

where he won the South Carolina Press Association's first Freedom of Information Award. He serves as the paper's publisher today, as well as chairman of USC's Intercollegiate Activities Committee and member of the board of trustees of the South Carolina Athletic Hall of Fame. He is also a longtime member of the USC board of trustees.

12

1943 – 1945

THE WORLD WAR II YEARS

Back in '42, given the effects of the war upon our student population, the University had protested to the Southern Conference that the rule banning freshmen from varsity competition no longer made sense, that we needed our freshmen just to field a team. As a result, the rule was rescinded for the duration of the war.

Still, athletic conditions were terrible in 1943. For a while it looked as though we would not be able to assemble a football squad even with freshmen. In fact, we didn't even have a coach. Rex Enright had enlisted in the Navy and was coaching down at Georgia Pre-Flight.

But then at the last moment our Naval V-12 program (a sort of Naval ROTC) saved the day. Students from all over America were enrolled in this Naval officers training program, and now they were being assigned to USC for their training. Among them were several outstanding athletes who had starred at other institutions before coming here. In early '43 the War Department gave them permission to play football for Carolina, so it was with a combination of seventeen-year-old freshmen,

V-12s, and 4-Fs that we finally put together the '43 squad. Even then, because of frequent transfers, we never knew from one week to the next who our starting lineup would be.

Ironically, under the direction of volunteer coach Lt. James P. Moran, we ended up with one of our best records in years. We lost only to a powerful service team, the 176th Infantry and to a very strong team from UNC. We beat Newberry, Presbyterian, the Charleston Coast Guard, and Orange Bowl-bound Wake Forest.

In fact, we even beat Clemson this year, though it should be noted that the Tigers fielded one of their poorest teams in history. They had no Naval V-12 program, and their Army trainees were not allowed to play football, so the team was entirely composed of 4-Fs and freshmen.

In the end, it was USC 33, Clemson 6, but the game was even more lopsided than the score. Phil Cantore gained 103 yards rushing on the day for the Gamecocks, which was 102 more than the entire Tiger team. Incredibly, Clemson made zero yards passing and only one yard rushing for the

Cary Cox

THE WORLD WAR II YEARS

game—their worst-ever offensive performance, and, conversely, USC's best-ever defensive performance.

But the real highlight of the Clemson game—and of our '43 season—was the story of our center, Cary Cox. Cary Cox has the supreme distinction of being the only man since the beginning of time to have served as a game captain for the Carolina Gamecocks and team captian for the Clemson Tigers.

Only something as tumultuous as World War II could have made it happen, but Cox shrugs it off as "really no big deal." Hoping to avoid the draft until he finished college, Cox made the mistake of signing up for the Naval V-12 program. He was promptly called up in the summer of '43 and assigned to the University of South Carolina for training. He was also ordered to report

for football practice.

He did well enough to become captain for the Clemson game, but then the week before Big Thursday, the thought of playing against his old teammates placed him in a moral dilemma. When he explained the situation to his V-12 commander, he was told, "Cox, I can't promise you'll get your commission if you play Thursday, but I can damn well promise that you won't get it if you don't play."

"It's amazing what a little counseling can do to assuage a troubled conscience," Cox explains, then continues: "So then I called Coach Howard and told him I felt bad about playing against Clemson. But ol' Coach just told me to do what I had to do: go out there and play my heart out."

At one point in the game, Carolina executed a line shift which placed the center

Phil Cantore wriggling free from hapless Tiger defender in 1943.

at end and thus eligible to receive a pass—which Cox did for a 28-yard reception. When the play was over and he was disentangling himself from the pile, he felt someone give him a swift kick in the seat of the pants. He jumped to his feet to face his assailant. It was Coach Howard.

"Can you believe he ran out on the field in front of 20,000 people and did that? Then he yelled, 'Son, I told you to play your heart out, but I didn't say nothing about catching no passes.'"

Cox, who still cherishes the game ball used that day, completed the war as captain of a landing craft in the Pacific, then returned to Clemson in 1946. He became a sports immortal when he became captain of the 1947 Clemson Tigers.

1944 – 1945

In 1944 we had essentially a new team—what with most of the '43 players now fighting in Europe or the Pacific—and a new head coach, William "Doc" Newton.

Our season was not as bad as our 3-4-2 record would indicate. We beat Newberry, UNC, and Presbyterian, while tying Miami and the Charleston Coast Guard. And three of our losses—to Rex Enright's Georgia Pre-Flight, Clemson, and Wake Forest—were by one touchdown or less. Our only real beating came at the hands of Duke, 34-7.

We then headed into the 1945 season, our first since the war ended in August of that year, with yet another new coach, Johnnie McMillan, our third in as many years. McMillan had been an outstanding player for USC in 1938, then coached at Sumter High. He came to us in '45 as the youngest head coach in America.

With the war over at last and our young men returning home, our football fortunes began to rise once more. Bobby Giles, a great running back, returned in midseason

as a welcome addition to our team, and we also had Bryant Meeks, an All-Southern center, who could have played for anybody in the country. But individual players and records aside, 1945 takes its hallowed place in the annals of Gamecock football as the first year we were invited to a bowl game.

We opened the '45 campaign inauspiciously with a thrashing at the hands of the '44 Sugar Bowl champion Duke, but the next week, led by fleet halfback Dutch Brembs' twenty-two points, we got into the win column with a 40-0 rout of Presbyterian. Then Brembs scored fourteen more the following Saturday in a 20-6 win over the Camp Blanding Gunners.

It turned out that we didn't win another game all year, but that really isn't as bad as it sounds. We managed three ties—against Clemson (0-0), Miami (13-13), and a strong Wake Forest team (13-13). Meanwhile, our only two other losses were to Alabama and Maryland.

It was at this point, after finishing with a 2-3-3 record, that a wonderful story began to unfold. On December 2 *The State* reported that a new bowl game was in the works. It would be played annually in Columbia's Municipal Stadium, would be called the Tobacco Bowl, and would feature the state champion of South Carolina versus an opponent from out of state.

But, coincidentally, city officials in Jacksonville, Florida, were toying with the same idea. And thanks to the influence of Rex Enright (now athletic director at Jacksonville Naval Air Station), those good people extended to the Gamecocks an invitation to play in the inaugural Gator Bowl (though it was as yet unnamed) against the Deacons of Wake Forest. After some debate, our boys voted to ignore the Tobacco Bowl in favor of a free trip to Florida, especially since the invitation—not just a proposal—was in hand.

Following the Gamecocks' decision, state

In 1944, for the first time ever, the rain came on Big Thursday.

and city officials found themselves in a dilemma—all dressed up with no place to go. They considered inviting Clemson to play but discarded the idea when no opponent could be found to face the Tigers on such short notice. Finally they announced that the first Tobacco Bowl would be postponed for a year. That postponement is now in its forty-fifth year.

As for the bowl game in Jacksonville, Coach McMillan was facing a problem of strategy. We had already faced Wake Forest (under legendary Peahead Walker) earlier in the season and found their forward wall to be impenetrable. As McMillan put it, "We can't do much moving against that Wake Forest line. We found out last time the only way we could go against them is to go over them, and that's what we'll try to do again."

It worked for a while. With our passing attack in gear, Bobby Giles scored to give us a 7-6 lead at halftime. Unfortunately, Wake Forest stormed back with twenty second-half points to win the game, 26-14.

Despite the unspectacular record for '45, we placed five men on the All-State team: Dutch Brembs, Phil Ball, George McDonald, Bobby Giles, and Bryant Meeks. Team captain Meeks also made the All-Southern team.

The 1945 season brought to a close what has come to be called the early era of Gamecock football. Our overall record to date was 197-192-28, a winning record if ever there was one!

13

1946 – 1951

Bogus Tickets, the Bishop and the Cadillac

Nineteen forty-six saw a return to normalcy in our football program. Coach Enright had returned after three years in the Navy, and we had a fine nucleus of players returning from our bowl team of '45. Bobby Giles at halfback, Dom Fusci at tackle, and Bryant Meeks at center were considered three of the finest players in the Southern Conference. In addition, we had a young freshman, Harold "Bo" Hagan, who was reputed to be one of the best T-formation quarterbacks in the South.

We took Newberry 21-0 in the opener, a game in which Bo Hagan ran fifty-eight yards for a touchdown the first time he ever touched the ball. Then we looked a lot like "the same old Gamecocks" as we lost a really tough one to Alabama and their great quarterback Harry Gilmer (14-6). We bounced back with gratifying wins over Furman, 14-7, The Citadel, 19-7, and Maryland, 21-17, but then lost the final two games of the season, to Duke and Wake Forest.

But the game we remember most from that '46 season was the big postwar shootout with the Clemson Tigers. Not only was this game sold out well in advance, but it was discovered just hours prior to kickoff that an additional 10,000 tickets had been counterfeited and sold by a shady printing outfit in Pennsylvania to unsuspecting fans everywhere.

By game time parking lots at Municipal Stadium were overflowing. Some 35,000 ticket-holding fans swarmed around a stadium that had just been enlarged to hold 26,000, and by now the word was out some tickets were real, some phony. But no one could tell which was which. The word was also out that the ticket-takers working the gates were admitting fans on a first-come, first-served basis. Frantic, fans started pushing and shoving. Fist fights broke out. But at last the stadium was full and the gates closed.

The bogus ticket scandal of 1946 had the sidelines overflowing for the USC – Clemson game.

It was at that point that one of the darndest spectacles in the long history of Carolina football took place. Ten thousand enraged ticket-holders rushed the gates, battering them to the ground, then swarmed into the stadium like killer bees.

Clemson's coach Frank Howard later recalled:

I'd look around for a substitute and there'd be fifty people between me and my bench. I believe something like 10,000 people crashed in that day. Most of the people on ground level just sat around talking to old friends because they couldn't see a thing out on the field. Two of these hawkers came up to me and tried to sell me their wares during the game. I heard one fellow say when he was leaving the game, 'That was the best game I never saw'!

Jimmy Byrnes, Secretary of State under Truman, would later recall that he gave up his box seat when fans came piling in. He made his way down to the field, he says, got down on his hands and knees, then watched the game from between the legs of Carolina players on the sideline.

But it was a great game. With only a minute left in the first quarter, and the score knotted at 0-0, Bobby Giles dashed sixty-two yards for a Carolina touchdown and we took the lead at 6-0. Bobby Gage, Clemson's All-American tailback, led them on two impressive drives in the second quarter, but we held both times.

Then it was Bo Hagan's turn. He completed pass after pass to Bobby O'Harra, Earl Dunham, Pat Thrash, and Doug Hinson on a 75-yard march. Red Harrison bullied his way over from the one, and our lead went to 12-0. But with only seconds remaining before the half, Bobby Gage hit Henry Walker for twenty-four yards, then Chip Clark for thirty-six and a Clemson score. We went to the sidelines holding a 12-7 lead.

At that point a Clemson Cadet ran out on the football field and wrung a rooster's neck. A riot ensued, and footballers from both schools stopped what they were doing to watch the most vicious fighting of the day unfold before their startled eyes. It took fifty state police fifteen minutes to restore order. To open the third quarter, Bobby Gage ran and passed the Tigers down to our one, from where Gerald Leverman pushed it over, and Clemson went ahead 14-12. But in the fourth quarter, behind the running of Whitey Jones, Red Harrison, and Earl Dunham, and the passing of Bo Hagan and Droopy Atwell, we finally broke through and took a 19-14 lead. On the next very series, Red Wilson took it over from the Clemson seven, and we won the game, 26-14.

Who could imagine a better way to kick off the modern era than to be 1-0 against the Clemson Tigers!

1947

The year 1947 marked the arrival in our backfield of a freshman sensation from Mullins, South Carolina, named Bishop Strickland, or simply The Bishop, as he soon came to be called.

After scoring 165 points (then a state record) his senior year at Mullins High, Strickland immediately won a starting position with the Gamecocks, and would start in thirty-nine consecutive games over the next four years.

He joined an outstanding veteran team in '47. At one halfback was Red Harrison, the 1946 recipient of the Jacobs Blocking Trophy and an All-Southern selection. At the other half was Ed Pasky, and at fullback was the great Bobby Giles. At quarterback were James "Droopy" Atwell and Bo Hagan, who, everyone agreed, could have been one of the finest quarterbacks in the country had it not been for a bad knee. Our line featured

Bishop Strickland

such great returnees as team captain Neil Allen, Al Faress, Roger Wilson, Bobby O'Harra, Phil Alexander, and Brick Bradford.

We opened with an easy 27-6 win over Newberry, but then came losses to Ole Miss and Maryland. We were far from discouraged, though. Indeed, it would be roughly a year before we would lose again. The streak began on Homecoming Day when we played our old nemesis Furman. This time, led by the smashing runs of Ernie Lawhorne, we routed them, 26-8.

Next came Clemson on Big Thursday,

Fullback Harry DeLoache rambles for yardage against The Citadel in '47.

led by their great wingback Ray Mathews and All-America tailback Bobby Gage. But the Tigers were still a year away from their undefeated team of '48, and this game was rated a tossup.

It proved to be just that. Eight minutes into the game, The Bishop took a pitchout from Droopy Atwell and dashed thirty-nine yards around left end for a touchdown. But on the next series Ray Mathews took the ball sixty-six yards to close the gap to 7-6.

As the quarter drew to a close, we were facing fourth and six at the Clemson nineteen. Strickland took a hand-off, started wide, then cut back inside and rammed it down to the two. From there Atwell took it over to widen our lead to 14-6. Clemson came right back again to score just before halftime, and we went to the sidelines nursing a 14-12 lead.

After a scoreless third quarter, Bobby Giles intercepted a Gage pass and returned it to the Clemson one, then took it over on the next play for a 21-12 lead. Clemson scored again, but it was too little too late, and we earned our third consecutive win over the Tigers, 21-19.

We closed out the season in memorable fashion. We shut out Miami and The Citadel, then earned a 0-0 tie against a Duke team that was favored by thirty points. In the finale, we whipped tough Wake Forest, 6-0, on the strength of a 30-yard TD dash by The Bishop.

Many fans called the '47 edition of the Gamecocks the best ever. We not only enjoyed a fine 6-2-1 record, but we held our last four opponents scoreless.

1948

Our optimism as we faced the 1948 season was greatly enhanced when it was

Freshman Steve Wadiak in '48 (not yet wearing his famous number 37).

Steve was a pro when he came down here. The first time we practiced, somebody knocked him down and he jumped back up and ran for a touchdown. That was legal in pro ball back then but not in college. Coach Enright had to step in real fast and stop him from doing things like that."

Soon Wadiak's gliding style and amazing acceleration earned him the descriptive appellation "Wadiak the Cadillac," a nickname USC fans latched onto wholeheartedly. With The Bishop at the other half, USC had one of the most feared backfield duos in the South. With the other great veterans from our '47 team who were back for another year, it looked like '48 might be the big year we'd been waiting for. Unfortunately, such was not the case. We opened with wins over Newberry and Furman. Then came a loss to Tulane, 14-0, and it was time to get ready for Big Thursday. In 1948 the Tigers fielded one of their greatest teams ever. Led by All-American Bobby Gage, they ran undefeated through ten regular-season opponents, then upset Missouri, 24-23 in the Gator Bowl. Still, we didn't exactly play dead. The first time he touched the ball, Wadiak rambled forty-three yards to the Clemson twenty-five. Two plays later Bo Hagan rifled a pass to Red Wilson in the end zone, and we took a 7-0 lead. That's the way the half ended.

Carol Cox scored for the Tigers on the last play of the third quarter, but a missed extra point kept us a point ahead. Then, on the ensuing kickoff, Wadiak took off on a beautiful run down to the Clemson seventeen, and our lead was looking better and better. Strickland rambled thirteen yards down to the Clemson four, but on the next play Wadiak fumbled a pitchout, and the Tigers recovered for a crucial turnover.

Clemson finally beat us when, just before the final whistle, Phil Prince blocked a Hagan punt and Oscar Thompson scooped the ball up and took it for a touchdown.

revealed that Coach Enright had landed a player who was potentially the greatest running back in America—Steve Wadiak, a twenty-year-old who had been dazzling fans in a semi-pro league in the Chicago area with his incredible speed and quickness.

Bill Milner, a former USC lineman now playing for the Chicago Bears, had watched Wadiak play and persuaded him to visit the Carolina campus. Coach Enright was impressed with Wadiak's performance during a practice drill conducted especially for him and quickly offered him a scholarship. In a recent interview, backfield mate Bishop Strickland recalled his association with Wadiak: "Well, we didn't advertise it, but

Demoralized, we went on to lose to both West Virginia and Maryland before recovering to beat a highly ranked Tulsa team, 27-7. In the finale we were back down, losing badly to Wake Forest, 38-0.

So we finished what should have been an excellent year with a truly disappointing 3-5 record. Still, we were cheered that Red Wilson and Bishop Strickland were named to the All-State team. And Steve Wadiak averaged 8.2 yards per carry in 1948, still number one in the the USC record book.

1949

Strickland and Wadiak were back in the saddle again in '49, joining a truly talented team. Bo Hagan returned for his senior season at quarterback, along with John Boyle, a tremendous passer up from the freshman team, and Ed Pasky. Also in the backfield were Bill Rutledge, Ed Jackson, Harry DeLoache, and Ashley Phillips. Also there were two other new stars in our backfield in '49: James "Blackie" Kincaid and Chuck Prezioso.

At ends we had Dick Fagan, Red Wilson (four times All-State), Cecil Woolbright, Jim Pinkerton, and Harry Bryson; at tackle Bob Dockery and Lamar Collie; at guard Roy Skinner, Vince Gargano, and Dave Sparks.

Given our talent, it was all the more distressing to open the season with three straight losses. On September 24, for the first time in history, our boys boarded a DC-3 for a flight to Waco, Texas. No more trains for us. But it really didn't matter as we took it on the chin from Baylor, 20-6, then followed with losses to Furman and UNC.

On Big Thursday, Clemson jumped off to a quick 13-0 lead, but that's when Bo Hagan, so hobbled by shattered knees that doctors said he would never play again, limped onto the field. From then on, led by

Bo Hagan, who, with two bad knees, came off the bench to lead the comeback win over Clemson in '49.

Hagan's passes, and Wadiak's and Strickland's amazing runs, we came back and stunned the Tigers 27-13.

This was also the day our "Phantom Tackler" made his debut. During substitutions, one of our players who left the field was Ed Dew, our giant left guard. Once he arrived on the sideline, however, he noted that we had only ten men on the field and that his place had not been filled. Just as he frantically dashed back onto the field, Clemson's Jackie Calvert took off on an end sweep. Calvert had taken only about three steps when Dew nabbed him from behind and threw him for a five yard loss. The referees failed to see Dew race in from the sidelines to make the tackle, and the play

Ed Pasky on his then-record 101-yard interception return for a touchdown against Wake Forest in 1949.

stood as a five-yard sack for Ed Dew.

After a loss to Maryland the next week, we traveled to Milwaukee and spoiled Marquette's homecoming game, in a fine defensive struggle, by a score of 6-3.

Then, after losses to Miami and Georgia Tech, we finished the year on a winning note, taking Wake Forest, 27-20, and The Citadel, 42-0. By the way, Bayard Pickett intercepted four passes in the Citadel game, an all-time USC record.

Recapitulating the high points of this disapointing 4-6 season, Ed Pasky had 159 yards in pass interception return yardage for an all-time record at USC. Bo Hagan was named All-State, All-Southern, and Honorable Mention All-American. Bishop Strickland, Steve Wadiak, and Red Wilson were All-State and All-Southern. Dave Sparks was named All-State.

1950

Despite the high expectations of Gamecock fans, 1950 proved to be another frustrating season for Carolina. Bishop Strickland, now a senior, and Steve Wadiak, a junior, were the best in the South, and they were joined by a company of Carolina players who could have made anybody's team. Yet we could never seem to win more than three or four games a year.

With Dave Sparks as team captain, and with Ed Pasky and Dick Balka at quarterback, we headed into our opener—a shootout against highly touted Duke. We were outgunned, 14-0. But we bounced back the next week with an "Enright upset," beating a fine Georgia Tech team, 7-0, on a Wadiak touchdown late in the game. Our Don Earley was voted Southern Conference Lineman of the Week for his stellar play against the Jackets.

Against Furman the next week, The Bishop scored on a 36-yard dash, and The

Cadillac motored for a 34-yarder to lead USC to a 21-6 win. So we were 2-1 going into Big Thursday, but Clemson was undefeated and unscored on as game day approached.

The first time he touched the ball that day, Wadiak rambled from our eleven all the way to the Clemson twenty-three, where speedy tackle Bob Hudson finally brought him down. The Bishop took it to the five, and Wadiak ran it across for a surprising 7-0 lead. But only a minute before the half, a Matthews-to-Hair pass tied the game at 7-all.

We jumped back in front in the third quarter when Wadiak, on the most sensational play of the day, broke through two tacklers at the line of scrimmage and dashed seventy-seven yards for the score. In the fourth quarter the Tigers again roared back to tie the score, but Wadiak still wasn't through. On the next series he took a pitchout and raced forty-four yards to the Clemson twenty-two. Unfortunately, our subsequent field goal attempt sailed wide, and the game ended in a 14-14 tie.

Wadiak rushed for 256 yards that day, an average of 13.5 yards per carry. Both these figures represented new Southern Conference single-game records and helped Steve win Southern Conference Player of the Year honors.

In our win against George Washington the next week, Wadiak gained another 181 yards, while Strickland tacked on 114. Wadiak, by the way, had a 96-yard TD run from scrimmage, still a USC record. After a tie with Marquette the next week, our record stood at 3-1-2, and hope was high for a winning season.

But then we were upset by The Citadel, the "breather" on our schedule, and that game was followed by losses to both UNC and Wake Forest. Our hopes were down the drain, and, despite our all-star lineup, we ended our season at 3-4-2.

We were nonetheless well represented on the All-State team by Strickland,

Wadiak finds the hole in USC's big win against Georgia Tech.

Wadiak, Larry Smith, Lamar Collie, Don Earley, and Dave Sparks. In addition to Wadiak being named Southern Conference Player of the Year, Strickland and Sparks were selected to play in the North-South All-Star game.

Despite being somewhat overshadowed by Wadiak, Bishop Strickland finished his career with 1,965 yards on 365 carries for a 5.2 yards-per-carry average. He's still considered one of the top ten running backs in USC history.

1951

It was bound to be a remarkable season. Senior Steve Wadiak was backed up by a veritable Carolina all-star team: Larry Smith, Harry Jabbusch, Billy Stephens, Paul Stephens, Don Earley, Vince Gargano, Bobby Drawdy, John "Lip" LaTorre, Clyde Bennett, Leon Cunningham, Chuck Prezioso, Johnny Gramling, Dick Balka, Hootie Johnson, Gene Wilson, Fred Duckett, and Bob Kahle. As for Wadiak, he had set a new Southern Conference record in 1950 with 998 yards rushing. He was averaging almost six yards per carry during his three years so far, despite the fact that teams had learned to stack their defenses against him.

However, as the season approached, loud rumblings of discontent could be heard throughout the state over Enright's failure to produce a really great season. In his ten years at the helm, his won-loss record stood at 38-47-7, including a 4-5-1 record against Clemson. Still, Enright would remain as head coach through the 1955 season.

Indeed, after USC was thrashed by Duke in the season opener (and Wadiak held to just twenty-six yards), Enright was blasted in *The State* by sports editor Jake Penland. But Penland, along with disgruntled fans, was somewhat appeased when USC ran off

two successive victories over Furman and The Citadel. Johnny Gramling was coming into his own as a passer, while Chuck Prezioso was complementing Wadiak as a running back. The next week, however, UNC held Wadiak to just twenty-two yards and beat us 21-6.

Then came Big Thursday, and as usual the Tigers entered the game as heavy favorites. But the oddsmakers reckoned without Billy Stephens, a small, third-string quarterback who, because of a series of injuries, suddenly found himself starting at safety for the Gamecocks that day. They could not foresee that late in the first quarter, little Stephens would take a Clemson punt on the twenty-six, juke a couple of burly Tiger defenders, and streak seventy-six yards for a touchdown. Dick Balka also scored before the half, and we went to the sidelines leading 14-0.

In the fourth quarter, with USC still nursing its 14-0 lead, Harry Jabbusch intercepted a Billy Hair pass and ran it back for what proved to be the final score of the game. The Gamecocks had prevailed, 20-0, and Billy Stephens was named MVP. Clemson now had not beaten us since 1948, but this was the first time we had held the Tigers scoreless since 1911.

Consistently inconsistent, we lost to George Washington the next week, clobbered West Virginia the following Saturday, then lost a close one to Virginia, 28-27, and ended the season with a win over Wake Forest, 21-0. In his last outing as a Gamecock, "Wadiak the Cadillac" was the leading rusher on the field and scored two touchdowns.

Wadiak was drafted by the Pittsburgh Steelers and doubtlessly would have made a great pro running back. But he had fallen in love with South Carolina and South Carolina with him. Upon graduation, he said, "I'm going back to Chicago to see my parents, and then I'm coming back to South

Hootie Johnson plows into the Ploughboy line on Big Thursday, 1951.

Carolina to spend the next fifty years."

But he would never make it to graduation day. He was killed in an automobile accident on March 10, when he and some friends were apparently returning from a trip to Augusta. He was so beloved among sports fans in South Carolina that grown men wept openly at his funeral.

Wadiak rushed for 2,878 yards during his career at Carolina, still third all-time behind only George Rogers and Harold Green.

14

1952 – 1955

THE WANING OF THE ENRIGHT ERA

We lost some great players in 1951, but the '52 roster offered plenty of grounds for optimism. In the backfield we had Johnny Gramling, Dick Balka, Bill Wohrman, Hootie Johnson, Bobby Drawdy, Bob Korn, and Gene Wilson. Linemen included Frank "Friendly Bear" Mincevich, Don Earley, Jess Berry, Leon Cunningham, Fred Duckett, Clyde Bennett, and co-captains Walt Shea and Lip LaTorre.

A curious new face on the field was that of Buddy Morrell, who stood five-seven and weighed 155. Enright gave him a one-semester scholarship (as a favor to his high school coach, Skimp Harrison, a former USC player), but still feared Buddy would be killed were he to take the field with all those big guys.

In the opening game, against lightweight Wofford, Enright put Morrell in just to see what would happen. What happened was that Buddy carried the ball three times for eighty-three yards in USC's 33-0 win. By year's end, Morrell would rush fifty-five times for 264 yards; he was then given a four-year scholarship.

After our opening win, we traveled to West Point and lost to a favored Army team, 28-7. Johnny Gramling's TD pass to Clyde Bennett was the only bright spot in an otherwise dismal afternoon. We rebounded against Furman with a big 27-7 win, but then bowed to a tough Duke team, 33-7.

Now it was time to face the Tigers on Big Thursday. Clemson had been to the Orange Bowl in '50 and to the Gator Bowl in '51, but it was a relatively new, inexperienced eleven that arrived in Columbia for this year's edition. Needless to say, though, Clemson would be no pushover.

Clemson, by the way, had broken Southern conference rules by accepting a bid to the Gator Bowl in '51, and, as a result,

Gene Wilson snares a Johnny Gramling pass for the only score in the '52 Clemson game.

Coach Enright gets a ride from Lip LaTorre and Leon Cunningham after USC's comeback win against Virginia.

they were prohibited from playing any Southern Conference teams in '52, including USC. Consequently, our state legislature stepped up and passed a law requiring Clemson and South Carolina to play each other every year. Since state law superseded conference rules, we held our game as usual.

We won the toss, and standing in safety for us, nervously awaiting the kickoff, was a face no one had seen before. It was little Carl Brazell, a last-minute addition to Carolina's starting team. Brazell fielded the ball on our ten and ran it back to the thirty-four, not bad for a young man of seventeen who had been given a varsity number only four days earlier.

After a Clemson series that went nowhere, USC drove for what would prove the only score of the game. It came on a short pass from Gramling to Gene Wilson, who pulled it down in the end zone. The final score was 6-0, and we remained unbeaten against the Tigers since 1948. Leon Cunningham was named MVP of the game for his outstanding defensive play.

One of our all-time great wins came the very next week against Virginia in Norfolk. With his team down 14-0 and only four minutes to play, Enright substituted Dick Balka for badly battered Gramling. After a Gayle Kerr interception of a Cavalier pass, Balka completed a desperation fourth-down pass to keep the Gamecocks alive. Three plays later, Balka found Clyde Bennett in the end zone to cut the lead in half.

The Cavaliers fumbled the ensuing kickoff, and a few seconds later freshman Mike Caskey pounded over for the tying score. Immediately thereafter, with Virginia in possession at their six, Gene Witt pulverized the Cavalier quarterback and caused a fumble. Bob King pounced on the ball in the end zone, and the Gamecocks had their third touchdown in under two minutes—surely the most spectacular comeback win in USC history.

Still euphoric, we throttled The Citadel the next week, 35-0, with Gramling throwing three TD passes in the first half. The win made us 5-2 on the season with three games to play. Was this going to be the big year?

Nope. We dropped all three—to UNC, West Virginia, and Wake Forest—and wound up at 5-5 for the year. Enright's record overall stood at 48-56-7, but he was now 6-4-1 against Clemson. Perhaps that was more important.

Despite our disappointing record, we had seven All-State players in '52, and a few of our boys received higher awards. Leon Cunningham was Player of the Year in South Carolina and named to the All-Southern team. Don Earley, Johnny Gramling, John LaTorre, and Norris Mullis were also All-Southern selections, and Norris Mullis made second team All-America.

1953

Nineteen fifty-three saw the formation of the Atlantic Coast Conference, motivated largely because of the Southern Conference's stringent restrictions on participation in post-season bowl games. The original members of the new conference were Maryland, UNC, NC State, Duke, Wake Forest, Clemson, and South Carolina. The new year also brought to Coach Enright the best season he would have at Carolina. After an opening loss to Duke in our first-ever ACC game, we reeled off wins over The Citadel, Virginia, Furman, and Clemson—our third straight victory over the Tigers.

On Big Thursday, we entered the game at full strength for the first time in several years, and our backfield was particularly strong: Johnny Gramling at quarterback, Gene Wilson and Carl Brazell at half, and the tremendous blocker Bill Wohrman at fullback.

Gene Wilson's long punt return against the Tigers was nullified by a clipping penalty.

Quarterback Johnny Gramling on a keeper against number-one ranked Maryland. Inset is Joe Silas.

But Clemson, needless to say, would prove no patsy. The only score of the first half came when quarterback Gramling uncorked a beautiful 45-yard pass to Clyde Bennett, and the Gamecocks took a 7-0 lead to the locker room.

In the third quarter, reserve quarterback Harold Lewis lofted a 21-yard pass to Joe Silas in the corner of the end zone to give us a 14-0 lead. Clemson managed to score late in the game, but we held on for a 14-7 win. We lost the following week to Jim Tatum's Maryland team (which went on to win the national championship that year), but then marched over UNC, squeezed by Sugar Bowl-bound West Virginia, and walloped Wofford. Had we beaten Wake Forest in the finale, we would have matched the 8-2 mark of our great 1903 team, but the Deacons nipped us 19-13. Still our 7-3 season constituted our best record since Branch Bocock's 1925 squad posted the same numbers.

Johnny Gramling concluded his USC career in record-setting style. His 1,045 yards passing was the most ever in a single season for a Gamecock; and his 2,007 yards for the '51-'53 seasons set a new record for career passing.

His favorite target, Clyde Bennett, set a new record for most passes caught in a season (34), most in a career (64), and most receiving yardage in a season (502).

1954

Graduation took Gramling and Bennett from us, but we still fielded a tough, veteran team in 1954. Sophomore Mackie Prickett was the new quarterback, but he was supported by Carl Brazell and Mike Caskey at halfback and workhorse Bill Wohrman at full. The line featured Joe Silas and Spec Granger at end, Harry Lovell and Sam

Harold Lewis knocks a pass away from the great Bob Kyasky in USC's big upset of Army.

THE WANING OF THE ENRIGHT ERA

DeLuca at tackle, Frank Mincevich and Dick Covington at guard, and Leon Cunningham at center—a strong front wall if ever we had one.

We opened at West Point's Michie Stadium against an Army team that, as usual, was considered the cream of Eastern football. The Black Knights of the Hudson were favored over our poor Birds by at least three touchdowns. But before this day was over, we would achieve one of our great all-time wins, upsetting Army 34-20. Behind superior blocking from the entire line, and especially from fullback Wohrman, Prickett, Brazell, and Caskey ran wild all day, amassing 472 total yards.

The win catapulted Carolina into the limelight with a number-15 national ranking in the Associated Press the next week. Needless to say, that was more prosperity than we could handle, and we immediately lost to West Virginia, 26-6. Our other losses that year came at the hands of Maryland, UNC, and Duke.

But in addition to Army, we had wins in '54 over Furman, Virginia, Wake Forest, and The Citadel. Most important of all, we also beat Clemson for the fourth consecutive year, our longest-ever win streak over the Tigers.

Fans still remember the '54 game as one of the most exciting ever between the two ancient rivals. Clemson drew first blood with a safety in the second period, but Mackie Prickett led us on a long drive that culminated when he took it over from the two. Then, with only a minute left in the half, Brazell took a pitchout at midfield and streaked all the way to the 3-yard line. Prickett again took it over, and we had staked ourselves to a 13-2 halftime lead.

After a scoreless third period, Clemson's Joel Wells lofted a halfback pass to Joe

Frank "the Friendly Bear" Mincevich, Gamecock All-American in 1954.

Pagliei, who caught it on the 45 and raced unmolested for a touchdown. With the score now 13-8, Tiger fans were showing their fangs, but the Gamecocks held on until time expired. It had now been six years since we had lost to the Tigers.

After this 6-4 campaign, several of our players earned post-season honors beyond the All-State level. Frank Mincevich was named to Football Writers of America's All-America team; Leon Cunningham was All-ACC and an AP third team All-American; Mackie Prickett was the Player of the Year in South Carolina and an NEA honorable mention All-American; and Bill Wohrman won the ACC Jacobs Blocking Trophy.

Gamecock great Mike Caskey running into heavy traffic against Wofford.

THE WANING OF THE ENRIGHT ERA

1955

On paper at least, we returned a fine team in 1955, and led by our fireplug running backs, Brazell and Caskey, we opened with a solid 26-7 win over Wofford. But the schedule took a turn for the tougher, and we lost in successive weeks to Wake Forest and Navy. Fans couldn't help wondering if three winning seasons in a row was too much to hope for.

We managed to shut out Furman, 19-0, the next week, and then it was time for what had become our annual Tiger-taming. We were 5-0-1 against Clemson over the past six seasons, but the Tigers were declaring that enough was enough.

Sure enough, early in the game Clemson scored on a 55-yard pass from Charlie Bussey to Willie Smith, and just moments later Joe Pagliei took it over from the three to stake Clemson to a 14-0 lead. Joel Wells ran all over us in the third quarter, finally scoring to up the lead to 21-0, and it looked like a rout might be on.

But Carolina staged a rally. Second-teamers Bobby Bunch and Carroll McClain keyed a drive that culminated in a 15-yard TD dash by McClain in the third quarter; then Eddie Field scored in the fourth quarter to cut the lead to 21-14. But the final touchdown was scored by the wrong team, and Clemson came away with a 28-14 victory to break its long drought.

The loss to Clemson sent us reeling to three straight subsequent defeats—to Maryland, UNC, and Duke—though we managed to save some face by beating Virginia in the final game of the season. To our immense relief, Brazell returned a Cavalier punt ninety-five yards for the winning score in that game.

Carl Brazell finished his career with a four-year average of 5.7 yards per carry, still tops in the Carolina record book. His cohort Mike Caskey averaged a phenomenal 6.7 yards per carry in '54 (still second only to Steve Wadiak's 8.2 average in 1948), and compiled a career average of 5.5 yards per carry, fifth-best in Gamecock history.

Even before this disappointing 3-6 season, Rex Enright had indicated that 1955 would be his last as USC's head coach, and his resignation became official at the end of the season. Enright, in whose honor our athletic center is named, would remain as athletic director until his death in 1960. With a career mark of 64-69-7, he holds the distinction of being both our winningest and losingest coach in history.

All-time great Carl Brazell, whose career average of 5.7 yards per rushing attempt is still tops in the USC record book.

15

1956 – 1960

Warren Giese and the Ground Game

Rex Enright chose as his successor a young man named Warren Giese, who had been the main assistant to Maryland's highly successful Jim Tatum. Giese enjoyed a reputation as a stern disciplinarian and a man with an eye for detail. He believed in control football, emphasizing the ground game and resorting to the forward pass only in dire emergencies. It was during Giese's tenure as head coach that the term "three yards and a cloud of dust" came into vogue at the university. It must be noted, though, that during his five years at USC, the Gamecocks suffered but one losing season.

Our opening game against Wofford was not the stuff of which inspirational songs are written, however. We finally pulled away in the second half to win, 26-13, but our fans left the stadium wondering how we would fare against the likes of Duke, Miami, Clemson, and Maryland.

We would find out shortly, as Duke came to town the next week, led by the great

Sonny Jurgensen. Duke had never lost an ACC game and didn't plan to start now, but the 30,000 fans jammed into Carolina Stadium were treated to a first. Late in the second quarter King Dixon, a youngster from Laurens, would cross the Duke goal line to give us a 7-0 lead, one we would preserve until the final gun sounded.

We did lose to Miami the following week, 14-6, but quickly bounced back to take the Tarheels of UNC, 14-0. Then, against Virginia, future great Alex Hawkins scored his first two touchdowns as a Gamecock to stake us to a 13-0 halftime lead. Late in the game, as we held an edgy 20-13 lead, fans were amazed when our great passer, Mackie Prickett, was actually allowed to throw a pass. It was good for another score and we prevailed, 27-13. The win gave us a 4-1 record going into the Clemson game, and it was speculated that the Clemson-USC winner would represent the ACC in the Orange Bowl.

Julius Derrick about to pull in the Mackie Prickett pass that would sew up the win against Virginia.

If statistics never lie, we beat Clemson that day. We had seventeen first downs to their eleven; ninety-four yards passing to their zero; and they lost two fumbles. Also, we thought we'd tied the game late when Don Johnson apparently bolted into the end zone for a score. But a split second before he crossed the goal line, the ball squirted from his hands and into the arms of Clemson's Charlie Bussey. That's the way the day went, and Clemson won, 7-0.

The following week, in a game in which we gained twenty-four yards passing, we squeezed past stubborn Furman, 13-6. Then, after a tough loss to NC State (and another big twenty-plus yards through the air), we finished with two straight shutouts, 13-0 over both Maryland and Wake Forest.

So in Coach Giese's first year we finished with a very respectable 7-3 record. Our controlled offense scored only 126 points, but our defense, the best in the ACC, allowed only sixty-seven.

Co-captains Mackie Prickett and Buddy Frick would be lost from this team, but in King Dixon and Alex Hawkins we had discovered another great running duo, one that in time would rival the best we'd ever had at USC.

1957

Expectations were high for the '57 season. Halfbacks Carroll McClain and Frank Destino could have been starters for almost any team in the South, but as the year got under way, they found themselves playing backup to an even better tandem of King Dixon and Alex Hawkins. And with a strong line anchored by co-captains Nelson Weston and Julius Derrick, there seemed no reason not to improve on last year's 7-3 mark.

Unfortunately, a Duke team hungry for revenge was the first game on the schedule. We played them tough for a half, but Bob

One of the great running back tandems in Gamecock history: Alex Hawkins and King Dixon.

Brodhead and his squad finally prevailed, 26-14. We got into the win column the next week, however, with a 26-0 thumping of Wofford, and so were in a better frame of mind to face national power Texas, in Texas, perhaps the biggest game on the '57 schedule. It proved to be one of USC's all-time great upset wins.

As the whistle blew to start play, 40,000 Longhorn fans were stunned to watch King Dixon take the kickoff and race ninety-eight yards for a touchdown. But Texas overpowered us from that point on and held a 21-7 lead as the third period came to a close. Instead of quitting, though, Carolina commenced on a long drive that ended with Hawkins scoring to cut the lead. Four minutes later, Hawkins hit Dixon with a 36-yard pass, and we now trailed by one, 21-20. And then in the final minutes it was Hawkins again, this time scoring on an 18-yard run to seal the victory 27-21.

An easy win against Furman the next week gave us three in a row and a 3-1 record heading into our Big Thursday, where a record crowd of 40,000 anticipated our breaking our two-game losing streak to the Tigers. But they were disappointed. With both Bobby Bunch and Dixon injured, we fell 13-0.

We continued the slide for two more weeks, losing to Maryland and UNC, then rebounded with a win over Virginia—our first conference win of the year. Next came NC State, the only undefeated team in the ACC, and—along with Texas—our other great game of the '57 campaign.

On the strength of touchdowns by Sammy Vickers, Stan Spears, and Don Johnson, we were up 19-7 at halftime. But by the time State's great Dick Christy scored his fourth touchdown of the afternoon, the Wolfpack had pulled ahead, 26-19. Then, with five minutes remaining, we tied it on a 40-yard pass from Hawkins to Julius Derrick. State took possession and moved down to our 35, but then time expired, and this classic duel had ended in a tie.

But wait! It seems Carolina was guilty of pass interference on the final play. The referees marched off a 15-yard penalty, and from there Christy booted a 35-yard field goal to win the game after the clock had run out. For Wolfpack fans it was an incredible victory, especially considering that Dick Christy had scored all twenty-nine NC State points. We salvaged a modicum of respectability by beating Wake Forest, 26-7, to finish the season at 5-5. However, it was far from what our fans had hoped for following the suc-cess of '56, and already a crack was beginning to appear in Coach Giese's porcelain exterior.

1958

The 1958 season saw us get back on the right track. Our seven wins included victories over Duke (8-0) and Georgia (24-14), and we also beat Clemson for the first time since 1954. We then went on to take Furman, Virginia, NC State, and Wake Forest and finished second in the ACC.

We lost close games to North Carolina (6-0) and Maryland (10-6) and only suf-

John Saunders takes a Bobby Bunch hand-off in the tough loss to Maryland.

fered one blowout on the year—to a powerful Army team led by All-American Pete Dawkins.

In the Big Thursday classic this year we turned in one of our best performances ever. Clemson, with the previous year's 7-3 team practically still intact, came into the game with a 4-0 record and a number-ten national ranking. And when Clemson scored first, late in the first quarter, it looked like it might be another long afternoon for Gamecock fans.

But Bobby Bunch went to the air and opened up the Tiger defense for fullback John Saunders, who then pounded the Tiger line until he went over for a TD with just seconds left in the half. In the second half we used our three-yards-and-a-cloud-of-dust offense to batter the Tiger line into submission. First we employed a 14-play,

Hawkins, ACC Player of the Year in '58, rolls through the Clemson Tigers.

54-yard drive that ate up eight and a half minutes and gave us the lead. Behind the hard running of Hawkins and Saunders, the same strategy resulted in two more fourth-quarter scores, and the final score was 26-6. Our passing game, by the way, covered thirty-four yards that day.

The other notable game on the '58 schedule was the finale against Wake Forest—notable because halfback Alex Hawkins, to the amazement of everyone in the stadium, threw three TD passes to King Dixon. After the game, when Coach Giese was asked if he planned to use Hawkins' halfback passes more in the upcoming season, he looked annoyed and turned away without answering.

Nevertheless, we finished with a 7-3 record and ranked fifteen in the nation in the Associated Press. Also, several of our players distinguished themselves with post-season laurels. John Saunders was All-ACC, led the conference in rushing yardage, and

won the ACC Jacobs Blocking Trophy. Hawkins was named captain of the All-ACC team, ACC Player of the Year, and AP third team All-American. Tackle Ed Pitts was another All-ACC selection, and guard Jake Bodkin was earned ACC Sophomore of the Week honors. King Dixon was voted USC's Most Valuable Player.

1959

Nineteen fifty-nine was a mixed bag of a year for the Gamecocks. We beat some great teams (and lost to some not-so-great ones); we faced some of the nation's premier quarterbacks; and we continued to live and die by the running game.

Despite the loss of Hawkins and Dixon, Coach Giese had a deep and talented team in '59, and our horses came out of the starting gate like thoroughbreds. First, using touchdown runs by Steve Kopian and Ken

Jack Morris follows Bob Farmer around end in the final Big Thursday game, 1959.

Norton, we beat Duke, 12-7. On the downside, we lost our fine fullback John Saunders for most of the year with a shoulder injury. We crushed Furman the next week, then prepared to meet Georgia, which would win the SEC with its all-time great quarterback Fran Tarkenton. A blocked punt by our Jake Bodkin led to the game's first score, and by the time Phil Lavoie had scored twice, USC led 21-0 in the third period. Tarkenton threw for a touchdown to cut into the lead, but by game's end Lavoie had a third touchdown and USC had a huge 30-14 win.

At this point we were 3-0 and had already beaten the best that either the ACC or SEC had to offer. Wasn't it time to dream of an undefeated season, a top national ranking, a major bowl bid? The very next week we lost to UNC, 19-6, and, while we were at it, lost both Steve Kopian and Sammy Fewell to injuries.

October 22, 1959 marked the end of a

Tackle Ed Pitts, USC All-American in 1959.

long and storied tradition. This was the day of the last Big Thursday shootout. Henceforth the Carolina-Clemson game would be played on a home-and-home basis, as the final game of the season for both teams.

Some 43,000 fans packed Carolina Stadium to see who would take this final classic, and most of them came away disappointed. Led by the passing of their superb Harvey White, the Tigers badly outclassed the Gamecocks, taking the game 27-0.

We picked ourselves up off the canvas, though, and scored nice wins over both Maryland and Virginia, thanks largely to the nice running of Steve Satterfield and Phil Lavoie. But then we had to face the Miami Hurricanes and another brilliant quarterback, Fran Curci. Again we were reminded of the virtues of the passing attack, with Curci completing thirteen of seventeen tosses for two TDs, and the 'Canes blew us out of town, 26-6.

Behind Ken Norton's two touchdowns, we managed to slip by NC State the next week, 12-7, despite our first look at sophomore quarterback Roman Gabriel. But in the finale we fell to Wake Forest and yet another great quarterback, Norman Snead. We led at the half, 20-18, but then their offense exploded and we got shelled, 43-20.

For a growing number of critics the Wake Forest game illustrated the weakness of our grind-'em-out style of play. With no passing attack, we invited opponents to stack their defenses against the run and, as Wake effectively did, to thereby shut us down. It happened to us in game after game, yet Giese steadfastly refused to concede that the forward pass might be a viable offensive weapon.

Despite the Gamecocks' 6-4 record in '59, Giese and Jake Penland, sports editor of *The State*, finally went public with their long-standing feud. Giese had fallen from Penland's favor immediately upon his arrival in Columbia when he closed Gamecock practices to the press and public. It wasn't long before Penland was using his Sunday column to assail Giese's dull, unimaginative style of play.

Giese, for his part, made no secret of his loathing for Jake Penland, but he had no ready soap box from which to broadcast his opinions. His best and only way to silence his severest critic was to come up with a great season in 1960. It was not to be.

Despite being touted as favorites to take the ACC championship, the Gamecocks dropped their first three games—to Duke, 31-0, to Georgia, 38-6, and to Miami, 21-6. They rebounded to beat UNC, 22-6, but then came bitter losses to Maryland, LSU, and Clemson.

So now we were 1-6 on the year and averaging fewer than six points per game. Part of the problem, no doubt, was that we simply lacked the big, rugged athletes necessary for Giese's physical brand of football. But it was also true that our pass defense had sunk to an all-time low. Since we threw no passes ourselves, it may be that our defense had little opportunity to practice against the pass. Whatever, it's worth noting that in the very first game of the season, Duke quarterback Don Altman completed eleven passes to end Tee Moorman alone.

It's not that we didn't have many outstanding players in 1960. In fact, it was our very wealth of talent that led people like Penland to believe that with a more wide-open offense we could have fielded an awesome team that year. Instead, after a tie with NC State and wins over Wake Forest

Billy Gambrell, all-time great Gamecock running back, crosses the Tar Heel goal line in 1960.

and Virginia, we ended a miserable year at 3-6-1.

It might be pointed out in Giese's defense that he was wearing three hats in 1960. Following the death of Rex Enright that year, Giese was named athletic director, as well as chairman of the Physical Education Department. With so much work—not to mention the scorn of Penland and his ilk—weighing upon him, it is not surprising that Giese resigned as head coach at the end of the '60 season, turning the position over to his former chief assistant Marvin Bass.

But Giese finished his five years at the helm with a 28-21-1 record, and only one losing season. Despite the detractors, his supporters were—and still are—legion.

16

1961 – 1965

MARVIN BASS AND DEACON DAN

If Warren Giese had an opposite number anywhere in the world, it must have been his successor, Marvin "Moose" Bass, a big, lumbering, friendly guy to whom informality was a way of life. A native of Petersburg, Virginia, Bass had been an outstanding tackle at William and Mary. After coaching stints at his alma mater, the Washington Redskins, and UNC, he joined Giese at USC in 1956. He served the '60 season under Bobby Dodd at Georgia Tech, then returned to USC upon Giese's resignation.

A solid squad greeted Bass upon his arrival in 1961. At quarterback were veterans Jim Costen and Dave Sowell, and we had three tremendous running backs in Billy Gambrell, Ed "Punky" Holler and Dickie Day. John Caskey and Ken Lester were at end, and the interior line featured Jim Moss, Joel Goodrich, Johnny Jones, and Richard Lomas.

Our schedule, on the other hand, was tougher than we were. In the opener we lost by one point to powerful Duke, 7-6, and after a nice win, 10-7 over Wake Forest, we lost again, this time to always potent Georgia.

Now at 1-2 on the year, we had to face one of the best teams in the country, Paul Dietzel's Bengal Tigers of LSU. We badly needed an upset before the home crowd to restore our waning confidence, but it wasn't to be. The Tigers, shored up by their famous Chinese Bandits defensive unit, crushed our poor Birds, 42-0.

It didn't get any better the next week, as we were again shut out, this time 17-0 by UNC. We came back to beat Maryland, 20-10, but then handed Virginia its first victory against an ACC opponent in three years when we fell to the Cavaliers, 28-20.

Clemson came to town next, bringing a 3-4 record to pit against our 2-5 mark. Before the game got underway, however,

Marvin Bass, USC head coach, 1961 – 65.

fans were treated to a still-memorable pre-game show.

As the crowd of 45,000 eagerly awaited the start of the game, here came the orange-clad Tigers barreling onto the field, led by their legendary coach Frank Howard. The customary cannons boomed, and the band broke into "Hold That Tiger Rag." But as the Tigers circled up for calisthenics, things seemed to go awry. Instead of the side-straddle hop, the players were doing the Bunny Hop. Then they paired off, and while one player used his fingers to create a likeness of an udder, his partner proceeded to start milking them. Several players broke ranks, went to the sideline, and commenced to blow kisses to the men in the stands. Coach Howard, meanwhile, was walking around spitting tobacco juice all over everything and everybody.

Then one of our country cousins, brighter than the average Clemson fan, shouted, "Them ain't our boys!" Sure enough, those

trusting Clemson bumpkins had once again fallen victim to a cruel city-slicker hoax. The "Tigers" were actually members of USC's Sigma Nu fraternity, who had borrowed uniforms from nearby Orangeburg High School and managed to pull off one of the most delightful pranks in the history of the series.

For USC fans, the game proved equally delightful. We scored first when Billy Gambrell carried the ball six straight times until he finally hit paydirt. Clemson, though, came back with two scores of its own to take a 14-7 lead in the third quarter.

Our Jimmy Costen sneaked over from two yards out for what should have been the tying score, but Clemson blocked the point-after kick to hold onto a 14-13 lead. But in the fourth quarter we got the big break we needed. As Dickie Day smashed into the Tiger line, the ball squirted out of his arms

Fullback Ed "Punky" Holler will bat this pass away before it gets to Tiger receiver. Great defense saved the game for the Gamecocks in '61.

and straight into the hands of Jimmy Costen, who had made the original hand-off. As the stunned Tigers watched, Costen then breezed down the sideline for what proved the winning score. The Tigers rallied courageously in the final moments, only to have the clock expire after they had advanced to our one-yard line.

We finished the season with a loss to Roman Gabriel's NC State team, followed by a much-needed win over Vanderbilt, and thus posted a 4-6 record for the year. Not great, but Marvin Bass was still enjoying his honeymoon at USC, and, besides, it was an improvement over the year before.

Two of our boys were selected for the All-ACC team that year—tackle Jim Moss and halfback Billy Gambrell—and our quarterback Jim Costen was signed by the Washington Redskins.

1962

Nineteen sixty-two marked the appearance of one of the finest athletes ever to enroll at Carolina: sophomore quarterback "Deacon Dan" Reeves from Americus, Georgia. He would team with senior Billy Gambrell to give us one of the finest offensive punches in the South.

Once again, however, our record for '62 would not reflect the caliber of our individual performers. We opened with losses to Northwestern and Duke, then salvaged a 7-7 tie against the Georgia Bulldogs. Our first victory of the year, against Wake Forest, was followed by losses to UNC and Maryland.

We righted ourselves at that point and ran off victories over Virginia, NC State, and Detroit, so that we were 4-4-1 as we faced Clemson in the final game of the year. It was our second trip to Death Valley, and it was a great game, but a Rodney Rogers field goal in the closing minutes left us winless at Clemson and with an-

In 1962, Billy Gambrell was named Player of the Year in the ACC as well as All-American.

other losing season.

But despite the disappointing record, several of our players earned high post-season honors. Billy Gambrell was the ACC Player of the Year, an honorable mention All-American, and the MVP of the Blue-Gray Game. Jim Moss was the All-State Lineman of the Year, All-ACC, and the winner of the Jacobs Blocking Trophy. John Caskey was another All-ACC performer.

1963

Much to our chagrin, 1963 turned out to be our most forgettable season since 1897, when we won none and lost three. Not only

J. R. Wilburn, one of the best receivers in Gamecock history, tries to elude UNC All-American Bob Lacey.

Deacon Dan Reeves ready to heave a long one against the Duke Blue Devils.

did we go 1-8-1 on the year, but we also earned the distinction of being the only team in history to break the two longest losing streaks in the nation in the same year.

On November 2, Tulane came to Columbia with a 17-game losing streak in tow, having beaten no one since 1961. They took us 20-7 on our home court. After the game, Coach Bass was nonplussed: "What can you say? You can't explain fumbles and penalties and guys not playing football. We just didn't play."

Two weeks later we met Wake Forest, which now led the nation with eighteen straight losses. By game's end, however, the Deacons had taken our measure, 20-19, and our name was forever etched in the NCAA record book.

Because of the assassination of President Kennedy on November 22 of that year, a Friday, our game with Clemson (like most of the nation's games) was postponed until Thanksgiving Day, the following Thursday. Prior to the game, Clemson coach Howard typically moaned that USC undoubtedly had the finest 1-7-1 team in the nation, and that it would require expert coaching to keep his team on the same field with the Gamecocks.

He was almost right. Carolina surprised everyone by taking a 14-7 halftime lead, but Clemson came back in the second half to take the game by a closer-than-expected score of 24-20.

How much difference it made cannot be known, but it should be noted that Dan Reeves suffered a severe eye injury during the first game of the season and played the rest of the year with his vision badly impaired.

1964

In 1964, Reeves' final season at USC, we again suffered through a dismal season. We tied Duke and Georgia while losing to Maryland, Nebraska, Florida, UNC, and NC State.

But we finished the season in fine fashion, reeling off victories against The Citadel, Wake Forest, and—most gratifyingly—the Clemson Tigers. If that seemed to bode well for the future, so did the appearance of sophomore defensive back Bobby Bryant, who would become a bright star in the Gamecock firmament.

J. R. Wilburn, an outstanding receiver and favorite target of Reeves, remembers the '64 season and Deacon Dan in a recent interview:

"I had the misfortune of poor timing many times in my career," Wilburn says. "At USC (1963-65) we suffered through some bad years; we didn't see daylight ahead until it was time for me to graduate."

Wilburn had the pleasure of playing with a pair of outstanding quarterbacks—Dan Reeves and Mike Fair at USC. He said that "Mike has always been one of my favorite people. He was smart and could throw the hound out of that football. Dan was the most intense competitor I've ever seen. He always used his ability to the utmost and had a lot of football savvy. He was simply a winner."

Wilburn related a story to illustrate Reeves' competitiveness:

"He and I used to frequent a place in Five Points that had pinball machines," he said. "Well, Dan knew the odds were overwhelmingly against his winning, but he would stand there and drop every cent he had in that thing, just to show the machine it couldn't beat him.

"The guy who owned the place came over one night and said, 'Son, you'd better stay away from anything that stands on four legs, backs itself into a corner, and takes on all comers.' That was good advice, but of course we didn't listen."

As for Deacon Dan, he would go on to an

Quarterback Mike Fair leads USC to a big win over Clemson (and a share of the ACC crown) in 1965.

outstanding career as a running back with the Dallas Cowboys. Today he is head coach of the Denver Broncos.

1965

Nineteen sixty-five witnessed the return of two-platoon football, which had been outlawed by the NCAA back in 1953. Now a player no longer had to go both ways and could specialize in either offense or defense. Coincidentally, Bobby Bryant also came along in '65 and eventually became one of the finest defensive backs ever for the university. On offense we fielded two dazzling new runners in Benny Galloway and Ben Garnto.

As for quarterback, Ted Wingard, a complete unknown, came off the bench to lead us to two second-half touchdowns and a come-from-behind win over The Citadel. But the following week, against Duke, eventual number-one quarterback Mike Fair made his first appearance. He played brilliantly, but his twelve completions weren't enough, and we fell by a score of 20-15.

We came back to beat NC State, 13-7, on Ben Garnto's 74-yard touchdown scamper, but then lost to mighty Tennessee, 24-3, despite J. R. Wilburn's new USC record of seven catches in a single ballgame. We played like national champions the next week against Wake Forest, clobbering the Deacons, 38-7. Ben Garnto had an 89-yard run from scrimmage, the longest non-scoring run in the USC record book, and J. R. Wilburn broke his own record with nine catches for 105 yards.

This up-and-down season went back down the next week. We gave ninth-ranked LSU a good scare (it was 7-7 late in the third quarter), but finally fell 21-7. And we stayed down the following week before our own Homecoming crowd, committing seven turnovers in a 27-14 loss to Maryland.

We bounced back to take Virginia, 17-7, but then had to face Orange Bowl-bound Alabama and their great quarterback Steve Sloan in Tuscaloosa. We hung in there at 7-7 through most of three periods, but then they exploded for twenty-eight quick points. The Clemson game that year was a honey, maybe the most exciting ever. This year we were both playing for all the marbles. A Clemson win would give them the ACC championship outright; a Carolina win would make us co-champions with Duke.

Clemson took an early 3-0 lead, then added another seven with only three minutes left in the half. But in the ensuing series, Carolina came to life when Fair eluded a vicious pass rush and heaved a long pass to Wilburn, who took it to the Clemson 25. Just a couple of plays later, Jule Smith bulled over to cut the lead to 10-7.

In the third quarter Jimmy Poole tied the game with a 21-yard field goal, and in the final period, behind the running of Phil Branson and Bob Harris, the Gamecocks went ahead 17-10. But Clemson wasn't through. With only forty seconds remaining, Tommy Ray hit Phil Rogers with a TD pass to pull within one. Frank Howard was not about to go for the tie, and on the two-point attempt Tommy Addison threw to Bo Ruffner in the end zone. The pass was on the money, but at the last second linebacker Bob Gunnels stuck out a hand and deflected the ball: USC 17, Clemson 16.

This was Coach Bass's third win over Clemson in five years, and the co-championship of the ACC was the first championship of any kind that the Gamecocks had ever won. Unfortunately, several months later we were forced to forfeit this game to the Tigers (they refused to accept it) and the ACC crown for recruiting violations. It was nice while it lasted.

USC's 5-5 record in 1965 gave Coach Bass a rather unenviable 17-29-4 record over five years. Perhaps his program was about to turn the corner, but we can only speculate. That spring Marvin Bass resigned to take the head coaching job of the Montreal franchise in the new Continental Pro Football League.

17

1966 – 1974

PAUL DIETZEL ARRIVES

It was a deal made in heaven. The illustrious Paul Dietzel would now take the wayward Gamecocks in hand and lead us to that great promised land of football prominence that had eluded us for seventy-five years.

He was clearly the man to do it, based on his impressive record. He had arrived at LSU in 1955 and within three years had led them to a national championship and been named NCAA Coach of the Year. In fact, between 1955 and 1962, he had won the Southeastern Conference championship twice, played in the Sugar Bowl twice, and gone to the Orange Bowl once. Obviously, Dietzel was just what the doctor ordered for USC's ailing program.

Upon arriving in Columbia, Dietzel wisely cautioned eager Carolina fans that success couldn't come overnight, that it would take him probably three years to turn Carolina into a national champion. Gamecock fans, on the other hand, whose hope, optimism, and patience had already proved boundless, took his warnings with a smile and began putting money aside for their big trip to Miami on New Year's Day.

Fleet defensive back Bobby Bryant was a bright spot in an otherwise dark year.

But Dietzel was telling the truth. His first season was not just a loser; it was an absolute disaster, our worst year in history. We went 1-9 on the year, including losses to LSU, Memphis State, Georgia, Wake Forest,

Sensational Warren Muir makes his presence felt against Duke in 1967.

Tennessee, Maryland, Florida State, Alabama, and, of course, Clemson.

Our lone win came in the fourth week of the season against NC State. It was a memorable win in a forgettable season, especially since Bobby Bryant set an all-time USC record by returning a punt ninety-eight yards for a touchdown.

In fact, Bryant, despite the atrocious season, received honorable mention All-America honors in 1966, then went on to a highly successful career with the Minnesota Vikings.

1967

Most of the team was back for 1967, including a sensational young fullback, Warren Muir, who had transferred from West Point. The new season also saw the emergence of a new split end, Roy Don Reeves, younger brother of Deacon Dan.

Muir wasted no time demonstrating his worth. In the opening game against highly ranked Iowa State, Muir made his debut in the second half, gained seventy-nine yards

over those thirty minutes, scored two touchdowns, and led us to a great 34-3 victory.

The next week we kept up the good work. Behind the explosive running of Muir and Garnto, we took a 16-10 lead in the third quarter. Late in the game, UNC recovered a fumble on our 26, but our sophomore defensive end Dave Lucas broke through on four successive plays to sack the Tarheel quarterback and preserve the win.

Next came Duke. Could we make it three in a row? We were down 10-7 in the third quarter when Mike Fair pulled a beautiful bootleg for a score, but Duke came right back to regain the lead with but five minutes left in the game. Then Fair went to work again, engineering a long drive and hitting Fred Zeigler three times in the process. Finally Muir took it over for the TD and a big 21-17 win. It was the first time we'd beaten Duke in Durham since 1930.

Our euphoria ended abruptly the next week when we lost to tough Georgia, 21-0, and followed that with another loss to Florida State, 17-0. Our offense was still on vacation through the first half of our Homecom-

Andy Chavous heads upfield with a Mike Fair pass in our losing effort against Clemson.

ing game against Virginia, and we were down again, 17-0. But suddenly Pat Watson returned a Cavalier punt sixty-seven yards for a score, and minutes later Fair hit Garnto with a TD strike. A two-point conversion brought us to within two points.

The Cavs scored again to make it 23-15, but Muir retaliated with a 14-yard scoring plunge up the middle. We got the ball back on downs, but our drive stalled out on the Virginia 35. That's when Jimmy Poole came in and kicked a 45-yarder to win the game, 24-23.

A 31-0 whitewashing of Maryland the next week gave us a 4-0 mark in ACC play and assured us of at least a break-even season. A win against Wake Forest the next week would give us the ACC crown. But again it wasn't to be. Mike Fair scored twice, but it

wasn't enough, and we bowed before the Deacons, 35-21.

A subsequent loss to Cotton Bowl-bound Alabama meant that everything would hinge on the Clemson game in the finale—our first winning season in recent memory and the ACC championship. But Clemson chose this day to put twenty-three points on the board before we opened our eyes, and the Tigers denied us our cherished title.

1968

During Coach Dietzel's first two years he had progressed from 1-9 to 5-5. Given such improvement, we figured '68 would be the year we had been waiting for.

Instead, we had another one of those all too typical Carolina seasons, winning four and losing six. But this was a young team that seemed to get better as the year progressed. We lost five of the first six, then came on strong to beat Virginia and Wake Forest. Pat Watson intercepted four passes in the Wake game, tying an all-time USC record. After a loss to VPI, 17-6, it was time

Tyler Hellams' 73-yard punt return for a touchdown to beat the Tigers in '68.

Tommy Suggs to Fred Zeigler, one of Carolina's all-time great combinations. Suggs threw five TD passes against Virginia in 1968. Zeigler caught three of them, along with 12 receptions overall for 199 yards. These are all all-time USC passing records.

for the showdown with Clemson.

Now it was time for Dietzel's young sophomores to show what they had leared. With little Tommy Suggs now at quarterback and Rudy Holloman and Benny Galloway at running back, we moved the ball well all afternoon. We just couldn't seem to score. In fact, Clemson led 3-0 at halftime.

But early in the third quarter, Tyler Hellams gained instant immortality when he took a Tiger punt at our 27 and raced seventy-three yards for a touchdown. He was hit a dozen times but simply wouldn't go down. Clemson desperately went to the air in the waning moments, but our sometimes maligned defensive backs came through, preserving the 7-3 victory.

Could it really be a taste of things to come?

1969

It happened. What we might have termed our "75-year rebuilding program" finally came to fruition in 1969. We had the talent, and, for once, put together a season that reflected it. Certainly it was high time. We had not had a winning season since 1958 and had never, ever, won a conference championship.

We opened with a big win over Duke in Columbia, 27-20. Among the many heroes, Tommy Suggs and Rudy Holloman stood out. Suggs scored on a 48-yard rollout and racked up 205 yards in total offense. Holloman accounted for 115 yards, including a 60-yard sprint for a score.

We played barely well enough to win the next week against UNC, but then got pounded by Georgia—luckily, a non-conference opponent. Back in conference play the following Saturday, Jim Mitchell returned a Wolfpack punt seventy-two yards for a score to nip NC State.

Then, against VPI, we were trailing 16-14 with a minute to play and in possession of the ball on our own 32. It was time for Tommy Suggs to go to work. He passed for forty-nine yards in forty-nine seconds, leaving nine more on the clock. Tiny Billy Dupre strode onto the field and calmly booted a then-record 47-yard field goal for the victory.

We followed this great win with a gratifying shutout of Maryland, but then lost badly to Florida State, 34-9. Now 5-2 on the year, we traveled to Knoxville to meet third-ranked Tennessee. We played them tough, scoring with only nine minutes remaining to cut the lead to 16-14, but the mighty Vols scored twice in the waning moments to take a 29-14 win.

The next week came the historic victory. We swamped Wake Forest, 24-6, to win the ACC championship, our first title in

Rudy Holloman, getting a Tiger hug here, caught two TD passes to help beat Clemson in '69.

ACC champion USC slugs it out against West Virginia in the 1969 Mud (i.e., Peach) Bowl.

seventy-five years of collegiate competition. Tommy Suggs tossed three touchdown passes in the game, and Muir had 101 yards rushing. Now we were 6-3 on the year and thinking that a win over Clemson in the finale would get us a bowl game invitation. It turned into quite a shootout.

We scored the first three times we had the ball to take a 17-0 lead early in the second quarter. Two Clemson scores narrowed our lead to 17-13 at the half, but the ten points scored in the second half all went up on our side of the scoreboard. We collected 287 yards on the ground and another 230 in the air for a total of 517—a Carolina record that would stand until 1985. As was the case so often throughout the season, Suggs, Zeigler, and Holloman were the offensive stars.

Five days earlier had come the announcement that USC would meet West Virginia in the 1969 Peach Bowl at Grant Field in Atlanta.

Game day was a weatherman's nightmare—and a football team's. Cold rain, and then freezing rain, turned Grant Field into a bowl of slush, and even the players were happy when it was all over. West Virginia, under Jim Carlen, handled the mud better than we did and took the victory, 14-3.

Still, 1969 was a great year. In addition to the championship, Warren Muir became our second player to be named to a first-string All-America team. And Fred Zeigler, who came to the Gamecocks as a walk-on, broke all conference records with 146 catches during his illustrious career.

1970

Three of our finest players—Muir, Zeigler, and Holloman—were lost to graduation, but 1970 saw the return of such stalwarts as Jimmy Poston, Dave DeCamilla,

All-American kick return specialist Dickie Harris.

PAUL DIETZEL ARRIVES

Jim Mitchell, Al Usher, Billy Ray Rice, Dickie Harris, Billy Dupre, and our great quarterback Tommy Suggs. And considering the team's accomplishments in '69, fans understandably had high expectations of the 1970 edition.

Our season opened at Grant Field in Atlanta against highly touted Georgia Tech. We saw this game as an opportunity for an impressive win and some national recognition, and we almost pulled it off. We led 20-17 going into the final quarter, but Tech's terrific quarterback Eddie McAshan—who passed for 202 yards on the day—moved his team downfield for a game-winning score.

Against Wake Forest the next week, however, we did look like a national power, racking up 522 total yards and clobbering the Deacons 43-7. But this big win was followed by a disappointing tie against winless NC State, so we were now 1-1-1 on the young season.

Backup quarterback Jackie Young led us to a 24-7 win over VPI; then we played a great game to take undefeated UNC. We led 21-7 at the half, only to see the Heels tie the game up with seven minutes to play. Again Jackie Young came in for the ailing Tommy Suggs, and on his first play tossed a long TD pass to tight end Doug Hamrick. Moments later Billy Ray Rice raced sixty-five yards for another Gamecock score, and we prevailed 35-21.

Now with hopes surging for another ACC crown, the proverbial wheels fell off. We lost five straight, to Maryland, Florida State, Georgia, Tennessee, and Duke.

Somehow, with our season in ruins at our feet, we managed to beat Clemson in the finale. Tommy Suggs, playing his last game as a Gamecock, could not be stopped. He completed nineteen passes for three touchdowns to vault us to a huge 38-32 win. Rather than the undefeated national championship season we'd hoped for, we

Billy DuPre, Carolina's ace kicker, 1968 – 70.

finished at 4-6-1. Our offense did the job, putting a then-record 285 points on the board, but the defense made the record book as well, allowing 253 points. For the first time in recent memory, frustrated fans began to boo the team at halftime.

Nevertheless, some impressive individual honors came our way following the '70 season. Dickie Harris established a new NCAA record with 880 yards in thirty kickoff returns and subsequently was named an All-American.

Tommy Suggs broke all our passing records during his days at USC, and his new marks stood for fifteen years, until the era of the great Todd Ellis. He was named team MVP for 1970 and went on earn MVP honors in the Blue-Gray game as well.

By the way, 1970 was our last year as a member of the ACC. Coach Dietzel, chafing under the more stringent academic requirements of the conference, convinced the board of trustees that he could recruit more effectively if USC were an independent and thus answerable only to NCAA guidelines.

1971

Following 1970, a season when fans had expected so much, Dietzel critics became a dime a dozen. But even his greatest detractors admitted that the man had a genius at least for the administrative part of his work, and most will admit, in retrospect, that it was Paul Dietzel's ambition and vision that truly put USC on the road to national prominence.

His efforts were in evidence the night we opened the '71 season against Georgia Tech before a sellout crowd of 54,842 in recently enlarged Carolina Stadium. Both the larger stadium and the sellout were products of Dietzel's promotional abilities.

Tech was nationally ranked that year and a heavy favorite to beat the Gamecocks, but the oddsmakers reckoned without Dickie Harris. Our star defensive back blocked a punt in the second quarter—which Jim Nash ran in for a touchdown—and in the third quarter he returned a punt seventy-seven yards for another score. It was a great 24-7 upset win for USC, and after the game Dietzel exulted, "At last we have the kind of defense we've always waited for."

The win was all the sweeter in that, after the debacle of 1970, the ground under Coach Dietzel was getting a little shaky. He needed a big year, and he needed it now.

It looked like he was going to get it. After a loss to Duke, we reeled off four impressive wins in a row—over NC State (a game in which Tommy Bell kicked a record 52-yard field goal), Memphis State, Virginia, and Maryland. We were 5-1 at that point and starting to think about New Year's Day.

We should have checked the remainder of the schedule. Over the next five weeks we lost to Florida State, Georgia, and Tennessee, beat Wake Forest, then lost to Clemson in our final game of the season. So we posted a winning mark, yes, but 6-5 was not the

All-American safety Dickie Harris with some of his booty at the Gamecocks' awards banquest in '71.

record we were hoping for.

In the Wake Forest game, with tailback Billy Ray Rice hampered by an injury, Dietzel moved "the Darter," Dickie Harris, to running back. He delighted the crowd and won the game by rushing for 108 yards and three touchdowns.

The versatile Harris continues to hold all records for punt and kickoff returns at Carolina, and at this point they still appear untouchable. During his career he returned seventy-seven punts for 825 yards and seventy-three kickoffs for another 1,946 yards. He was named team captain and team MVP in '71 and was again an All-American.

1972

If USC faithful were disappointed with

Quarterback Bill Troup flies over a couple of Yellow Jackets.

Bobby Marino's last-minute field goal to upset Florida State in '72.

1971's 6-5 record, they shouldn't have been. The '72 season proved to be a disaster. Of the year's two bright spots, the first occurred during the halftime of our opening game, when Carolina Stadium became Williams-Brice stadium.

As for the game itself, it was a fateful omen for the season; we were upset by a weak Virginia team, 24-16. This despite quarterback Bill Troup's new records of twenty-four completions and forty-seven attempts. We followed with two more lopsided losses, to Georgia Tech, 34-6, and Ole Miss, 21-0.

We bounced back for two straight wins, though, and found a new hero in the process. Redshirt sophomore Dobby Grossman threw three TD passes to Mike Haggard to key a 34-7 beating of Memphis State; then, against Appalachian State, he hit Haggard twice more en route to another victory.

But before we could even our record, we suffered two more losses, first to Dietzel's alma mater, Miami of Ohio, and to NC State. We then beat Wake Forest, 35-3, and Wake coach Tom Harper was fired immediately afterward. As *The Garnet and Black* cynically editorialized, "Apparently Wake Forest trustees felt that if Tom Harper lost to South Carolina, he couldn't beat anybody."

Against VPI the next week, the Gamecocks were overmatched by the great passing of Don Strock, who would lead the nation in total offense that year. We also got our first look at freshman quarterback Jeff Grantz, who came in late in the game and led us to two touchdowns. But it wasn't enough that day, as we fell to the Gobblers, 45-20.

Powerful Florida State visited Williams-Brice Stadium the next Saturday, and, quite unexpectedly, supplied the season's second highlight. Neville Files intercepted three

Seminole passes, Dobby Grossman heaved three TD passes, and with 1:30 left on the clock, freshman Bobby Marino kicked a 38-yard field goal to give us a startling 24-21 victory.

The long season came to an end in Clemson, with both teams taking a rain-swept field with 4-6 records. In a fitting conclusion, we lost, 7-6, by virtue of a failed two-point conversion.

Again we were forced to seek consolation in individual post-season honors. Defensive stalwart John LeHeup was named all-American and played on both the Hula Bowl and the East-West Game. Neville Files, the team MVP, was selected to play in the Blue-Gray Game; team captain Rick Brown was chosen for the Senior Bowl; and Mike Haggard played in the All-America Bowl.

As for Coach Dietzel, his overall record now stood at 31-42-1. But if his coaching credentials were losing their luster, he was without peer as athletic director. Our athletic program was on a par with the best in the country, and, thanks solely to his efforts, Williams-Brice Stadium was one of the finest facilities in the nation.

1973

Call it the year of the veer. With the extremely talented Jeff Grantz available to handle the ball, Coach Dietzel scrapped his pro-type offense in favor of the veer formation. Dietzel seemed to have a knack for recruiting great quarterbacks, and the young sophomore Grantz could run the veer as though he had invented it.

Including backfield mates Jay Lynn Hodgin and Russ Jackson, Grantz and Company burst onto the national scene in '73 by whipping a good Georgia Tech team, 41-28. Grantz, in his debut as a starter, rushed for 102 yards and two touchdowns

and passed for seventy-nine yards and another two scores. For his efforts the NCAA named him National Back of the Week.

Also in that game, Mel Baxley, part of a rejuvenated defensive backfield that called itself the "Soul Patrol," picked off a Tech pass and returned it 102 yards for a score, tying an all-time USC record.

Grantz missed the second half of play in a 27-19 loss to Houston, then had an uncharacteristically unproductive outing in a 13-11 loss to Miami. Next, however, we churned out 478 total yards to take a close one from VPI, 27-24.

Against Ohio University the following weekend, Grantz had the day of his—or anybody's—career. He rushed twenty-four times for 260 yards, breaking Steve Wadiak's old record of 256. He also returned a kickoff eighty-five yards for a touchdown and passed for another twenty-five. The Associated Press named him Back of the Week.

Grantz graciously allowed another hero to step forward against Wake Forest. Jay Lynn Hodgin rushed for 143 yards on just nineteen carries and completed three of three halfback passes for sixty-four yards and two touchdowns. Final score: USC 28, Wake Forest 12.

The following week, in what *The State* called the finest football game ever played in Columbia, the Gamecocks took on the 6-0 Tigers from LSU, ranked eighth in the country. Grantz was magnificent, piling up 276 yards in total offense and engineering a 29-26 lead with three minutes to play. It just wasn't quite enough. LSU scored at the last minute to steal the win, 33-29.

An ankle injury to Grantz forced Dietzel to bring Ron Bass up from the freshman team to start against NC State. Bass looked good, but Lou Holtz's Wolfpack looked better, finally upending our Gamecocks, 56-35. Still at the helm the next week against Appalachian State, Bass accounted for 264 total yards in our 35-14 win. And if

Jeff Grantz looks upfield against Ohio.

anybody still doubted his effectiveness, Bass led us to an impressive 52-12 win over Florida State the following Saturday.

Now, with a 6-4 record, it was time to face Clemson. Would we end up with an outstanding year or a barely winning season? Grantz, now back in action, answered that question in no uncertain terms. By day's end, he had rushed for 185 yards, thrown for 121 more, and scored two touchdowns to lead us to victory.

So we concluded our season at 7-4 and had high hopes for a Peach Bowl bid. But since Georgia Tech could not beat Georgia, we had to stay home on New Year's. It was nonetheless a fine year, and it took a great deal of heat off of Paul Dietzel.

With Grantz on the sideline, Ron Bass led USC to a 52 – 12 walloping of Florida State.

1974

If 1973 had been a good year, 1974 proved to be a miserable one, both on the football field and in the press.

Following an opening-game loss to Georgia Tech, Herman Helms of *The State* wrote: "After one game of a season which Dietzel predicted would be a good one, Carolina fans are not celebrating a victory. Instead, they are . . . once again playing that frustrating old waiting game with Paul Dietzel. Waiting and wondering how long . . . it will be before Carolina realizes some return on the long and costly investment the school has in him."

The next week brought a loss to Duke in a game we were supposed to have won, and Dietzel suddenly announced his resignation. "After the first game," he explained in his press release, "the cauldron-stirrer had it ready. Obviously, he [i.e., Helms] had worked on it all summer. I figure there's no sense in having our squad, our wives and families subjected to it all year."

Following this announcement, the Gamecocks suffered three more losses, to Georgia, Houston, and VPI, so that after five games we had beaten no one. We then picked up victories over Ole Miss and UNC before NC State handed us our sixth loss of the season. We managed to defeat relatively weak teams from Wake Forest and Appalachian State, then lost our last game of the season to Clemson, 39-21.

Immediately following the Clemson game, NC State's Lou Holtz declined to take on the vacant Carolina job. Our offer to him was rumored to include a $60,000 salary, a TV show, cars, a new home, and free educations for his four children. Holtz said that the offer was tempting, but he preferred to remain at State.

Other candidates for the job included former quarterback Dan Reeves, who eagerly

An agonized Coach Dietzel resigned after two games in 1974.

sought the position, and Lower Richland High coach "Mooney" Player, who lobbied for the job by stating in the press, "Give me two years, and if I'm not winning, you won't have to ask me to leave."

But the position went to Jim Carlen, a former player at Georgia Tech, who had fielded successful teams at both West Virginia and Texas Tech. Dietzel, meanwhile, assumed that the athletic director's job was still securely his, but such was not the case. In addition to head football coach, Carlen was named athletic director for football, while basketball coach Frank McGuire became athletic director for basketball.

After a less than spectacular nine-year career at the Gamecock helm, Paul Dietzel packed his bags and moved on to the position of commissioner of the Ohio Valley Conference.

18

1975 – 1981

JIM CARLEN AND GEORGE ROGERS

Diametrically opposed to his predecessor, Jim Carlen was a big, blunt country boy from Tennessee who was known for telling it like it is. The players seemed to respond to the new coach, for Carlen's first season turned out to be far more successful than anyone dared hope.

Surely it helped, though, that Jeff Grantz was back for his senior year. In the opening game, Grantz ran for one TD and passed for two others in a big upset win over Georgia Tech, 23-17. A second upset followed when we beat a good Duke team in Durham, 24-16. Grantz scored twice, while Clarence Williams rushed for 118 yards and Kevin Long ran for eighty-five more.

After a tough loss to Georgia, 28-20, we took on reigning SWC champion Baylor, which had tied number-three Michigan the week before. Once again we were clearly underdogs, but behind Williams and Long, who combined for 244 yards rushing, we

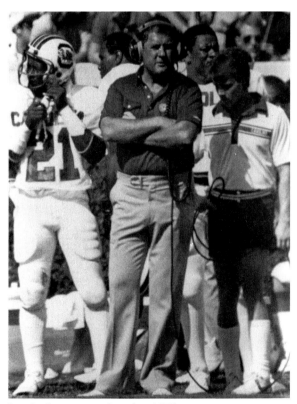

Jim Carlen came on board in 1975.

Kevin Long was one of the heroes against Clemson in '75.

upset the Bears, 24-13.

And we weren't through yet. After a 41-14 thrashing of Virginia, we traveled to Jackson to take on the Rebels of Ole Miss. We lost a big lead in the game and were down 29-28 with a minute to play. But starting at our own 19, Grantz completed five straight passes to move us to the Rebel 28. Then, with 0:23 on the clock, he hit Phil Logan for the game-winner.

At that point, however, we crashed and burned. We turned the ball over six times and lost to LSU, then got beat the next week when NC State scored with only nine seconds left in the game. Unfortunately, we hadn't bottomed out yet. The next Saturday tiny Appalachian State, a team we should have beaten easily, came down to Columbia and whipped us on our own field, 39-34.

Mercifully, we got back on track against Wake Forest, humbling the Deacons, 37-26. Kevin Long rushed for ninety-five yards on the day, making him the first USC running back ever to surpass a thousand yards in a single season.

So even despite our late-season swoon, we were a somewhat surprising 6-4 at this point, and looking forward to the Clemson Tigers. The experts were predicting a close game, but we whipped the Striped Beasts by the score of 56-20! Clarence Williams rolled up 160 yards rushing to become the second USC player to pass the 1,000-yard mark, and Jeff Grantz tied Tommy Suggs' all-time USC record by throwing five touchdown passes.

Our fine 7-4 record earned us an invitation to the Tangerine Bowl in Orlando, but the less said about that game the better. Though we went into the game with an offense ranked fourth in the nation, we simply couldn't find the goal line and lost to Miami of Ohio, 20-7.

It was a tough way for Jeff Grantz to

Backfield in motion: Kevin Long throws the block, Ron Bass carries the ball, and Clarence Williams looks for the pitch-out.

finish his USC career, but a number of post-season honors came his way. He was named team MVP, then played in the Hula Bowl, the East-West Shrine Game, and the Japan Bowl. Best of all, he was named to the AP All-America second team.

1976

So the great Jeff Grantz was gone, but ready to take his place for the '76 season was another talented Paul Dietzel recruit, Ron Bass. We also had both Kevin Long and Clarence Williams back for another year.

We opened the season by avenging last year's humiliating loss to Appalachian State, then rolled to impressive wins over Georgia Tech and Duke. But then came two heartbreakers in a row. We lost to seventh-ranked Georgia, 20-12, and the following week saw Baylor score eighteen fourth-

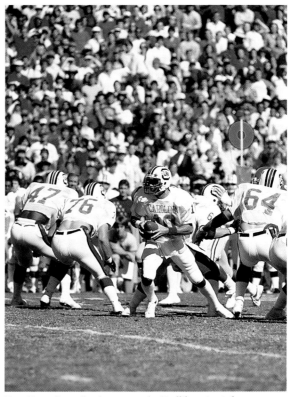

Ron Bass drops back against the Bulldogs in Athens.

quarter points to eke out an 18-17 victory. We bounced back to demolish Virginia, 35-7, in a game in which Bass completed an amazing thirteen of fifteen passes, then squeezed past Ole Miss, 10-7. Now at 5-2 on the year, we found ourselves edging into the national spotlight with a number nineteen national ranking, and at the same time preparing to take on the twelfth-ranked Irish of Notre Dame. It was a good, hard-fought game, but we came out on the short end of the 13-6 score.

We picked ourselves up with a decisive 27-7 win over a good NC State team the next week, but then were knocked back down by our old *bête noire*, inconsistency. We lost to a mediocre Wake Forest team, 10-7, and with that loss, our fourth, went our bowl hopes as well.

Already down, we took a gratuitous butt-kicking from Clemson to conclude the season. Throwing off the shackles of a terrible 2-6-2 season, the Tigers mauled us, 28-9.

1977 – 1978

After two successive winning seasons, Coach Carlen was forced to walk a dark valley in '77 and '78. We upset Georgia Tech in '77, but that was our only notable win. Of our seven losses, five were by seven points or less, but they were still losses. The epitaph for the season was written when we traveled to Honolulu to play Hawaii for our final game. Hawaii would be an easy mark, of course, and the trip would be a nice reward for a year of gridiron work. The Islanders beat us, 24-7.

The '78 season was a slight improvement, and after beating both Georgia and Ole Miss and tying Kentucky, we took some pleasure in considering ourselves SEC champions. But again the close games seemed to go the other way, and three of our five losses were by a total of nine points. We went 5-5-1 in '78, giving us twelve losses

Gamecock defense stifles Georgia in '78.

The incomparable George Rogers came into his own as a sophomore in '78.

Ben Cornett dives for the ball against Wake Forest in '79.

over this dismal two-year period.

There was a glimmer of light, though. In our 37-14 win over Wake Forest in '78, a young sophomore named George Rogers caught everyone's eye when he rushed for 237 yards and two touchdowns.

It should also be remembered that Max Runager, one of the nation's best punters, played in the '78 Canadian-American Bowl and went on to a pro career with the Philadelphia Eagles and Kansas City Chiefs.

1979

Despite missing three games with injuries, George Rogers rushed for 1,006 yards during his sophomore year, so it was with good reason that Gamecock fans were looking for a turnaround in 1979. And they got one, as USC won eight games for the first time since 1903.

In the opener, a 28-0 whitewashing at the hands of UNC, we looked like were still playing the '78 season, but we then proceeded to reel off five wins in a row, including our first win over Georgia in Athens in twenty-one years.

We lost to Notre Dame, 18-17, in the last minute of play, whipped NC State 30-28, then were soundly beaten by an undefeated Florida State team, 27-7. We clobbered Wake Forest, 35-14, and began preparing for our grudge match against Clemson.

The Tigers were 8-2 and nationally ranked coming into the game and had defeated mighty Notre Dame the week before coming to Columbia. We were 7-3 and looking for revenge. In a tough game that hinged largely on field position, fifteen of the twenty-two total points came on field goals. Luckily, the one touchdown belonged to the Gamecocks, and we prevailed, 13-9.

Then came a bid to play Missouri in the

Tight end Willie Scott stars in Carolina's big win over the Tigers in 1979.

JIM CARLEN AND GEORGE ROGERS

Hall of Fame Bowl in Birmingham. Coach Carlen told the team not to be misled by Missouri's 6-5 record, and he told the truth. On a cold night in Alabama with the rain falling so hard we could hardly see the field, the Tigers roared back from an early deficit to take the game, 24-14.

George Rogers finished the year with 1,681 yards rushing and was named to the All-America team.

1980

In 1980, with both George Rogers and Johnnie Wright back for another year, we had the finest running duo in the history of Carolina football. Wright was a big, fleet, exceptionally talented fullback who had the misfortune of having to play in the shadow of Rogers. Even so, he rushed for 2,589 yards during his career, fourth on Carolina's all-time rushing list.

With Garry Harper again running the offense, we opened with easy wins over the University of the Pacific and Wichita State. (The 73-0 romp over Wichita State remains our biggest score ever in the modern era.)

We then took on fourth-ranked Southern Cal, led by the great Marcus Allen. We lost a tough one, 23-13, but Rogers had 141 yards rushing to Allen's 103 and thus did nothing to hurt his chances for the Heisman Trophy.

With barely time to catch our breath, it was on to Ann Arbor to face highly ranked Michigan before 104,213 highly partisan fans. The odds were far from in our favor, and the experts were congratulating themselves when the Wolverines took a 14-0 halftime lead. But in the third quarter, Eddie Leopard put us on the board with a field goal, and, after a fumble recovery, Rogers hauled it across to cut the lead to 14-10.

The big play came early in the fourth quarter. Michigan, with fourth and

inches on their own 30, faked a punt and tried to sweep the end for the first down. But cornerback Chuck Finney stayed home on the play and dumped Michigan for a one-yard loss. Six plays later we took the lead, 17-14, when Wright went over for the score.

Michigan wasn't through, though, and with eighteen seconds left, they had advanced to our three. But on third down defensive end Hal Henderson dumped their quarterback for a yard loss, and then Chuck Finney came through again, batting down a fourth-down pass to preserve the win.

Rogers rushed for 142 of our 172 yards on the ground, and Garry Harper kept the defense off balance with 206 yards passing. It was a great team win, and considered to be one of USC's six greatest wins of all time.

Still euphoric, the Gamecocks rolled to three easy wins in a row—over NC State, Duke, and hapless Cincinnati. Then came our old nemesis, Georgia, down at Sanford Stadium. Down 13-10 late in the fourth quarter, we drove to the Bulldog 16. Rogers, who had already carried the ball thirty-four times on the day, crashed off-tackle for what looked like another first down, but he was hit dead-on and the ball was jarred loose. Georgia recovered, and that was the game. After wins over The Citadel and Wake Forest, we trooped to Death Valley to take on the despised Striped Beasts. We were 8-2 on the year and had already accepted a bid to play Pittsburgh in the Gator Bowl. A win over Clemson would produce our finest season ever.

It wasn't to be. Despite Rogers' 168 yards, our only points came on two Leopard field goals, and Clemson prevailed, 27-6. Still, it was a much closer game than that. Late in the third quarter the score was tied at six, but two Garry Harper interceptions

Dynamic Duo: George Rogers and Johnnie Wright.

on consecutive possessions led to two Tiger touchdowns, and suddenly the game was effectively over.

In the Gator Bowl, our chance for a record ninth victory slipped away again. We were overmatched by the tough Pitt Panthers and went down, 37-9.

Still, it was another fine season, and our sixteen wins over two years set a new Carolina record.

As for Rogers, he rushed for more than a thousand yards for the third consecutive year and finished his career with an all-time USC record of 5,204 yards. His thirty-three touchdowns constitute another Carolina record. He led the NCAA in rushing for 1980 and was named to every All-America team. Most important, he became the first collegiate player in the state of South Carolina to win the Heisman Trophy. Rogers was the first-round pick of the New Orleans Saints and went on to a distinguished pro career with both New Orleans and Washington.

1981

Needless to say, the departure of George Rogers created a huge hole in the Carolina attack, so it came as no surprise that the 1981 season was marked by inconsistency, confusion, and uncertainty on the offensive side of the line. In fact, Terry Bishop, who opened at quarterback, ended the season as a backup wide receiver. The brightest spot for '81 was the return of Johnnie Wright for his senior season.

The first half of the year was predictably mediocre. We beat Wake Forest, lost to Ole Miss, beat Duke, then lost to both Georgia and Pitt. But we surprised ourselves by taking four games in a row—over Kentucky, Virginia, UNC, and NC State.

The win over UNC, by the way, came at Kenan Stadium at a time when the Tarheels were ranked third in the nation. But quarterback Gordon Beckham played like a man possessed that day, completing sixteen of seventeen passes for a .941 completion percentage (still a USC record). Johnnie Wright weighed in with 115 yards rushing, and we won convincingly, 31-13.

But after the win over NC State the next week, our Gamecocks looked like bedraggled chickens, losing to widely unheralded University of the Pacific, 23-21. Then we bowed before Clemson (which was on its march to the 1981

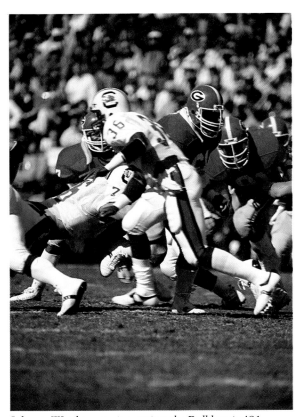

Johnnie Wright motoring against the Bulldogs in '81.

national championship), 29-13.

We were 6-5 following the Clemson game, a winning if not a spectacular season. Unfortunately, however, Coach Carlen had scheduled a twelfth game for 1981, against Hawaii. Presumably, he had anticipated an easy addition to the "W" column, but in fact we suffered a humiliating drubbing, 33-10. Not a winning season after all.

Then, on top of everything else, the university announced that Carlen had been fired. Back in July he had been given a three-year extension on his contract; now, for reasons never made clear, he was out.

But regardless of the circumstances of his firing, it must be said of Jim Carlen that he enjoyed the affection of his players, he compiled a record of 45-36-1

Quarterback Gordon Beckham keeps it for a first down against the Tigers.

against some of the toughest teams in the nation, and he took us to bowl games three times in seven years.

1982

For the 1982 season, the Gamecock reins were passed to Carlen's assistant, Richard Bell, a man best remembered as a nice guy who deserved better. Suffice it to say that Bell inherited some severe organizational problems which tended to manifest themselves on Saturday afternoons.

Behind quarterback Gordon Beckham (who would be named Academic All-American and be a candidate for a Rhodes Scholarship), we managed to defeat some of the lightweights on the '82 schedule (Pacific, Richmond, Cincinnati, and Navy), but that was about it. We lost not only to Duke, NC State, Georgia, LSU, Florida State, and Clemson; we lost even to creampuff Furman. In fact, Richard Bell was dismissed immediately following the Clemson game, but it was widely believed that the loss to Furman was what sealed his fate.

If there was a ray of light during this dark year, it was the play of defensive tackle Andrew Provence. He was named All-American and has had a fine pro career with both Atlanta and Denver. Also, freshman running back Thomas Dendy rushed for 848 yards in '82 (still a freshman record) and gave us at least one reason to look forward to 1983.

JIM CARLEN AND GEORGE ROGERS

19

1983 – 1985

JOE MORRISON THE MAN IN BLACK

A native of Ohio, Joe Morrison was a record-setting quarterback at Cincinnati University before signing a pro contract with the New York Giants. He was thrice named Most Valuable Player for the Giants and set a number of offensive records during his fourteen-year pro career.

As a collegiate football coach, he quickly became known as the Magic Man. At mediocre UT–Chattanooga he went 9-1 in both '77 and '78, and at New Mexico he produced a 10-1 record in '82. At that point USC athletic director Bob Marcum decided that Morrison was the man he was looking for.

Morrison immediately installed the veer formation as our new offensive set, raising the question of who would run it. Last year's quarterback Bill Bradshaw had undergone knee surgery in the off-season and was now being challenged by redshirt sophomore Allen Mitchell. On the plus side, we had

seventeen starters returning from the '82 squad, but with a schedule rated by *Sporting News* as the toughest in the country, we would certainly need them.

After an opening loss to UNC, we defeated Miami of Ohio for Coach Morrison's first win, then came back from a 14-0 halftime deficit to beat Duke the next week. Young Mitchell came off the bench to engineer the fine comeback, completing fourteen of twenty passes for two touchdowns. But the clinching score came via a 90-yard drive featuring the great running of Thomas Dendy and Kent Hagood.

Then came a 31-13 loss to Georgia in Athens, but the next week against Southern Cal, before a capacity-plus crowd at Williams-Brice, the Gamecocks pulled off one of those inexplicable upsets that they've become famous for over the years. Thanks to a ferocious defense that forced several Southern Cal fumbles, we scored an amazing

Joe Morrison, "the man in black," arrives in Columbia in 1983.

twenty-four points during a nine-minute run in the second half to take the game from the demoralized Trojans, 38-14. Dendy scored twice and led all rushers with 101 yards.

It was as a result of this game that our "Fire Ant" defense began to enjoy national notoriety. The name was appropriate not only because of the unit's blitzing, wide-open, damn-the-torpedoes style of play, but also because Morrison, with a sharp eye for publicity, outfitted the team all in red, both jerseys and pants.

Our thrill was soon gone, however, as we lost the next two, to Notre Dame and LSU. We then beat NC State, thanks to Thomas Dendy's 47-yard sprint for a go-ahead touchdown, but lost the following week to Florida State.

We bombed Navy, 31-7, when our Fire Ants simply wouldn't allow the Middies

and their All-American tailback, Napoleon McCallum, to get off the deck. Hagood, on the other hand, rushed for 121 yards. The win made us 5-5 on the year, and, given our deadly schedule, Gamecock fans weren't complaining.

Clemson, under Danny Ford, was 8-1-1 coming into our big clash, but was going nowhere on New Year's Day because of NCAA sanctions against them for recruiting violations. We mustn't say that we were happy to see our country cousins in trouble with the authorities, but it is true that a popular bumper sticker in Columbia that year read, "I told on Danny."

The Tigers stifled our laughter, though, with a 22-13 victory, their seventh win over the Gamecocks in the past eight years.

So we finished the season with a losing record of five wins and six losses, hardly a portent of what was about to happen.

1984

There can be only one explanation for what happened to the Gamecocks in 1984: Black Magic.

It started in the first game of what every football publication predicted would be another mediocre 6-5 season for the Gamecocks. With two minutes to play, The Citadel kicked a field goal to tie the game at 24-all, and Gamecock fans had to wonder, if we couldn't beat this team, where in the world we were going to find five victories.

But with 1:12 left on the clock, we pulled a desperation halfback pass. Quinton Lewis lofted a wobbly 40-yarder to Chris Wade, who streaked the distance for the tie-breaker.

We easily beat Duke the next week, 21-0, but then had to face the mighty Georgia Bulldogs, who came to Columbia with a 2-0 record and favored by two touchdowns. We surprised the oddsmakers by leading 10-3 at the half, but Georgia tied it up late in the third quarter. Time for a little Black Magic. Mike Hold, an untried junior college transfer from Arizona, replaced Allen Mitchell at quarterback, and on the fourth play from scrimmage he threw a perfect 62-yard strike

Earl Johnson and the Fire Ants record another blocked punt in USC's win over Kansas State.

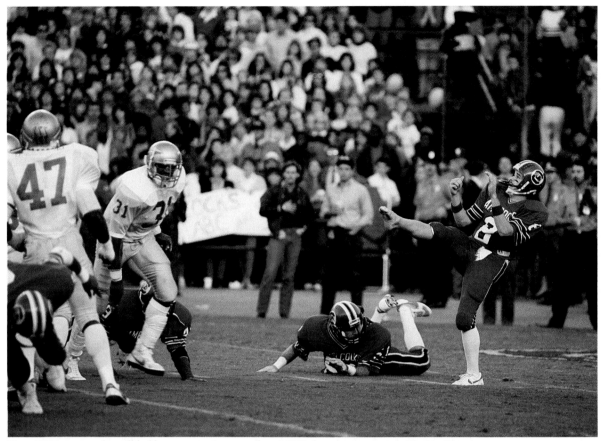

Tom O'Connor, who still holds most punting records at USC, booms one against Florida State.

to Ira Hillery, down to the Georgia six. A play later he took it over himself for the game-winner.

Against Kansas State, the same incantation produced the same result. With seven seconds remaining in the first half, Hold came off the bench and immediately hit Eric Poole with a 47-yard touchdown pass. In the second half our Fire Ants turned it into a rout, blocking two punts en route to a 49-17 shellacking.

We were now 4-0, our best start since 1928, and ranked fourteenth in the nation. But with potent Pitt coming to town, we had to wonder if there was any Black Magic left. Incredibly, there was. We were tied, 14-14, late in the second period when Morrison once again made the magic move. Hold came in and—yes—on the very first play hit Chris Wade for a 31-yard touchdown pass. Then in the third quarter, Hold hit Wade

again for a two-touchdown lead.

But that wasn't all. After Pitt had closed the gap in the fourth quarter to 28-21, Morrison, in touch with forces only he could fathom, sent Mitchell back in at quarterback. Mitchell responded by immediately hitting Wade with yet another TD strike. Thomas Dendy's subsequent 43-yard touchdown dash pretty well iced the cake, and USC went on to post a huge 45-21 victory.

Only the Gamecock teams of 1902 and 1928 had gotten off to a 5-0 start, and when the polls came out on Tuesday morning, we found ourselves at number eleven.

But things were not going to get any easier. Our next date was within the unforgiving environs of South Bend, Indiana. And as a packed stadium of Irish faithful and a national TV audience looked on, it looked like the streak was over. We trailed at the half, 17-14, and with our Fire

Mike Hold about to pitch to Quinton Lewis in the incredible one-point win over Clemson.

Ants getting pushed around, we gave up another nine points in the third quarter.

That's when Morrison made the move to Mike Hold. He failed to produce the scoring strike on first down, but the methodical 73-yard drive followed by the two-point conversion was just as magical, and the lead was cut to 26-22. Eight minutes later on the Irish 33, Hold couldn't find a receiver, so he dashed up the middle for another score, giving us a 29-26 lead.

Was it voodoo? Instead of launching one of their vaunted comebacks, the Irish fumbled the kickoff, and our Rick Rabune recovered at the 17. Three plays later Quinton Lewis bolted over from the four to give us the padding we would need. Final score: USC 36, Notre Dame 32.

Then came wins over East Carolina, 42-20, and NC State, 35-28. (It should be noted, though, that we trailed East Caro-

lina, 10-7, in the second quarter when Mike Hold entered the game. Guess what? On his first play he hit Ira Hillery with a 71-yard scoring pass.)

We were now 8-0 and ranked fifth in the country with Florida State coming to Williams-Brice. If we could get past this game, we would have clear sailing to an undefeated regular season. Rising to the occasion, we played like contending national champs. Entering the second half with a 17-7 lead, our Raynard Brown broke the back of the Seminoles with a 99-yard kickoff return for a touchdown. Also, Bryant Gilliard tied an all-time USC record with four interceptions on the day.

The final score was 38-26, yet another impressive win. Thomas Dendy scored twice, and Mitchell threw two touchdown passes in an offensive effort that covered 464 total yards. By now Morrison had our team—and himself— attired completely in black, and our slogan, "Black Magic," was known throughout the land.

So we were 9-0, number two in the polls, second only to Nebraska, and looking forward to a weak, 3-6 Navy team the next week. Once we got by the Middies, only Clemson would stand in the way of a perfect regular season.

And certainly, sadly, catastrophically, that's what the Gamecocks were thinking. They clearly were not focused on Navy, and they paid the price of a lifetime. Black Magic turned into Black Saturday as we were totally torpedoed by the Midshipmen, 38-21. It wasn't even that close, since Navy led 38-7 early in the fourth quarter.

If the loss weren't already bitter enough, Nebraska also lost that day, to Oklahoma, so that a win over Navy would have made us the number-one team in the nation.

Some of the magic returned the next week against Clemson. Behind 21-3 late in the second period, we began, at last, to shake off our doldrums. Quinton Lewis scored to make the score 21-10 at the half, and a safety in the third period shaved the Tiger lead by another two. With seven minutes to play, a Scott Hagler field goal made it 21-15, and then Mike Hold took the team on an 86-yard march for the winning score. It came with fifty seconds remaining and provided us with a heart-stopping 22-21 win.

After our loss to Navy, the Orange, Sugar, and Cotton Bowls lost interest in us, and we were again wooed and won by our old suitor the Gator Bowl. We would face the 9-2 Cowboys of Oklahoma State, and surely we would win our first bowl game in history.

No. In spite of a great comeback from a 13-0 halftime deficit to give us a 14-13 lead in the fourth quarter, the Cowboys tagged us with our sixth straight bowl loss.

The "man in black," Joe Morrison, was named National Coach of the Year, but it looked like the magic spell was over.

1985

Mike Hold, a sharpshooting passer and dangerous scrambler cut in the mold of Jeff Grantz, replaced Allen Mitchell at starting quarterback for the '85 season, and he was backed up by such accomplished runners as Thomas Dendy, Kent Hagood, and Raynard Brown. But we had lost three big All-Americans—offensive guard Del Wilkes, linebacker James Seawright, and defensive back Bryant Gilliard—and their absence was a source of concern as the season got underway.

We opened with a sound thrashing of The Citadel, but in the second week we had to fight for our lives to hold off little Appalachian State, 20-13. Unfortunately, that struggle proved a harbinger of things to come.

And they came quickly. Mighty Michigan, with an offensive line that averaged 280 pounds per man, crushed us 34-3, and then Georgia, down in Athens, outgunned us in an offensive shootout, 35-21. Of note, a young receiver named Sterling Sharpe caught his first TD pass in this game—the first of many.

The next week we made it three in a row when we were thrashed by Pitt, 42-7. Our lone touchdown, though, came on one of our most remarkable plays of all time. With first down on our 20, Mike Hold dropped back to pass, was forced out of the pocket, and scrambled his way backward to the end zone. Then, with five Panthers latched onto his head, he fired a 30-yard pass to Anthony Smith. The ball hit Smith's shoulder pad and bounced fifteen yards across the field into the outstretched hands of Raynard Brown, who, without breaking stride, gathered it in and raced for the touchdown. We beat Duke the following Saturday in a

Linebacker Derrick Little about to crush Michigan quarterback.

Return man Raynard Brown leaves Tigers in the turf in 1985.

game that featured Sterling Sharpe's USC-record 100-yard return of a kickoff, and then smothered East Carolina 52-10. But two more losses followed, to NC State and Florida State.

Exactly one year too late we beat Navy, 34-31, but then lost to Clemson in our final game, 24-17.

The 5-6 record for 1985 was all the more disappointing in that several brilliant USC careers were now at an end. Mike Hold accounted for 1,959 yards in total offense that year, behind only Todd Ellis and Jeff Grantz in the single-season record book. Thomas Dendy amassed 2,767 rushing yards during his four-year career at Carolina, and his 5.6 yards-per-carry average is second only to Carl Brazell's 5.7 average. Finally, Kent Hagood rushed for 2,014 yards, and his 5.5 yard average is still fourth on the all-time list.

20

1986 – 1988

Morrison Finds a Quarterback

As the 1986 season approached, Carolina fans were very much aware that we had waiting in the wings one of the most heralded high school players in America to take over our quarterback slot: Todd Ellis, a redshirt freshman from Greensboro, North Carolina. Ellis was a magnificent athlete, and the entire Gamecock offense for the next four years would be structured around him and his golden arm.

Complementing Ellis's arm, the '86 squad included the all-time great Carolina receivers Sterling Sharpe and Ryan Bethea. Our running backs were Harold Green, Anthony Smith, and the veteran Raynard Brown.

To take advantage of Ellis's firepower, Morrison installed the run-and-shoot offense that year. Following our opening-game loss to Miami, some cynics were heard to joke, "Yeah, we're gonna run Morrison off and shoot Todd Ellis." But the truth was, for

freshman Ellis it wasn't a bad debut—277 yards passing against the third-ranked Hurricanes.

Two more losses, to Virginia and Georgia, were sandwiched around Ellis's first win, a 45-24 walloping of Western Carolina. Then third-ranked Nebraska came to Willliams-Brice Stadium favored by twenty-six points over the Gamecocks. But with Ellis winging the ball for 286 yards, the Huskers were lucky to escape Columbia with a 27-24 victory.

Against VPI the following Saturday Ellis was even better. Down 24-10 at the half, we came back to earn a tie, 27-27. Ellis broke all USC records that day by throwing for an incredible 394 yards. East Carolina came next, and Ellis recorded another 300-plus yard game, along with four touchdowns. Final score: USC 38, East Carolina 3.

The next week we lost to NC State after time had expired. We held them at our 38

Receiver Ryan Bethea flying away from grounded Bulldogs.

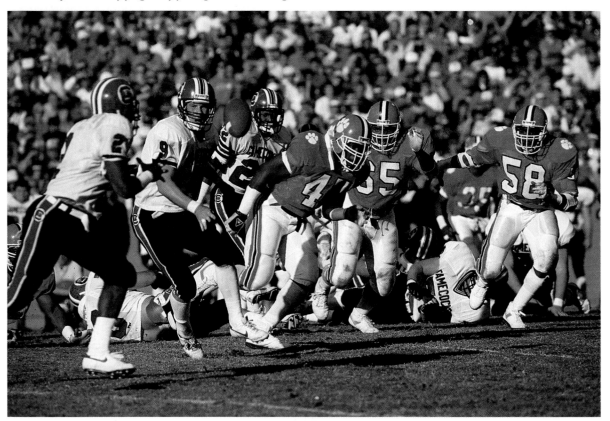

Freshman Todd Ellis pitches out to Sterling Sharpe against the Tigers in '86.

MORRISON FINDS A QUARTERBACK

on the final play of the game to preserve a 22-16 lead, but the referees called USC offsides on the play and gave State another crack at it. Sure enough, Erik Kramer hit Danny Peebles with a scoring strike, and the Pack pulled it out, 23-22. Ellis, by the way, slacked off that afternoon; he only passed for 297 yards.

We split the next two games, losing to Florida State and beating Wake Forest, then packed our gear for a trip to Death Valley. We thought we had bagged a Tiger, but a Treadwell field goal with three minutes left deadlocked the game at 21-all. Our Scott Hagler had a shot at it in the final seconds, but his 41-yard attempt sailed wide, and the game ended in a tie.

The year ended with a less than distinguished 3-6-2 mark, but even as a freshman Todd Ellis was beginning to rewrite the USC record book. He completed 205 passes out of 340 attempts for a .603

completion percentage, and his passes accounted for 3,020 yards and twenty touchdowns. All three figures (percentage, yardage, and touchdowns) are still tops in USC history for a single season.

His primary receiver, Sterling Sharpe, also still holds the records he set that year: seventy-four catches for 1,106 yards and ten touchdowns. Ellis and Sharpe were both named second-team All-Americans.

1987

The Todd Ellis-Joe Morrison combination began to click in 1987. Harold Green's running added great balance to Ellis's passing attack, and the fabled "Fire Ant" defense swarmed all over the opposition.

In the opener against Appalachian State, a 24-3 win, Ellis completed a record thirty

All-time great Gamecock receiver Sterling Sharpe crossing the goal line agai, this time against VPI.

passes for 329 yards. His total fell to 259 yards against Western Carolina, but his three touchdown passes were enough to post a 31-6 victory.

The word was that if our Fire Ants could hold highly ranked Georgia to two touchdowns, the Ellis Express would do the rest. But it didn't work out quite that way. Ellis passed for 306 yards, and we stayed inside the Bulldog 20 all night, but we just couldn't cross the goal line. Final score: Georgia 13, USC 6.

The next week against second-ranked Nebraska, Ellis's two touchdown passes staked us to a 21-13 lead going into the fourth quarter. But thanks to an untimely fumble and a backbreaking interception, the Cornhuskers came back to win, 30-21. It was a tough pill to swallow, but the Gamecocks showed no ill aftereffects. The following Saturday, we romped over VPI, 40-10, and followed that with a 58-10 thrash-ing of Virginia. In truth, USC was now on a roll the likes of which had seldom been seen in Columbia.

The next victim was East Carolina, which fell 34-12 when Ellis threw for a new-record 425 yards. Now, with two years still left to play, Ellis became our all-time passing leader with 5,201 yards to his credit. Then came NC State, and it was payback time for the one-point loss they'd pinned on us the year before. The fact that the Pack had just beaten seventh-ranked Clemson the week before raised the stakes even higher. With the Fire Ants swarming and Green notch-ing his third three-touchdown game of the year, we got a lifetime's worth of revenge, 48-0.

A 30-0 shutout of Wake Forest the next week earned us a Gator Bowl bid, and with that in hand, we prepared for Clemson to pay a visit. A crowd of 75,000 and a national TV audience were tuned in, and USC fans

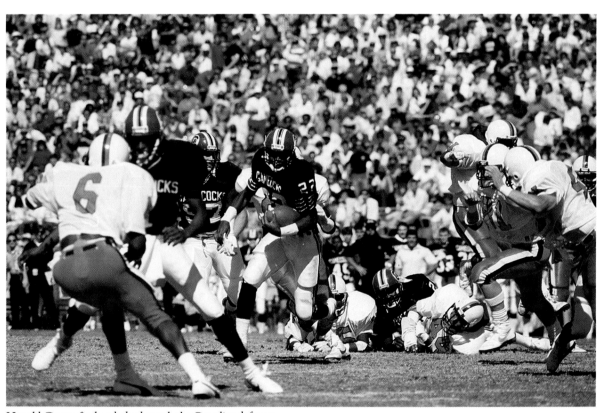

Harold Green finds a hole through the Cavalier defense.

MORRISON FINDS A QUARTERBACK

All-American defensive back Brad Edwards.

were not disappointed. Ellis hit Bethea with a 77-yarder to set up an early field goal, but the Tigers came back to take a 7-6 halftime lead. The Fire Ants shut them down from there, though, and we went ahead on a short plunge by Green. Late in the game our Brad Edwards picked off a desperation pass by Rodney Williams and returned it for a score to ice the win, 20-7.

Now ranked eighth in the nation, our 8-2 Gamecocks traveled to Miami to take on the second-ranked Hurricanes in another nationally televised game. In this game, however, our blitzing, bothersome Fire Ants played right into 'Canes quarterback Steve Walsh's hands. Rather than being rattled, Walsh stood tall and picked our man-to-man defense apart all night. Plus, Ellis suffered through the worst game of his career, covering only 141 yards through the air. Still we trailed only 14-13 at the half, and the game wasn't over until the final gun sounded with the Hurricanes holding a 20-16 lead.

Some spectators contended, by the way, that the referees occasionally appeared biased in favor of Miami. With nine minutes remaining, for example, Ellis threw a pass and appeared to be the victim of a late hit by two Miami linemen. No flag was thrown, but when the Carolina bench rushed onto the field to defend their quarterback, the ref did throw his flag— and penalized USC fifteen yards for unsportsmanlike conduct.

As for the Gator Bowl, let it only be said that seventh-ranked LSU rolled over our still-depressed Gamecocks, 30-13, for our seventh consecutive bowl loss.

All told, though, it was a banner year, certainly one in which we enjoyed more national recognition than had ever been lavished upon us before. And to cap it, both Sterling Sharpe and Brad Edwards were named All-American. Nose guard Roy Hart was named a second team All-American, and Mark Fryer was named to the Academic All-America team. Even Coach Morrison got in on the post-season glory, as the Southern Independent Coach of the Year. Harold Green scored sixteen touchdowns in '87, still an all-time USC record, and freshman kicker Collin Mackie scored 113 points, another all-time record.

Ellis continued his assault on the record book, completing 241 passes for 3,206 yards. As a sophomore, he now had 6,226 yards through the air, a phenomenal achievement. For the second year in a row, he was named team MVP.

1988

We started the 1988 season with the look of the national power we were supposed to be, reeling off routine wins over UNC, Western Carolina, and East Carolina. Then sixth-ranked Georgia came to Williams-Brice to take on our fourteenth-ranked Gamecocks. This was the game in which receiver Robert Brooks gained instant immortality with his sensational one-handed grab of an Ellis pass for the go-ahead touchdown. Fueling dreams of the Big Year, we routed the Bulldogs 23-10 and shot to number seven in the rankings. We easily beat Appalachian State the next week, but it was that game which to Gamecock fans seemed to mark the end of a great era. For reasons that remain mysterious, the team went flat following the ASU game, and even though we won three more games in '88, we never looked the same again.

The first—and very obvious—clue came the next week against VPI. Our vaunted

Freshman Eddie Miller about to wrap up an Ellis pass against Applachian State.

Mike Dingle goes over the top for a TD against Western Carolina.

offense mustered only one touchdown in this game, one which we should have won by thirty points, and our famous Fire Ants had completely lost their sting. Only by virtue of four Collin Mackie field goals and a TD kickoff return by Robert Brooks did we manage to escape with a 26-24 win.

Well, anybody can have an off day. Surely we would get back on track against Georgia Tech, a team that hadn't beaten a Division 1 opponent in fifteen tries. But on Grant Field that day, our dream of an undefeated season quickly turned into our worst nightmare. The lowly Jackets destroyed us 34-0, the first time we had been shut out in eighty-two games.

After a much-needed win over NC State, here came fifth-ranked Florida State, along with a national television audience—a perfect opportunity to redeem ourselves.

But we stepped on our own toes again, looking totally inept and suffering our worst home-game loss ever, 59-0. Ellis, by the way, had seventy-nine yards passing.

We did beat Navy the next week, thanks largely to four Collin Mackie field goals, and despite our recent horrors we were still 8-2 on the year (and only the sixth team in USC history to win eight games in a season). Also, the win over Navy earned us an invitation to the Liberty Bowl.

But first came Clemson, which turned into another disastrous loss, 29-10. So it was with our tail between our legs that we traveled to Memphis to take on Indiana. Unbelievably; the second-rate Hoosiers rolled up 575 total yards against our humiliated Fire Ants, to our team's total of 241, and took the victory, 34-10.

And that was it. The season was over,

Anthony Parlor stretches for a pass versus Georgia.

but the mystery remains.

As for Coach Morrison, he suffered a fatal heart attack in February of 1989. During his six years at Carolina he had become, percentage-wise, one of our winningest coaches ever with a 39-28-2 record, and he had taken us to three bowl games and considerable national prominence. His loss was deeply felt.

Sparky Woods at the Helm

The death of Joe Morrison marked the end of a memorable era in Gamecock football, and a new era began with the arrival of new coach Sparky Woods.

Woods, the highly successful young coach at Appalachian State, was recognized not only for winning games but for running a squeaky clean program, which was a matter of some importance to the university right then. An internal investigation had confirmed the truth of allegations by former lineman Tommy Chaikin that there was widespread steroid use on the USC team, so athletic director King Dixon was looking for a coach untouched even by a breath of scandal.

Woods, a graduate of Carson-Newman, had been an assistant at Tennessee, Kansas, Northern Alabama, Iowa State, and Appalachian State before becoming the nation's youngest head coach at ASU. There he compiled a 38-19-2 record, won the Southern Conference crown twice, and was thrice named the conference's Coach of the Year.

With Todd Ellis back for his senior season, the '89 campaign opened well enough. After beating Duke, tying VPI, and losing to a powerful West Virginia squad, we ripped off four wins in a row—over Georgia Tech, 21-10, Georgia, 24-20, East Carolina, 47-14, and Western Carolina, 24-3.

But the next week against NC State, Todd Ellis went down in the first quarter with a season-ending knee injury, dropping a sudden, sad curtain on what had been a brilliant college career. Backup Dick DeMasi filled in for the rest of the season, but things weren't quite the same.

We lost the NC State game, then lost again to Florida State before managing to beat weakling UNC. As for the Clemson game, which to our chagrin happened to be on national TV, the Tigers ripped us to shreds, 45-0.

New Gamecock coach Sparky Woods.

of 3,005 yards.

Also from the '89 team, tackle Mark Fryer made the Academic All-America team for the third consecutive year.

1990

Coach Woods had finished his first year with a respectable 6-4-1 record, but now Ellis and Green were gone, and we doubted that they could be replaced. But in 1990 we were introduced to one Bobby Fuller, a junior transfer from Appalachian State (where he played under Sparky Woods), who had given the Gamecocks fits in '86.

At one running back we had Mike Dingle, a six-three, 235-pound speedster whom defenders were generally anxious to avoid. At the other was one of the most exciting young backs we'd seen since the days of Wadiak the Cadillac. At five-ten, 200 pounds, Rob DeBoer was a fire hydrant who seemed to delight in attacking opposing linemen and who quickly earned the affection of Gamecock fans everywhere. In fact, DeBoer would set a record for freshmen by rushing for 165 yards against East Carolina.

The 1990 season proved to be another one of those up-and-down years that have become rather the hallmark of USC football. We opened with three wins—over Duke, UNC, and VPI—in the last of which Mike Dingle set a modern era record by scoring four touchdowns in a single game. But in the fourth game we were ambushed by eventual national champion Georgia Tech, and the season never quite righted itself.

We beat East Carolina the following week, but then, in one of those mystery games USC endures periodically, we were defeated—at home—by The Citadel, supposedly the breather on our schedule. Our

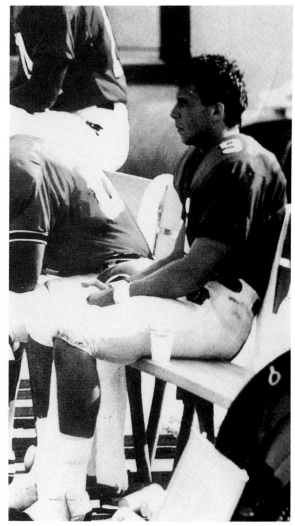

A dark curtain drops: Todd Ellis ends his career with a knee injury against NC State in '89.

Todd Ellis, despite missing half of his senior season, broke almost every Gamecock passing record. During his career he completed 747 passes for an incredible 9,953 yards (almost six miles) and forty-nine touchdowns. For comparison's sake, Tommy Suggs, our second-leading all-time passer, completed 355 passes for 4,916 yards and thirty-four TDs.

As for our great running back Harold Green, it was his misfortune to come along when USC lived and died by the pass. Nevertheless, he remains second only to George Rogers in career rushing with a total

Bobby Fuller takes control of the offense in 1990.

Mike Dingle takes to the air again.

Tough-running Rob DeBoer leaves East Carolinians looking for his footprints.

offense scored thirty-five points that day, but our defense gave up thirty-eight, and it was a dark omen of things to come.

We allowed thirty-eight points again in a loss to NC State, then topped that performance by giving up forty-one in a blistering at the hands of Florida State. So we were allowing an average of thirty-nine points over the past three games, and fans were beginning to long for the Fire Ants of old.

We beat Southern Illinois, then lost to Clemson to even our record for the year at 5-5 with one game remaining. The finale was against West Virginia and, before a national TV audience on ESPN, we did ourselves proud. Collin Mackie broke an all-time Carolina record by kicking five field goals, and we defeated a good Mountaineer team, 29-10.

In leading us to this 6-5 record, Bobby Fuller had a sensational year, completing 171 passes for 2,372 yards and thirteen touchdowns—second only to Ellis for single-season stats. His favorite receiver, Robert Brooks, now had 101 catches and fourteen touchdowns over three years, and we planned to enjoy watching those totals rise during 1991.

Collin Mackie, by the way, scored 330 points during his stellar career, an all-time USC scoring record.

1991

We had every reason to expect Coach Woods to put together his third consecutive winning season in 1991. Bobby Fuller was back for his senior year; we had talented, fleet receivers in Robert Brooks, Eddie Miller, and David Pitchko; and we had an exciting freshman tailback by the name of Brandon Bennett.

On the other hand, though, doomsayers might have pointed out that we had a young, inexperienced line, both offensively and defensively.

The opener against Duke set the tone for the season. We won for fifty-eight minutes, but somehow the Blue Devils scored fourteen points in the final two and emerged with a tie. It became a familiar pattern. In fact, if our games had lasted only forty-five minutes, we would have enjoyed a super season, but we seemed to collapse in the final quarter of game after game.

We wound up with a disappointing 3-6-2 record, beating only VPI, East Tennessee, and Georgia Tech, while losing to West Virginia, East Carolina, NC State, Florida State, UNC, and Clemson. Our second tie of the season, against Louisiana Tech, also came at the last minute.

Sensational freshman running back Brandon Bennett.

Had it not been for Fuller, we might have gone winless. During his two-year career, Fuller completed 373 passes for 4,896 yards, and his .588 career completion percentage is tops in the Gamecock record book.

As for Robert Brooks, he completed his career with 156 catches for 2,211 yards, making him second all-time in receptions and in receiving yardage (behind Sterling Sharpe). Also, his nineteen TD receptions established a new Gamecock career record.

Freshman Brandon Bennett, by the way, broke Jeff Grantz's single-game rushing record when he ran for 278 yards against East Tennessee. Gamecock fans can look forward with pleasure to his continued success.

Wolfpack defender will never get his hands on this loose ball.

SPARKY WOODS AT THE HELM

EPILOGUE

A glance back over the past hundred years reveals a history of great wins, tough losses, fascinating stories, and a lot of excitement for Gamecock fans everywhere. Under twenty-nine head coaches from Dixie Whaley to Sparky Woods, we've played big games against the big names and compiled an overall mark of 435 victories, 425 defeats, and forty-three ties—a winning record in anybody's book.

Our Gamecock Club, the chief fund raiser and right arm of the athletic department, has now enjoyed fifty years of steady growth and is considered one of the foremost such organizations in the nation. Under the leadership of executive director Art Baker, the Gamecock Club now raises more than five million dollars a year and supports all athletic activities at the university.

Prospects for 1992 are especially exciting. Along with Arkansas, USC joined the Southeastern Conference as of July, 1991.

We fall within the conference's newly designated East Division, where our foes will include Florida, Georgia, Kentucky, Tennessee, and Vanderbilt. The Western Division consists of Alabama, Arkansas, Auburn, LSU, Ole Miss, and Mississippi State.

Looking ahead, Coach Woods says, "My hope is for USC to become one of the premier football programs in the country. I want to consistently graduate our players, be in a bowl game every year, and have fun doing it.

"It won't be easy. The competition in the Southeastern Conference is strong. But anyone who plays this game enjoys competition. And I'm just crazy enough to believe that we can be the best in the country."

Still, win, lose, or draw, we can only say HERE'S A HEALTH, CAROLINA, FOREVER TO THEE!

Gamecocks Through the Years

1892   Won 0, Lost 1   No Coach
Furman 0-44   Dec.   24   at Charleston, S.C.

1893   No team

1894   Won 0, Lost 2   No Coach
Georgia 0-40   Nov.   3   at Columbia
Augusta Y 4-16   Nov.   11   at Columbia

1895   Won 2, Lost 1   No Coach
Columbia AA .... 20- 0   Nov.   2   at Columbia
Furman 14-10   Nov.   8   at Columbia
Wofford 0-10   Nov.   14   at Columbia

1896   Won 1, Lost 3   Coach W. H. Whaley
Charleston Y .... 4- 6   Oct.   31   at Charleston
Clemson .... 12- 6   Nov.   12   at Columbia
Wofford .... 4- 6   Nov.   19   at Columbia
Furman 0-12   Nov.   26   at Greenville, S.C.

1897   Won 0, Lost 3   Coach W. P. Murphy
Clemson 6-18   Nov.   11   at Columbia
Charleston Y .... 0- 6   Nov.   26   at Charleston, S.C.
Charleston Y .... 0- 4   Oct.   23   at Columbia

1898   Won 1, Lost 2   Coach W. Wertenbaker
Bingham .... 16- 5   Oct.   18   at Columbia
Clemson 0-24   Nov.   17   at Columbia
Davidson .... 0- 6   Nov.   24   at Charlotte, N.C.

1899   Won 2, Lost 3   Coach I. O. Hunt
Columbia Y .... 4- 0   Oct.   15   at Columbia
Clemson 0-34   Nov.   9   at Columbia
Bingham .... 11- 5   Nov.   15   at Columbia
Bingham 6-18   Nov.   22   at Asheville, N.C.
Davidson .... 0- 5   Nov.   30   at Charlotte, N.C.

1900   Won 4, Lost 3   Coach I. O. Hunt
Georgia .... 0- 5   Oct.   20   at Athens
Guilford .... 10- 0   Oct.   25   at Columbia
Clemson 0-51   Nov.   1   at Columbia
N.C. A&M .... 12- 0   Nov.   10   at Columbia
Furman .... 27- 0   Nov.   17   at Greenville, S.C.
Davidson .... 0- 5   Nov.   22   at Charlotte, N.C.
N.C. A&M .... 17- 5   Nov.   29   at Raleigh

1901   Won 3, Lost 4   Coach B. W. Dickson
Georgia 5-10   Oct.   12   at Augusta
Furman .... 12- 0   Oct.   22   at Columbia
Bingham .... 11- 6   Oct.   24   at Asheville, N.C.
Davidson 5-12   Oct.   30   at Columbia
Georgia Tech 0-13   Nov.   9   at Atlanta
N.C.M.A .... 47- 0   Nov.   12   at Columbia
Wofford 5-11   Nov.   18   at Spartanburg, S.C.

1902   Won 6, Lost 1   Coach C. R. Williams
Guilford .... 10- 0   Oct.   15   at Columbia
N.C.M.A .... 60- 0   Oct.   21   at Columbia
Bingham .... 28- 0   Oct.   25   at Columbia
Clemson .... 12- 6   Oct.   30   at Columbia
St. Albans .... 5- 0   Nov.   6   at Columbia
Furman 0-10   Nov.   14   at Greenville, S.C.
Charleston M.C .... 80- 0   Nov.   28   at Columbia

1903   Won 8, Lost 2   Coach C. R. Williams
Columbia Y .... 24- 0   Oct.   2   at Columbia
Welsh Neck .... 89- 0   Oct.   6   at Columbia
North Carolina 0-17   Oct.   10   at Columbia
Georgia .... 17- 0   Oct.   17   at Athens
Guilford .... 29- 0   Oct.   23   at Columbia
Tennessee .... 24- 0   Oct.   29   at Columbia
Davidson 29-12   Nov.   8   at Charlotte, N.C.
N.C. A&M .... 5- 6   Nov.   14   at Raleigh
Charleston .... 16- 0   Nov.   21   at Charleston, S.C.
Georgia Tech .... 16- 0   Nov.   26   at Atlanta

1904   Won 5, Lost 2, Tied 1   Coach Christie Benet
Welsh Neck .... 14- 0   Oct.   7   at Columbia
North Carolina 0-27   Oct.   15   at Chapel Hill
Guilford .... 21- 4   Oct.   20   at Columbia
Georgia .... 2- 0   Oct.   26   at Columbia
N.C. A&M .... 0- 0   Nov.   5   at Raleigh
Davidson .... 0- 6   Nov.   12   at Columbia
Charleston A.C. .... 24- 6   Nov.   19   at Charleston, S.C.
Wash. and Lee .... 25- 0   Nov.   24   at Sumter, SC

1905   Won 4, Lost 2, Tied 1   Coach Christie Benet
Welsh Neck .... 14- 0   Oct.   13   at Columbia
Bingham .... 19- 6   Oct.   20   at Columbia
N.C. A&M 0-29   Oct.   26   at Columbia
Davidson .... 6- 4   Nov.   4   at Charlotte, N.C.
Bingham .... 5- 5   Nov.   11   at Asheville, N.C.
Virginia Tech 0-34   Nov.   18   at Roanoke
The Citadel .... 47- 0   Nov.   30   at Charleston, S.C.

1906   No team — Trustees abolished football

1907   Won 3, Lost O   Coach Douglas McKay
Charleston .... 14- 4   Nov.   16   at Columbia
Georgia College .... 4- 0   Nov.   21   at Columbia
The Citadel .... 12- 0   Nov.   28   at Charleston, S.C.

1908   Won 3, Lost 5, Tied 1   Coach Christie Benet
Ridgewood .... 0- 0   Oct.   3   at Columbia
Charleston .... 17- 0   Oct.   10   at Columbia
Georgia 6-29   Oct.   17   at Athens
Charleston AA 4-15   Oct.   22   at Columbia
Davidson 0-22   Oct.   29   at Columbia
Georgia M.S. .... 19- 5   Nov.   4   at Augusta
Bingham 6-10   Nov.   7   at Columbia
North Carolina 0-22   Nov.   14   at Chapel Hill
The Citadel .... 12- 0   Nov.   26   at Charleston, S.C.

1909   Won 2, Lost 6   Coach Christie Benet
N.C.M.C .... 0- 5   Oct.   9   at Columbia
Georgia Tech 0-59   Oct.   16   at Atlanta
Wake Forest .... 0- 8   Oct.   23   at Columbia
Charleston 17-11   Oct.   28   at Columbia
Clemson .... 0- 6   Nov.   3   at Columbia
Davidson 5-29   Nov. ʼ13   at Davidson, N.C.
Mercer .... 3- 5   Nov.   20   at Macon, Ga.
The Citadel .... 11- 5   Nov.   25   at Charleston, S.C.

1910   Won 4, Lost 4   Coach John H. Neff

Charleston	8- 0	Oct.	8	at Columbia
Georgia M.S.	14- 0	Oct.	15	at Augusta
Lenoir	33- 0	Oct.	22	at Columbia
Wake Forest	6- 0	Oct.	27	at Columbia
Clemson	0-24	Nov.	3	at Columbia
Davidson	0-53	Nov.	12	at Davidson, N.C.
North Carolina	6-23	Nov.	19	at Durham, N.C.
The Citadel	0- 5	Nov.	24	at Charleston, S.C.

1911   Won 1, Lost 4, Tied 2   Coach John H. Neff

Georgia	0-38	Oct.	7	at Athens
Charleston	16- 0	Oct.	14	at Charleston, S.C.
Florida	6- 6	Oct.	21	at Columbia
Clemson	0-27	Nov.	2	at Columbia
North Carolina	0-21	Nov.	11	at Chapel Hill
Davidson	0-10	Nov.	18	at Columbia
The Citadel	0- 0	Nov.	30	at Charleston, S.C.

1912   Won 5, Lost 2, Tied 1   Coach N. B. Edgerton

Wake Forest	10- 3	Oct.	5	at Columbia
Virginia	0-19	Oct.	14	at Charlottesville
Florida	6-10	Oct.	19	at Gainesville
Charleston	68- 0	Oct.	26	at Charleston, S.C.
Clemson	22- 7	Oct.	31	at Columbia
North Carolina	6- 6	Nov.	9	at Chapel Hill
Porter	66- 0	Nov.	16	at Columbia
The Citadel	26- 2	Nov.	28	at Columbia

1913   Won 4, Lost 3   Coach N. B. Edgerton

Virginia	0-54	Oct.	4	at Charlottesville
Wake Forest	27-10	Oct.	11	at Columbia
North Carolina	3-13	Oct.	18	at Columbia
Clemson	0-32	Oct.	30	at Columbia
Florida	13- 0	Nov.	8	at Columbia
Davidson	10- 0	Nov.	15	at Davidson, N.C.
The Citadel	42-13	Nov.	26	at Columbia

1914   Won 5, Lost 5, Tied 1   Coach N. B. Edgerton

Mach. Mates	30- 7	Sept.	30	at Columbia
Georgia Tech	0-20	Oct.	3	at Atlanta
North Carolina	0-48	Oct.	12	at Chapel Hill
Virginia	7-49	Oct.	17	at Charlottesville
Newberry	13-13	Oct.	24	at Columbia
Clemson	6-29	Oct.	29	at Columbia
Wofford	25- 0	Nov.	4	at Spartanburg, S.C.
Wake Forest	26- 0	Nov.	7	at Columbia
Davidson	7-13	Nov.	14	at Columbia
Newberry	47- 6	Nov.	19	at Newberry, S.C.
The Citadel	7- 6	Nov.	26	at Columbia

1915   Won 5, Lost 3, Tied 1   Coach N. B. Edgerton

Newberry	29- 0	Oct.	2	at Columbia
Presbyterian	41- 0	Oct.	9	at Columbia
N.C. A&M	19-10	Oct.	21	at Raleigh
Clemson	0- 0	Oct.	28	at Columbia
Wofford	33- 6	Nov.	4	at Spartanburg, S.C.
Cumberland	68- 0	Nov.	6	at Columbia
Virginia	0-13	Nov.	13	at Columbia
Georgetown	0-61	Nov.	20	at Washington, D.C.
The Citadel	0- 3	Nov.	25	at Columbia

1916   Won 2, Lost 7   Coach Rice Warren

Newberry	0-10	Oct.	7	at Columbia
Wofford	23- 3	Oct.	14	at Columbia
Tennessee	0-26	Oct.	21	at Knoxville
Clemson	0-27	Oct.	26	at Columbia
Wake Forest	7-33	Nov.	4	at Columbia
Virginia	6-35	Nov.	11	at Charlottesville
Mercer	47- 0	Nov.	18	at Columbia
Furman	0-14	Nov.	23	at Greenville, S.C.
The Citadel	2-20	Nov.	30	at Columbia

1917   Won 3, Lost 5   Coach Dixon Foster

Newberry	38- 0	Oct.	6	at Columbia
Florida	13-21	Oct.	13	at Gainesville
Clemson	13-21	Oct.	25	at Columbia
Erskine	13-14	Nov.	3	at Columbia
Furman	26- 0	Nov.	8	at Florence, S.C.
Wofford	0-20	Nov.	17	at Spartanburg, S.C.
Presbyterian	14-20	Nov.	24	at Columbia
The Citadel	20- 0	Nov.	29	at Columbia

1918   Won 2, Lost 1, Tied 1   Coach Frank Dobson

Clemson	0-39	Nov.	2	at Columbia
Furman	20-12	Nov.	16	at Greenville, S.C.
Wofford	13- 0	Nov.	23	at Columbia
The Citadel	0- 0	Nov.	28	at Orangeburg, S.C.

1919   Won 1, Lost 7, Tied 1   Coach Dixon Foster

Presbyterian	0- 6	Sept.	27	at Columbia
Erskine	6- 0	Oct.	4	at Columbia
Georgia	0-14	Od.	11	at Athens
Davidson	0- 7	Oct.	18	at Columbia
Clemson	6-19	Oct.	30	at Columbia
Tennessee	6- 6	Nov.	8	at Columbia
Wash. and Lee	0-26	Nov	15	at Lexington, Va.
Florida	0-13	Nov.	22	at Columbia
The Citadel	7-14	Nov.	27	at Columbia

1920   Won 5, Lost 4   Coach Sol Metzger

Wofford	10- 0	Oct.	2	at Columbia
Georgia	0-37	Oct.	9	at Columbia
North Carolina	0- 7	Oct.	16	at Chapel Hill
Presbyterian	14- 0	Oct.	21	at Augusta, Ga.
Clemson	3- 0	Oct.	28	at Columbia
Davidson	0-27	Nov.	6	at Davidson, N.C.
Navy	0-63	Nov.	13	at Annapolis, Md.
Newberry	48- 0	Nov.	20	at Columbia
The Citadel	7- 6	Nov.	25	at Charleston, S.C.

1921   Won 5. Lost 1, Tied 2   Coach Sol Metzger

Erskine	13- 7	Oct.	1	at Columbia
Newberry	7- 0	Oct.	8	at Columbia
North Carolina	7- 7	Oct.	15	at Columbia
Presbyterian	48- 0	Oct.	22	at Columbia
Clemson	21- 0	Oct.	27	at Columbia
Florida	7- 7	Nov.	5	at Tampa
Furman	0- 7	Nov.	12	at Greenville, S.C.
The Citadel	13- 0	Nov.	24	at Columbia

1922   Won 5, Lost 4   Coach Sol Metzger

Erskine	13- 0	Sept.	29	at Columbia
Presbyterian	7- 0	Oct.	7	at Columbia
North Carolina	7-10	Oct.	14	at Chapel Hill
Wofford	20- 0	Oct.	20	at Columbia
Clemson	0- 3	Oct.	26	at Columbia
Sewanee	6- 7	Nov.	4	at Columbia
Furman	27- 7	Nov.	11	at Columbia
The Citadel	13- 0	Nov.	16	at Orangeburg, S.C.
Centre	0-42	Nov.	30	at Danville, Ky.

Gamecocks Through the Years

1923   Won 4, Lost 6   Coach Sol Metzger

Erskine	35- 0	Sept.	29	at Columbia
Presbyterian	3- 7	Oct.	6	at Columbia
N. C. State	0- 7	Oct.	13	at Raleigh
Newberry	24- 0	Oct.	19	at Columbia
Clemson	6- 7	Oct.	25	at Columbia
North Carolina	0-13	Nov.	3	at Columbia
Furman	3-23	Nov.	10	at Greenville, S.C.
The Citadel	12- 0	Nov.	15	at Orangeburg, S.C.
Wash. and Lee	7-13	Nov.	17	at Columbia
Wake Forest	14- 7	Nov.	29	at Columbia

1924   Won 7, Lost 3   Coach Sol Metzger

Erskine	47- 0	Sept.	27	at Columbia
Georgia	0-18	Oct.	4	at Athens
N. C. State	10- 0	Oct.	11	at Columbia
Presbyterian	29- 0	Oct.	17	at Columbia
Clemson	3- 0	Oct.	23	at Columbia
The Citadel	14- 3	Oct.	29	at Orangeburg, S.C.
North Carolina	10- 7	Nov.	1	at Chapel Hill
Furman	0-10	Nov.	8	at Columbia
Sewanee	0-10	Nov.	15	at Columbia
Wake Forest	7- 0	Nov.	27	at Columbia

1925   Won 7, Lost 3   Coach Branch Bocock

Erskine	33- 0	Sept.	26	at Columbia
North Carolina	0- 7	Oct.	3	at Columbia
N. C. State	7- 6	Oct.	11	at Raleigh
Wofford	6- 0	Oct.	16	at Columbia
Clemson	33- 0	Oct.	22	at Columbia
The Citadel	30- 6	Oct.	28	at Orangeburg, S.C.
Virginia Tech	0- 6	Oct.	31	at Richmond
Furman	0- 2	Nov.	14	at Greenville, S.C.
Presbyterian	21- 0	Nov.	20	at Columbia
Centre	20- 0	Nov.	28	at Columbia

1926   Won 6, Lost 4   Coach Branch Bocock

Erskine	41- 0	Sept.	25	at Columbia
Maryland	12- 0	Oct.	2	at Columbia
North Carolina	0- 7	Oct.	9	at Chapel Hill
Wofford	27-13	Oct.	15	at Columbia
Clemson	24- 0	Oct.	21	at Columbia
The Citadel	9-12	Oct.	28	at Orangeburg, S.C.
Virginia	0- 6	Oct.	30	at Columbia
Virginia Tech	19- 0	Nov.	6	at Richmond
Furman	7-10	Nov.	13	at Columbia
N. C. State	20-14	Nov.	20	at Columbia

1927   Won 4, Lost 5   Coach Harry Lightsey

Erskine	13- 6	Sept.	24	at Columbia
Maryland	0-26	Oct.	1	at College Park
Virginia	13-12	Oct.	8	at Charlottesville
North Carolina	14- 6	Oct.	15	at Columbia
Clemson	0-20	Oct.	20	at Columbia
The Citadel	6- 0	Oct.	27	at Orangeburg, S.C.
Virginia Tech	0-35	Nov.	5	at Richmond
Furman	0-33	Nov.	12	at Greenville, S.C.
N. C. State	0-34	Nov.	24	at Columbia

1928   Won 6, Lost 2, Tied 2   Coach Billy Laval

Erskine	19- 0	Sept.	22	at Columbia
Chicago	6- 0	Sept.	29	at Chicago, Ill.
Virginia	24-13	Oct.	6	at Charlottesville
Maryland	21- 7	Oct.	13	at Columbia
Presbyterian	13- 0	Oct.	19	at Columbia
Clemson	0-32	Oct.	25	at Columbia
The Citadel	0- 0	Nov.	1	at Orangeburg, S.C.
North Carolina	0- 0	Nov.	10	at Chapel Hill
Furman	6- 0	Nov.	17	at Columbia
N. C. State	7-18	Nov.	29	at Raleigh

1929   Won 6, Lost 5   Coach Billy Laval

Erskine	26- 7	Sept.	28	at Columbia
Virginia	0- 6	Oct.	5	at Columbia
Maryland	26- 6	Oct.	12	at College Park
Presbyterian	41- 0	Oct.	18	at Columbia
Clemson	14-21	Oct.	24	at Columbia
The Citadel	27-14	Oct.	31	at Orangeburg, S.C.
North Carolina	0-40	Nov.	9	at Columbia
Furman	2- 0	Nov.	16	at Greenville, S.C.
Florida	7-20	Nov.	23	at Columbia
N. C. State	20- 6	Nov.	30	at Raleigh
Tennessee	0-54	Dec.	7	at Knoxville

1930   Won 6, Lost 4   Coach Billy Laval

Erskine	19- 0	Sept.	20	at Columbia
Duke	22- 0	Sept.	27	at Durham, N.C.
Georgia Tech	0-45	Oct.	4	at Atlanta
Louisiana State	7- 6	Oct.	11	at Columbia
Clemson	7-20	Oct.	23	at Columbia
The Citadel	13- 0	Oct.	30	at Orangeburg, S.C.
Furman	0-14	Nov.	8	at Greenville, S.C.
Sewanee	14-13	Nov.	15	at Columbia
N. C. State	19- 0	Nov.	22	at Columbia
Auburn	7-25	Nov.	27	at Columbus, Ga.

1931   Won 5, Lost 4, Tied 1   Coach Billy Laval

Duke	7- 0	Sept.	26	at Columbia
Georgia Tech	13-25	Oct.	3	at Atlanta
Louisiana State	12-19	Oct.	10	at Baton Rouge
Clemson	21- 0	Oct.	22	at Columbia
The Citadel	26- 7	Oct.	29	at Orangeburg, S.C.
Furman	27- 0	Nov.	7	at Columbia
Florida	6- 6	Nov.	14	at Tampa
N. C. State	21- 0	Nov.	21	at Columbia
Auburn	6-13	Nov.	26	at Montgomery, Ala.
Centre	7- 9	Dec.	5	at Columbia

1932   Won 5, Lost 4, Tied 2   Coach Billy Laval

Sewanee	7- 3	Sept.	24	at Columbia
Villanova	7- 6	Oct.	1	at Philadelphia, Penn.
Wake Forest	0- 6	Oct.	8	at Charlotte, N.C.
Wofford	19- 0	Oct.	14	at Columbia
Clemson	14- 0	Oct.	20	at Columbia
Tulane	0- 6	Oct.	29	at New Orleans, La.
Louisiana State	0- 6	Nov.	5	at Columbia
Furman	0-14	Nov.	12	at Greenville, S.C.
The Citadel	19- 0	Nov.	19	at Columbia
N. C. State	7- 7	Nov.	24	at Raleigh
Auburn	20-20	Dec.	3	at Birmingham, Ala.

1933   Won 6, Lost 3, Tied 1   Coach Billy Laval

Wofford	31- 0	Sept.	23	at Columbia
Temple	6-26	Sept.	29	at Philadelphia, Penn.
Villanova	6-15	Oct.	7	at Columbia
†Clemson	7- 0	Oct.	19	at Columbia
The Citadel	12- 6	Oct.	26	at Orangeburg, S.C.
†Virginia Tech	12- 0	Oct.	28	at Blacksburg
Louisiana State	7-30	Nov.	5	at Baton Rouge, La.
†N. C. State	14- 0	Nov.	11	at Columbia
Furman	0- 0	Nov.	19	at Columbia
Auburn	16-14	Dec.	2	at Birmingham, Ala.

THE
HISTORY

Gamecocks Through the Years

1934   Won 5, Lost 4   Coach Billy Laval

Erskine	25- 0	Sept.	29	at Columbia
† V.M.I.	22- 6	Oct.	6	at Columbia
† N. C. State	0- 6	Oct.	13	at Raleigh
The Citadel	20- 6	Oct.	18	at Orangeburg, S.C.
† Clemson	0-19	Oct.	25	at Columbia
† Virginia Tech	20- 0	Nov.	3	at Columbia
Villanova	0-20	Nov.	10	at Philadelphia, Penn.
Furman	2- 0	Nov.	17	at Greenville, S.C.
† Wash. and Lee	7-14	Nov.	29	at Columbia

1935   Won 3, Lost 7   Coach Don McCallister

Erskine	33- 0	Sept.	21	at Columbia
† Duke	0-47	Sept.	28	at Durham, N.C.
† N. C. State	0-14	Oct.	5	at Columbia
Davidson	6-13	Oct.	12	at Davidson, N.C.
The Citadel	25- 0	Oct.	17	at Orangeburg, S.C.
† Clemson	0-44	Oct.	24	at Columbia
† Virginia Tech	0-27	Nov.	2	at Blacksburg
Furman	7-20	Nov.	16	at Columbia
† Wash. and Lee	2- 0	Nov.	23	at Columbia
Florida	0-22	Dec.	7	at Tampa

1936   Won 5, Lost 7   Coach Don McCallister

Erskine	38- 0	Sept.	19	at Columbia
† V.M.I.	7-24	Sept.	26	at Lexington, Va.
† Duke	0-21	Oct.	3	at Columbia
Florida	7- 0	Oct.	10	at Columbia
† Virginia Tech	14 -0	Oct.	17	at Columbia
† Clemson	0-19	Oct.	22	at Columbia
† The Citadel	9- 0	Oct.	30	at Orangeburg, S.C.
Villanova	0-14	Nov.	7	at Columbia
† Furman	6-23	Nov.	14	at Greenville, S.C.
† North Carolina	0-14	Nov.	21	at Columbia
Xavier (Ohio)	13-21	Nov.	26	at Cincinnati
Miami (Fla.)	6- 3	Dec.	11	at Miami

1937   Won 5, Lost 6, Tied 1   Coach Don McCallister

Emory & Henry	45- 7	Sept.	18	at Columbia
† North Carolina	13-13	Sept.	25	at Chapel Hill
Georgia	7-13	Oct.	2	at Columbia
Alabama	0-20	Oct.	9	at Tuscaloosa
† Davidson	12- 7	Oct.	16	at Columbia
† Clemson	6-34	Oct.	21	at Columbia
† The Citadel	21- 6	Oct.	29	at Orangeburg, S.C.
Kentucky	7-27	Nov.	6	at Lexington
† Furman	0-12	Nov.	13	at Columbia
Presbyterian	64- 0	Nov.	20	at Columbia
Catholic	14-27	Nov.	25	at Washington, D.C.
Miami (Fla.)	3- 0	Dec.	3	at Miami

1938   Won 6, Lost 4, Tied 1   Coach Rex Enright

Erskine	53- 0	Sept.	19	at Columbia
Xavier (Ohio)	6- 0	Sept.	24	at Cincinnati
Georgia	6- 7	Oct.	1	at Columbia
† Wake Forest	19-20	Oct.	8	at Columbia
† Davidson	25- 0	Oct.	14	at Sumter, S.C.
† Clemson	12-34	Oct.	20	at Columbia
Villanova	6- 6	Oct.	28	at Orangeburg, S.C.
Duquesne	7- 0	Nov.	5	at Columbia
† Furman	27- 6	Nov.	12	at Greenville, S.C.
Fordham	0-13	Nov.	19	at New York, N.Y.
Catholic	7- 0	Nov.	28	at Washington, D.C.

1939   Won 3, Lost 6, Tied 1   Coach Rex Enright

† Wake Forest	7-19	Sept.	23	at Wake Forest, N.C.
Catholic	0-12	Sept.	29	at Columbia
Villanova	0-40	Oct.	6	at Philadelphia, Penn.
† Davidson	7- 0	Oct.	13	at Sumter, S.C.
† Clemson	0-27	Oct.	19	at Columbia
West Virginia	6- 6	Oct.	27	at Orangeburg, S.C.
Florida	7- 0	Nov.	4	at Columbia
† Furman	0-20	Nov.	11	at Columbia
Georgia	7-33	Nov.	18	at Athens
Miami (Fla.)	7- 6	Nov.	25	at Columbia

1940   Won 3, Lost 6   Coach Rex Enright

Georgia	2-33	Oct.	5	at Columbia
Duquesne	21-27	Oct.	11	at Pittsburgh, Penn.
† Clemson	13-21	Oct.	24	at Columbia
Penn State	0-12	Nov.	2	at University Park
Kansas State	20-13	Nov.	9	at Columbia
† Furman	7-25	Nov.	16	at Greenville, S.C.
Miami (Fla.)	7- 2	Nov.	22	at Miami
† Wake Forest	6- 7	Nov.	28	at Charlotte, N.C.
† The Citadel	31- 6	Dec.	8	at Charleston, S.C.

1941   Won 4, Lost 4, Tied 1   Coach Rex Enright

† North Carolina	13- 7	Sept.	27	at Chapel Hill
Georgia	6-34	Oct.	4	at Athens
† Wake Forest	6- 6	Oct.	11	at Columbia
† Clemson	18-14	Oct.	23	at Columbia
† The Citadel	13- 6	Oct.	31	at Orangeburg, S.C.
Kansas State	0- 3	Nov.	8	at Manhattan
† Furman	26- 7	Nov.	15	at Columbia
Miami (Fla.)	6- 7	Nov.	21	at Miami
Penn State	12-19	Nov.	29	at Columbia

1942   Won 1, Lost 7, Tied 1   Coach Rex Enright

Tennessee	0- 0	Sept.	26	at Columbia
† North Carolina	6-18	Oct.	3	at Chapel Hill
West Virginia	0-13	Oct.	10	at Morgantown
† Clemson	6-18	Oct.	22	at Columbia
† The Citadel	14- 0	Oct.	30	at Orangeburg, S.C.
Alabama	0-29	Nov.	7	at Tuscaloosa
† Furman	0- 6	Nov.	14	at Columbia
Miami (Fla.)	6-13	Nov.	21	at Miami
† Wake Forest	14-33	Nov.	27	at Charlotte, N.C.

1943   Won 5, Lost 2   Coach J. P. Moran

Newberry	19- 7	Sept.	25	at Columbia
176th Infantry	7-13	Oct.	2	at Columbia
Presbyterian	20- 7	Oct.	9	at Columbia
† Clemson	33- 6	Oct.	21	at Columbia
Charleston C.G	20- 0	Oct.	29	at Orangeburg, S.C.
† North Carolina	6-21	Nov.	6	at Columbia
† Wake Forest	13- 2	Nov.	25	at Charlotte, N.C.

Gamecocks Through the Years

1944   Won 3, Lost 4, Tied 2   Coach William Newton

Newberry	48- 0	Sept.	23	at Columbia
Ga. Pre-Flight	14-20	Sept.	30	at Columbia
Miami (Fla.)	0- 0	Oct.	7	at Miami
† Clemson	13-20	Oct.	19	at Columbia
Charleston C.G	6- 6	Oct.	27	at Orangeburg, S.C.
† North Carolina	6- 0	Nov.	4	at Chapel Hill
Presbyterian	28- 7	Nov.	11	at Columbia
† Duke	7-34	Nov.	18	at Columbia
† Wake Forest	13-19	Nov.	23	at Charlotte, N.C.

1945   Won 2, Lost 4, Tied 3   Coach Johnnie McMillan

† Duke	0-60	Sept.	22	at Durham, N.C.
Presbyterian	40- 0	Sept.	29	at Columbia
Camp Blanding	20- 6	Oct.	6	at Columbia
Alabama	0-55	Oct.	13	at Montgomery
† Clemson	0- 0	Oct.	25	at Columbia
Miami (Fla.)	13-13	Nov.	9	at Miami
† Wake Forest	13-13	Nov.	22	at Charlotte, N C.
† Maryland	13-19	Dec.	1	at Columbia
Wake Forest	14-26	Jan.	1	at Jacksonville, Fla.

(1946 Gator Bowl)

1946   Won 5, Lost 3   Coach Rex Enright

Newberry	21- 0	Sept.	29	at Colurnbia
Alabama	6-14	Oct.	5	at Columbia
† Furman	14- 7	Oct.	11	at Greenville, S.C.
† Clemson	26-14	Oct.	24	at Columbia
† The Citadel	19- 7	Nov.	1	at Orangeburg, S.C.
† Maryland	21-17	Nov.	9	at College Park
† Duke	0-39	Nov.	16	at Columbia
† Wake Forest	0-35	Nov.	28	at Charlotte, N.C.

1947   Won 6, Lost 2, Tied 1   Coach Rex Enright

Newberry	27- 6	Sept.	20	at Columbia
† Maryland	13-19	Sept.	27	at Columbia
Mississippi	0-33	Oct.	4	at Memphis, Tenn.
† Furman	26- 8	Oct.	11	at Columbia
† Clemson	21-19	Oct.	23	at Columbia
Miami (Fla.)	8- 0	Oct.	31	at Miami
† The Citadel	12- 0	Nov.	7	at Orangeburg, S.C.
† Duke	0- 0	Nov.	15	at Durham, N.C.
† Wake Forest	6- 0	Nov.	27	at Charlotte, N.C.

1948   Won 3, Lost 5   Coach Rex Enright

Newberry	46- 0	Sept.	24	at Columbia
† Furman	7- 0	Oct.	1	at Greenville, S.C.
Tulane	0-14	Oct.	9	at New Orleans, La.
† Clemson	7-13	Oct.	21	at Columbia
West Virginia	12-35	Oct.	30	at Morgantown
† Maryland	7-19	Nov.	6	at Columbia
Tulsa	27- 7	Nov.	13	at Tulsa, Okla.
† Wake Forest	0-38	Nov.	25	at Columbia

1949   Won 4, Lost 6   Coach Rex Enright

Baylor	6-20	Sept.	24	at Waco, Texas
† Furman	7-14	Sept.	30	at Columbia
† North Carolina	13-28	Oct.	8	at Columbia
† Clemson	27-13	Oct.	20	at Columbia
† Maryland	7 44	Oct.	29	at College Park
Marquette	6- 3	Nov.	5	at Milwaukee, Wis.
Miami (Fla.)	7-13	Nov.	11	at Miami
Georgia Tech	3-13	Nov.	19	at Atlanta
† Wake Forest	27-20	Nov.	23	at Columbia
† The Citadel	42- 0	Dec.	3	at Columbia

1950   Won 3, Lost 4, Tied 2   Coach Rex Enright

† Duke	0-14	Sept.	23	at Columbia
Georgia Tech	7- 0	Sept.	30	at Atlanta
† Furman	21- 6	Oct.	6	at Greenville, S.C.
† Clemson	14-14	Oct.	19	at Columbia
† George Wash	34-20	Oct.	27	at Washington, D.C.
Marquette	13-13	Nov.	3	at Columbia
† The Citadel	7-19	Nov.	11	at Charleston, S.C.
† North Carolina	7-14	Nov.	18	at Columbia
† Wake Forest	7-14	Nov.	25	at Columbia

1951   Won 5, Lost 4   Coach Rex Enright

† Duke	6-34	Sept.	22	at Columbia
† The Citadel	26- 7	Sept.	29	at Columbia
† Furman	21- 6	Oct.	6	at Columbia
† North Carolina	6-21	Oct.	13	at Chapel Hill, N.C.
† Clemson	20- 0	Oct.	25	at Columbia
† George Wash	14-20	Nov.	3	at Columbia
† West Virginia	34-13	Nov.	10	at Morgantown
Virginia	27-28	Nov.	17	at Charlottesville
† Wake Forest	21- 0	Nov.	24	at Columbia

1952   Won 5, Lost 5   Coach Rex Enright

Wofford	33- 0	Sept.	20	at Columbia
Army	7-28	Sept.	27	at West Point, N.Y.
† Furman	27- 7	Oct.	4	at Greenville, S.C.
† Duke	7-33	Oct.	11	at Columbia
Clemson	6- 0	Oct.	23	at Columbia
Virginia	21-14	Nov.	1	at Norfolk
† The Citadel	35- 0	Nov.	8	at Charleston, S.C.
† North Carolina	19-27	Nov.	15	at Columbia
† West Virginia	6-13	Nov.	22	at Columbia
† Wake Forest	14-39	Nov.	29	at Winston-Salem, N.C.

1953   Won 7, Lost 3   Coach Rex Enright

* Duke	7-20	Sept.	19	at Columbia
The Citadel	25- 0	Sept.	26	at Columbia
Virginia	19- 0	Oct.	3	at Charlottesville
Furman	27-13	Oct.	10	at Columbia
* Clemson	14 -7	Oct.	22	at Columbia
Maryland	6-24	Oct.	31	at College Park
* North Carolina	18- 0	Nov.	7	at Columbia
West Virginia	20-14	Nov.	14	at Morgantown
Wofford	49- 0	Nov.	21	at Columbia
* Wake Forest	13-19	Nov.	26	at Charlotte, N.C.

1954   Won 6, Lost 4   Coach Rex Enright

Army	34-20	Sept.	25	at West Point, N.Y.
West Virginia	6-26	Oct.	2	at Columbia
Furman	27- 7	Oct.	9	at Greenville, S.C.
* Clemson	13- 8	Oct.	21	at Columbia
* Maryland	0-20	Oct.	30	at Columbia
* North Carolina	19-21	Nov.	6	at Chapel Hill
* Virginia	27- 0	Nov.	13	at Columbia
* Duke	7-26	Nov.	20	at Durham, N.C.
* Wake Forest	20-19	Nov.	27	at Columbia
The Citadel	19- 6	Dec.	4	at Charleston, S.C.

1955   Won 3, Lost 6   Coach Rex Enright

Wofford	26- 7	Sept.	17	at Columbia
*Wake Forest	19-34	Sept.	24	at Winston-Salem, N.C.
Navy	0-26	Oct.	1	at Columbia
Furman	19- 0	Oct.	8	at Columbia
*Clemson	14-28	Oct.	20	at Columbia
*Maryland	0-27	Oct.	29	at College Park
*North Carolina	14-32	Nov.	5	at Norfolk, Va.
*Duke	7-41	Nov.	12	at Columbia
Virginia	21-14	Nov.	26	at Charlottesville

1956   Won 7, Lost 3   Coach Warren Giese

Wofford	26-13	Sept.	15	at Columbia
*Duke	7- 0	Sept.	22	at Columbia
Miami (Fla.)	6-14	Sept.	28	at Miami
*North Carolina	14-0	Oct.	6	at Columbia
*Virginia	27-13	Oct.	13	at Richmond
*Clemson	0. 7	Oct.	25	at Columbia
Furman	13- 6	Nov.	3	at Greenville, S.C.
*N. C. State	7-14	Nov.	10	at Raleigh
*Maryland	13- 0	Nov.	17	at Columbia
Wake Forest	13- 0	Nov.	22	at Charlotte, N.C.

1957   Won 5, Lost 5   Coach Warren Giese

*Duke	14-26	Sept.	21	at Columbia
Wofford	26- 0	Sept.	28	at Columbia
Texas	27-21	Oct.	5	at Austin
Furman	58-13	Oct.	12	at Columbia
*Clemson	0-13	Oct.	24	at Columbia
*Maryland	6-10	Nov.	2	at Columbia
*North Carolina	6-28	Nov.	9	at Chapel Hill
*Virginia	13- 0	Nov.	16	at Charlottesville
*N. C. State	26-29	Nov.	23	at Columbia
*Wake Forest	26- 7	Nov.	30	at Winston-Salem, N.C.

1958   Won 7. Lost 3   Coach Warren Giese

*Duke	8- 0	Sept.	20	at Columbia
Army	8-45	Sept.	27	at West Point, N.Y.
Georgia	24-14	Oct.	4	at Athens
*North Carolina	0- 6	Oct.	11	at Chapel Hill
*Clemson	26- 6	Oct.	23	at Columbia
*Maryland	6-10	Nov.	1	at College Park
Furman	32- 7	Nov.	8	at Greenville, S.C.
*Virginia	28-14	Nov.	15	at Columbia
*N. C. State	12- 7	Nov.	22	at Columbia
*Wake Forest	24 -7	Nov.	27	at Columbia

1959   Won 6. Lost 4   Coach Warren Giese

*Duke	12- 7	Sept.	19	at Columbia
Furman	30- 0	Sept.	26	at Columbia
Georgia	30-14	Oct.	3	at Columbia
*North Carolina	6-19	Oct.	10	at Chapel Hill
*Clemson	0-27	Oct.	22	at Columbia
*Maryland	22- 6	Oct.	31	at Columbia
*Virginia	32-20	Nov.	7	at Charlottesville
Miami (Fla.)	6-26	Nov.	13	at Miami
*N. C. State	12- 7	Nov.	21	at Columbia
*Wake Forest	20-43	Nov.	28	at Charlotte, N.C.

1960   Won 3, Lost 6, Tied 1   Coach Warren Giese

*Duke	0-31	Sept.	24	at Columbia
Georgia	6-38	Oct.	1	at Athens
Miami (Fla.)	6-21	Oct.	14	at Miami
*North Carolina	22- 6	Oct.	22	at Columbia
*Maryland	0-15	Oct.	29	at College Park
Louisiana State	6-35	Nov.	5	at Baton Rouge
*Clemson	2-12	Nov.	12	at Clemson, S.C.
*N. C. State	8- 8	Nov.	19	at Columbia
*Wake Forest	41-20	Nov.	26	at Columbia
*Virginia	26- 0	Dec.	3	at Columbia

1961   Won 4, Lost 6   Coach Marvin Bass

*Duke	6- 7	Sept.	23	at Columbia
*Wake Forest	10- 7	Sept.	30	at Winston-Salem, N.C.
Georgia	14-17	Oct.	7	at Athens
Louisiana State	0-42	Oct.	14	at Columbia
*North Carolina	0-17	Oct.	21	at Columbia
*Maryland	20-10	Oct.	28	at Columbia
*Virginia	20-28	Nov.	4	at Charlottesville
*Clemson	21-14	Nov.	11	at Columbia
*N. C. State	14-38	Nov.	18	at Raleigh
Vanderbilt	23- 7	Nov.	25	at Nashville, Tenn.

1962   Won 4, Lost 5, Tied 1   Coach Marvin Bass

Northwestern	20-37	Sept.	22	at Evanston, Ill.
*Duke	8-21	Sept.	29	at Durham, N.C.
Georgia	7- 7	Oct.	6	at Columbia
*Wake Forest	27- 6	Oct.	13	at Columbia
*North Carolina	14-19	Oct.	20	at Chapel Hill
*Maryland	11-13	Oct.	27	at College Park
*Virginia	40- 6	Nov.	3	at Columbia
*N. C. State	17- 6	Nov.	10	at Columbia
Detroit	26-13	Nov.	17	at Detroit, Mich.
*Clemson	17-20	Nov.	24	at Clemson, S.C.

1963   Won 1, Lost 8, Tied 1   Coach Marvin Bass

*Duke	14-22	Sept.	21	at Durham, N.C.
*Maryland	21-13	Sept.	28	at Columbia
Georgia	7-27	Oct.	5	at Athens
*N. C. State	6-18	Oct.	12	at Columbia
*Virginia	10-10	Oct.	19	at Charlottesville
*North Carolina	0- 7	Oct.	26	at Columbia
Tulane	7-20	Nov.	2	at Columbia
Memphis State	0- 9	Nov.	9	at Memphis, Tenn.
*Wake Forest	19-20	Nov.	16	at Winston-Salem, N.C.
*Clemson	20-24	Nov.	28	at Columbia

1964   Won 3, Lost 5, Tied 2   Coach Marvin Bass

*Duke	9- 9	Sept.	19	at Columbia
*Maryland	6-24	Sept.	26	at College Park
Georgia	7- 7	Oct.	3	at Columbia
Nebraska	6-28	Oct.	10	at Lincoln
Florida	0-37	Oct.	17	at Gainesville
*North Carolina	6-24	Oct.	24	at Chapel Hill
*N. C. State	14-17	Oct.	31	at Raleigh
The Citadel	17-14	Nov.	7	at Columbia
*Wake Forest	23-13	Nov.	14	at Columbia
*Clemson	7- 3	Nov.	21	at Clemson, S.C.

Gamecocks Through the Years

1965   Won 5, Lost 5   Coach Marvin Bass

The Citadel	13- 3	Sept. 18	at Charleston, S.C.
*Duke	15-20	Sept. 25	at Columbia
*N. C. State	13- 7	Oct. 2	at Columbia
Tennessee	3-24	Oct. 9	at Knoxville
*Wake Forest	38- 7	Oct. 16	at Columbia
Louisiana State	7-21	Oct. 23	at Baton Rouge
*Maryland	14-27	Oct. 30	at Columbia
*Virginia	17- 7	Nov. 6	at Charlottesville
Alabama	14-35	Nov. 1	at Tuscaloosa
*Clemson	17-16	Nov. 2	at Columbia

1966   Won 1, Lost 9   Coach Paul Dietzel

Louisiana State	12-28	Sept. 17	at Baton Rouge
Memphis State	7-16	Sept. 24	at Columbia
Georgia	0- 7	Oct. 1	at Columbia
*N. C. State	31-21	Oct. 8	at Raleigh
*Wake Forest	6-10	Oct. 15	at Columbia
Tennessee	17-29	Oct. 22	at Knoxville
*Maryland	2-14	Oct. 29	at College Park
Florida State	10-32	Nov. 5	at Columbia
Alabama	0-24	Nov. 12	at Tuscaloosa
*Clemson	10-35	Nov. 26	at Clemson, S.C.

1967   Won 5, Lost 5   Coach Paul Dietzel

Iowa State	34 -3	Sept. 16	at Columbia
*North Carolina	16-10	Sept. 23	at Columbia
*Duke	21-17	Sept. 30	at Durham, N.C.
Georgia	0-21	Oct. 7	at Athens
Florida State	0-17	Oct. 14	at Tallahassee
*Virginia	24-23	Oct. 21	at Columbia
*Maryland	31- 0	Oct. 28	at Columbia
*Wake Forest	21-35	Nov. 4	at Winston-Salem, N.C.
Alabama	0-17	Nov. 18	at Tuscaloosa
*Clemson	12-23	Nov. 25	at Columbia

1968   Won 4, Lost 6   Coach Paul Dietzel

*Duke	7-14	Sept. 21	at Columbia
*North Carolina	32-27	Sept. 28	at Chapel Hill
Georgia	20-21	Oct. 5	at Columbia
*N.C. State	12-36	Oct. 12	at Raleigh
*Maryland	19-21	Oct. 19	at College Park
Florida State	28-35	Oct. 26	at Columbia
*Virginia	49-28	Nov. 2	at Charlottesville
*Wake Forest	34-21	Nov. 9	at Winston-Salem, N.C.
Virginia Tech	6-17	Nov. 16	at Columbia
*Clemson	7- 3	Nov. 23	at Clemson, S.C

1969   Won 7, Lost 4   Coach Paul Dietzel

*Duke	27-20	Sept. 20	at Columbia
*North Carolina	14- 6	Sept. 27	at Columbia
Georgia	16-41	Oct. 4	at Athens
*N. C. State	21-16	Oct. 11	at Columbia
Virginia Tech	17-16	Oct. 18	at Blacksburg
*Maryland	17- 0	Oct. 25	at Columbia
*Florida State	9-34	Nov. 1	at Tallahassee
Tennessee	14-29	Nov. 8	at Knoxville
*Wake Forest	24- 6	Nov. 15	at Winston-Salem, N.C.
*Clemson	27-13	Nov. 22	at Columbia
West Virginia	3-14	Dec. 30	at Atlanta, Ga.

(Peach Bowl)

1970   Won 4. Lost 6, Tied 1   Coach Paul Dietzel

Georgia Tech	20-23	Sept. 12	at Atlanta
*Wake Forest	43- 7	Sept. 19	at Columbia
*N. C. State	7- 7	Sept. 26	at Raleigh
Virginia Tech	24- 7	Oct. 3	at Columbia
*North Carolina	35-21	Oct. 10	at Chapel Hill
*Maryland	15-21	Oct. 17	at College Park
Florida State	13-21	Oct. 24	at Columbia
Georgia	34-52	Oct. 31	at Athens
Tennessee	18-20	Nov. 7	at Columbia
*Duke	38-42	Nov. 14	at Columbia
*Clemson	38-32	Nov. 21	at Clemson, S.C.

1971   Won 6, Lost 5   Coach Paul Dietzel

Georgia Tech	24- 7	Sept. 11	at Columbia
Duke	12-28	Sept. 18	at Durham, N.C.
N. C. State	24- 6	Sept. 25	at Columbia
Memphis State	7- 3	Oct. 2	at Memphis, Tenn.
Virginia	34-14	Oct. 9	at Columbia
Maryland	35- 6	Oct. 16	at Columbia
Florida State	18-49	Oct. 23	at Tallahassee
Georgia	0-24	Oct. 30	at Columbia
Tennessee	6-35	Nov. 6	at Knoxville
Wake Forest	24- 7	Nov. 20	at Columbia
Clemson	7-17	Nov. 27	at Columbia

1972   Won 4, Lost 7   Coach Paul Dietzel

Virginia	16-24	Sept. 9	at Columbia
Georgia Tech	6-34	Sept. 16	at Atlanta
Mississippi	0-21	Sept. 23	at Columbia
Memphis State	34- 7	Sept. 30	at Columbia
Appalachian St	41- 7	Oct. 14	at Columbia
Miami (Ohio)	8-21	Oct. 21	at Columbia
N. C. State	24-42	Oct. 28	at Raleigh
Wake Forest	35- 3	Nov. 4	at Columbia
Virginia Tech	20-45	Nov. 11	at Blacksburg
Florida State	24-21	Nov. 18	at Columbia
Clemson	6- 7	Nov. 25	at Clemson, S.C.

1973   Won 7, Lost 4   Coach Paul Dietzel

Georgia Tech	41-28	Sept. 15	at Columbia
Houston	19-27	Sept. 21	at Houston, Texas
Miami (Ohio)	11-13	Sept. 29	at Columbia
Virginia Tech	27-24	Oct. 6	at Blacksburg
Wake Forest	28-12	Oct. 13	at Winston-Salem, N.C.
Ohio Univ.	38-22	Oct. 20	at Columbia
Louisiana State	29-33	Oct. 27	at Columbia
N. C. State	35-56	Nov. 3	at Columbia
Appalachian St	35-14	Nov. 10	at Columbia
Florida State	52-12	Nov. 17	at Tallahassee
Clemson	32-20	Nov. 24	at Columbia

1974   Won 4, Lost 7   Coach Paul Dietzel

Georgia Tech	20-35	Sept. 14	at Atlanta
Duke	14-20	Sept. 21	at Columbia
Georgia	14-52	Sept. 28	at Athens
Houston	14-24	Oct. 5	at Columbia
Virginia Tech	17-31	Oct. 12	at Columbia
Mississippi	10- 7	Oct. 19	at Oxford
North Carolina	31-23	Oct. 26	at Columbia
N. C. State	27-42	Nov. 2	at Raleigh
Appalachian St	21-18	Nov. 9	at Columbia
Wake Forest	34-21	Nov. 16	at Columbia
Clemson	21-39	Nov. 23	at Clemson, S.C.

1975   Won 7, Lost 5   Coach Jim Carlen

Georgia Tech	23-17	Sept. 13	at Columbia
Duke	24-16	Sept. 20	at Durham, N.C.
Georgia	20-28	Sept. 27	at Columbia
Baylor	24-13	Oct. 4	at Columbia
Virginia	41-14	Oct. 11	at Columbia
Mississippi	35-29	Oct. 18	at Jackson
Louisiana State	6-24	Oct. 25	at Baton Rouge
N. C. State	21-28	Nov. 1	at Raleigh
Appalachian St	34-39	Nov. 8	at Columbia
Wake Forest	37-26	Nov. 15	at Columbia
Clemson	56-20	Nov. 22	at Columbia
Miami (Ohio)	7-20	Dec. 20	at Orlando, Fla.

(Tangerine Bowl)

1976   Won 6, Lost 5   Coach Jim Carlen

Appalachian St	21-10	Sept. 4	at Columbia
Georgia Tech	27-17	Sept. 11	at Atlanta
Duke	24- 6	Sept. 18	at Columbia
Georgia	12-20	Sept. 25	at Athens
Baylor	17-18	Oct. 2	at Waco, Texas
Virginia	35- 7	Oct. 9	at Columbia
Mississippi	10- 7	Oct. 16	at Columbia
Notre Dame	6-13	Oct. 23	at Columbia
N. C. State	27- 7	Oct. 30	at Columbia
Wake Forest	7-10	Nov. 13	at Columbia
Clemson	9-28	Nov. 20	at Clemson, S.C.

1977   Won 5, Lost 7   Coach Jim Carlen

Appalachian St	32-17	Sept. 3	at Columbia
Georgia Tech	17- 0	Sept. 10	at Columbia
Miami (Ohio)	42-19	Sept. 17	at Columbia
Georgia	13-15	Sept. 24	at Columbia
East Carolina	19-16	Oct. 1	at Columbia
Duke	21-25	Oct. 8	at Columbia
Mississippi	10-17	Oct. 15	at Oxford
North Carolina	0-17	Oct. 22	at Chapel Hill
N. C. State	3- 7	Oct. 29	at Raleigh
Wake Forest	24-14	Nov. 12	at Winston-Salem, N.C.
Clemson	27-31	Nov. 19	at Columbia
Hawaii	7-24	Nov. 26	at Honolulu

1978   Won 5, Lost 5, Tied 1   Coach Jim Carlen

Furman	45-10	Sept. 9	at Columbia
Kentucky	14-14	Sept. 16	at Columbia
Duke	12-16	Sept. 23	at Durham, N.C.
Georgia	27-10	Sept. 30	at Columbia
Georgia Tech	3- 6	Oct. 7	at Atlanta
Ohio Univ	24- 7	Oct. 14	at Columbia
Mississippi	18-17	Oct. 21	at Columbia
North Carolina	22-24	Oct. 28	at Columbia
N. C. State	13-22	Nov. 4	at Raleigh
Wake Forest	37-14	Nov. 18	at Columbia
Clemson	23-41	Nov. 25	at Clemson, S.C.

1979   Won 8, Lost 4   Coach Jim Carlen

North Carolina	0-28	Sept. 8	at Chapel Hill
Western Mich	24- 7	Sept. 15	at Columbia
Duke	35- 0	Sept. 22	at Columbia
Georgia	27-20	Sept. 29	at Athens
Oklahoma State	23-16	Oct. 6	at Columbia
Mississippi	21-14	Oct. 20	at Columbia
Notre Dame	17-18	Oct. 27	at Notre Dame, Ind.
N. C. State	30-28	Nov. 3	at Columbia
Florida State	7-27	Nov. 10	at Tallahassee
Wake Forest	35-14	Nov. 17	at Columbia
Clemson	13- 9	Nov. 24	at Columbia
Missouri	14-24	Dec. 29	at Birmingham, Ala.

(Hall of Fame Bowl)

1980   Won 8, Lost 4   Coach Jim Carlen

Pacific	37- 0	Sept. 6	at Columbia
Wichita State	73- 0	Sept. 13	at Columbia
Southern Cal.	13-23	Sept. 20	at Los Angeles
Michigan	17-14	Sept. 27	at Ann Arbor
N. C. State	30-10	Oct. 4	at Columbia
Duke	20- 7	Oct. 11	at Columbia
Cincinnati	49- 7	Oct. 18	at Columbia
Georgia	10-13	Nov. 1	at Athens
The Citadel	45-24	Nov. 8	at Columbia
Wake Forest	39-38	Nov. 15	at Columbia
Clemson	6-27	Nov. 22	at Clemson
Pittsburgh	9-37	Dec. 29	at Jacksonville, Fla.

(Gator Bowl)

1981   Won 6, Lost 6   Coach Jim Carlen

Wake Forest	23- 6	Sept. 5	at Winston-Salem, N.C.
Mississippi	13-20	Sept. 12	at Columbia
Duke	17- 3	Sept. 19	at Columbia
Georgia	0-24	Sept. 26	at Athens
Pittsburgh	28-42	Oct. 3	at Columbia
Kentucky	28-14	Oct. 10	at Lexington
Virginia	21- 3	Oct. 17	at Columbia
North Carolina	31-13	Oct. 24	at Chapel Hill
N. C. State	20-12	Oct. 31	at Columbia
Pacific	21-23	Nov. 7	at Columbia
Clemson	13-29	Nov. 21	at Columbia
Hawaii	10-33	Dec. 5	at Honolulu

1982   Won 4, Lost 7   Coach Richard Bell

Pacific	41- 6	Sept. 4	at Columbia
Richmond	30-10	Sept. 11	at Columbia
Duke	17-30	Sept. 18	at Columbia
Georgia	18-34	Sept 25	at Columbia
Cincinnati	37-10	Oct. 2	at Columbia
Furman	23-28	Oct. 16	at Columbia
Louisiana State	6-14	Oct. 23	at Baton Rouge
N. C. State	3-33	Oct. 30	at Raleigh
Florida State	26-56	Nov. 6	at Columbia
Navy	17-14	Nov. 13	at Columbia
Clemson	6-24	Nov. 20	at Clemson, S.C.

Gamecocks Through the Years

THE
H I S T O R Y

1983   Won 5, Lost 6   Coach Joe Morrison

North Carolina	8-24	Sept.	3	at Columbia
Miami (Ohio)	24- 3	Sept.	10	at Columbia
Duke	31-24	Sept.	17	at Durham, N.C.
Georgia	13-31	Sept.	24	at Athens
Southern Cal	38-14	Oct.	1	at Columbia
Notre Dame	6-30	Oct.	8	at Columbia
Louisiana State	6-20	Oct.	22	at Baton Rouge
N. C. State	31-17	Oct.	29	at Columbia
Florida State	30-45	Nov.	5	at Tallahassee
Navy	31- 7	Nov.	12	at Columbia
Clemson	13-22	Nov.	19	at Columbia

1984   Won 10, Lost 2   Coach Joe Morrison

The Citadel	31-24	Sept.	8	at Columbia
Duke	21- 0	Sept.	22	at Columbia
Georgia	17-10	Sept.	29	at Columbia
Kansas State	49-17	Oct.	6	at Columbia
Pittsburgh	45-21	Oct.	13	at Columbia
Notre Dame	36-32	Oct.	20	at South Bend
East Carolina	42-20	Oct.	27	at Columbia
N. C. State	35-28	Nov.	3	at Raleigh, N.C.
Florida State	38-26	Nov.	10	at Columbia
Navy	21-38	Nov.	17	at Annapolis
Clemson	22-21	Nov.	24	at Clemson
Oklahoma State	14-21	Dec.	28	at Jacksonville, Fla.

(Gator Bowl)

1985   Won 5, Lost 6   Coach Joe Morrison

The Citadel	56-17	Aug.	31	at Columbia
Appalachian State	20-13	Sept.	7	at Columbia
Michigan	3-34	Sept.	21	at Columbia
Georgia	21-35	Sept.	28	at Athens
Pittsburgh	7-42	Oct.	5	at Pittsburgh
Duke	28- 7	Oct.	12	at Columbia
East Carolina	52-10	Oct.	26	at Greenville
North Carolina St.	7-21	Nov.	2	at Columbia
Florida State	14-56	Nov.	9	at Tallahassee
Navy	34-31	Nov.	16	at Columbia
Clemson	17-24	Nov.	23	at Columbia

1986   Won 3, Lost 6, Tied 2 Coach Joe Morrison

Miami, Fla	14-34	Aug.	30	at Columbia
Virginia	20-30	Sept.	7	at Charlottesville
Western Carolina	45-24	Sept.	13	at Columbia
Georgia	26-31	Sept.	27	at Columbia
Nebraska	24-27	Oct.	4	at Columbia
Virginia Tech	27-27	Oct.	11	at Blacksburg
East Carolina	38- 3	Oct.	25	at Columbia
North Carolina St.	22-23	Nov.	1	at Raleigh
Florida State	28-45	Nov.	8	at Columbia
Wake Forest	48-21	Nov.	15	at Columbia
Clemson	21-21	Nov.	22	at Clemson

1987   Won 8, Lost 4   Coach Joe Morrison

Appalachian State	24 - 3	Sept.	5	at Columbia
Western Carolina	31- 6	Sept.	12	at Columbia
Georgia	6-13	Sept.	26	at Athens
Nebraska	21-30	Oct.	3	at Lincoln
Virginia Tech	40-10	Oct.	10	at Columbia
Virginia	58-10	Oct.	17	at Columbia
East Carolina	34-12	Oct.	24	at Columbia
North Carolina St.	48- 0	Oct.	31	at Columbia
Wake Forest	30- 0	Nov.	14	at Winston-Salem
Clemson	20- 7	Nov.	21	at Columbia
Miami, Fla	16-20	Dec.	5	at Miami
Louisiana State	13-30	Dec.	31	at Jacksonville

(Mazda Gator Bowl)

1988   Won 8, Lost 4   Coach Joe Morrison

North Carolina	31-10	Sept.	3	at Columbia
Western Carolina	38- 0	Sept.	10	at Columbia
East Carolina	17- 0	Sept.	17	at Columbia
Georgia	23-10	Sept.	24	at Columbia
Appalachian State	35- 9	Oct.	1	at Columbia
Virginia Tech	26-24	Oct.	8	at Blacksburg
Georgia Tech	0-34	Oct.	15	at Atlanta
North Carolina St	23- 7	Oct.	29	at Raleigh
Florida State	0-59	Nov.	5	at Columbia
Navy	19- 7	Nov.	12	at Columbia
Clemson	10-29	Nov.	19	at Clemson
Indiana	10-34	Dec.	28	at Memphis

(Liberty Bowl)

1989   Won 6, Lost 4, Tied 1 Coach Sparky Woods

Duke	27-21	Sept.	2	at Columbia
Virginia Tech	17-17	Sept.	9	at Columbia
West Virginia	21-45	Sept.	16	at Morgantown
Georgia Tech	21-10	Sept.	23	at Columbia
Georgia	24-20	Sept.	30	at Athens
East Carolina	47-14	Oct.	7	at Columbia
Western Carolina	24- 3	Oct.	21	at Columbia
North Carolina St.	10-20	Oct.	28	at Columbia
Florida State	10-35	Nov.	4	at Tallahassee
North Carolina	27-20	Nov.	11	at Chapel Hill
Clemson	0-45	Nov.	18	at Columbia

1990   Won 6, Lost 5   Coach Sparky Woods

Duke	21-10	Sept.	1	at Columbia
North Carolina	27- 5	Sept.	8	at Columbia
Virginia Tech	35-24	Sept.	22	at Blacksburg
Georgia Tech	6-27	Sept.	29	at Atlanta
East Carolina	37- 7	Oct.	13	at Columbia
The Citadel	35-38	Oct.	20	at Columbia
North Carolina St.	29-38	Oct.	27	at Raleigh
Florida State	10-41	Nov.	3	at Tallahassee
Southern Illinois	38-13	Nov.	10	at Columbia
Clemson	15-24	Nov.	17	at Clemson
West Virginia	29-10	Nov.	22	at Columbia

† Southern Conference Game
* Atlantic Coast Conference Game

Gamecock Lettermen

A

Abel, Trevor: 1925-26
Abraczinskas, Don: 1973-74
Adair, Bryant: 1929-30-31
Adam, Dave: 1959-60-61
Adams, Ed: 1955
Adams, Frank: 1990
Adamski, Jacyn: 1973-74-75-76
Addison, Dennis: 1987
Addison, Joe: 1985-86-87-88
Addison, Tommy: 1955-56-57
Alexander, Clay (Bud): 1933-34-35
Alexander, Kale: 1946-47-48
Alexander, Phil: 1946-47-48
Allen, Chuck: 1977,1980
Allen, Gus: 1919-20
Allen, Gus: 1949-50
Allen, Neil: 1942-43; 1946-47
Ambs, A. G.: 1923
Amick, Jamie: 1989
Amrein, Tom: 1972, 1974-75
Amsler, Buddy: 1950
Ancrum, Calhoun: 1902
Anderson, Erik: 1989-90
Anderson, Sammy: 1961-62-63
Andrews, Jones: 1985-86-87
Andrews, Lee: 1971
Anthony, Rick: 1971-72-73
Antley, Gene: 1975
Applegate, Bill: 1939-40-41
Armstrong, Mike: 1987
Arnold,. Danny: 1985
Arrowsmith, Dewitt: 1938, 1940-41
Ary, T. S.: 1943
Ashton, Jack: 1957-58-59
Attaway, Tommy: 1940-41
Atwell, James (Droopy): 1946-47
Aubin, Jerry: 1981
Aubrey, W. B.: 1919
Austin, Darrell: 1971-72-73
Austin, Mark: 1979-80-81-82
Auten, Frank: 1951

B

Bacon, Emory: 1982-83-84
Baggott, Bob: 1943
Bailey, Anthony: 1983
Bailey, Don: 1968-69-70
Bailey, John: 1977-78, 1980
Bailey, Leroy: 1965-66
Baker, Marty: 1988-89-90
Baker, Red: 1933
Balka, Dick: 1950-51-52
Ball, Phil: 1944-45
Bame, Scott: 1986
Bank, Chris: 1968-69-70
Barber, Charlie: 1974, 1976
Barfield, Woody: 1960-61-62
Bargiacchi, Fred: 1947
Barnes, Dabney: 1918
Barnhill, Bill: 1982-83-84
Barrett, Bob: 1955-56-57
Bartell, Henry: 1921-22-23
Baskin, Weems III: 1956-57-58
Bass, Ron: 1973-74,1976-77
Bauer, Ernest: 1942-43
Baughn, James: 1943
Bauknight, Hank: 1933

Baxley, Ed: 1979-80
Baxley, Mel: 1972-73
Beach, Jake: 1943
Beake, Chip: 1990
Beall, Carlye: 1928
Beall, Eddie: 1956-57-58
Beall, Julian: 1927-28-29
Beall, Ted: 1918
Beard, Jim: 1971-72-73
Beasley, Chan: 1971-72
Beasley, Luke: 1956
Beckham, Gordon: 1980-81-82
Behrens, Bill: 1954-55
Belk, George: 1921
Bell, Hugh: 1952-53-54-55
Bell, Hugh, Jr.: 1974, 1976
Bell, Ted: 1899-1900
Bell, Tommy: 1970-71-72
Bell, Wayne: 1989
Belser, Irvine: 1909
Belser, Ritchie Hugh: 1907-08-09
Bembery, Cedric: 1990
Benet, Christie: 1897-98
Bennett, Bralyn: 1990
Bennett, Buddy: 1958-59-60
Bennett, Clyde: 1951-52-53
Berkeley, Fred: 1981
Bernish, Steve: 1977-78-79
Berry, David: 1964-65-66
Berry, Jess: 1951-52
Berry, Todd: 1981-82
Bethea, Ryan: 1985-86-87
Bethune: 1910
Bethune, J.: 1937
Beverly, Benjamin: 1908-09
Bice, Tim: 1966-67-68
Biggs, J. T.: 1937, 1939
Bing, Keith: 1986-87-88-89
Bingham, Ray: 1984
Biondi, Lou: 1977-78-79
Bishop, Terry: 1981-82
Black, Greg: 1971-72
Blackburn, John: 1909
Blackman, Scott: 1975-76-77
Blackmon, Steve: 1973-74
Blackwell, Patrick: 1988-89-90
Blackwell, Robert: 1900
Blasingame, Dominique: 1981-82
Blouin, Harvey: 1939-40-41
Blount, Gerard: 1930
Blount, Miles: 1929-30-31
Boatwright, W. H.: 1923
Bobo, Don: 1975-76
Bodkin, Jake: 1958-59-60
Boineau, Ed ("Bru"): 1928-29-30
Bolton, Eddie: 1968
Bolton, Ray: 1986-88
Bond, Brett: 1977-78-79
Bostwick, Frank: 1929-30-31
Botkins, Henry A.: 1945
Boulware, J. H.: 1916
Boulware, M. B.: 1912-13
Bowen, Pat: 1979-80-81-82
Bowman, Jim: 1958-59
Boyd, Candler: 1967, 1969-70
Boyd, Curtis: 1977
Boyd, W. M.: 1924-25-26
Boyle, John: 1977
Boyle, William: 1903

Boyte, Billy: 1969-70-71
Bradford, Jack (Brick): 1943-44, 1946-47
Bradshaw, Bill: 1982-83-84
Bramlet, Osgood: 1935-36
Branch, Dany: 1988-89-90
Branson, Phil: 1964-65
Brant, Don: 1970
Brantley, Tom: 1931
Braswell, Charlie: 1944
Brazell, Carl: 1952-53-54-55
Breeden, John: 1963-64-65
Brembs, Dutch: 1944-45
Bretz, A.: 1937
Brice, T. H.: 1922-23
Bridges, Mark: 1978, 1980
Brigham, William: 1929-30
Brinker, Jack: 1975
Brockington, Heyward: 1917-18-19-20
Brooker, A. H.: 1898-99
Brooker, N. W.: 1896
Brooks, Joe: 1983-84-85
Brooks, Robert: 1988-89-90
Broussard, Arthur: 1978-79
Brown: 1909
Brown, Allen: 1968
Brown, Allen: 1932-33-34
Brown, Aubrey, Jr.: 1935
Brown, Bobby: 1988-89-90
Brown, Chick: 1933
Brown, Eldridge (Buster): 1953
Brown, Eric: 1990
Brown, George: 1917-18
Brown, Hardin: 1985-86-87-88
Brown, Jackie: 1970-71-72
Brown, John: 1986
Brown, Mark: 1982
Brown, Ned: 1951-52-53
Brown, Raynard: 1983-84-85-86
Brown, Rick: 1970-71-72
Brown, W.: 1917
Brunson, Mason: 1897
Brunson, Robert: 1951-52
Bryant, Bobby: 1964-65-66
Bryson, Harry: 1948-49
Buckner, Don: 1967-68-69
Buie, Lewis: 1911
Bullard, Bill: 1955-56-57
Bunch, Bobby: 1955, 1957-58
Bunch, Randy: 1990
Bunch, Ron: 1967-68
Burger, Gary: 1979-80
Burgess, Nat: 1940-41
Burke, S. F.: 1925-26
Burns, John: 1936-37-38
Burton, Leonard: 1984-85
Byers, Tony: 1955-56
Byrd, Sonny: 1944

C

Cain, Francis: 1909
Camp, Charlie: 1951-52-53
Campbell, Dale: 1988
Campbell, Matthew: 1990
Candler, Stan: 1976
Cantore, Phil: 1943
Carpenter, Al: 1973-74
Carpenter, Dana: 1971-72-73
Carpenter, Ray: 1982,1984-85-86

Gamecock Lettermen

Carr, Bill: 1945
Carter, Berte: 1908-09
Carter, Casper: 1973;1975-76-77
Carter, Elmore (Bobo): 1940-41, 1946
Cartwright, George: 1907
Cash, Dave (Junior): 1971-72-73
Caskey, John: 1960-61-62
Caskey, Mike: 1952-53-54-55
Chaikin, Tommy: 1984-85-86-87
Chalmers, Fred: 1981-82
Chambliss, James: 1983
Chappelle, Chap: 1921-22
Chastain, Randy: 1973-74-75
Chatman, Roy: 1961-62-63
Chavous, Andy: 1967,1969
Chivers, DeWayne: 1980-81
Clancy, Danny: 1976-77-78
Clark, J. R. (Red): 1943
Clark, Spencer: 1977-78-79
Clarke, Babe: 1916-17
Clarke, Sumpter: 1915-16-17
Clarke, Warren: 1951-52-53
Clarkson, William: 1904-05-06-07
Clary, Buford: 1940-41
Clary, Ed: 1936-37-38
Clary, Wilburn: 1933-34-35
Clary, Earl: 1931-32-33
Cline, Mike: 1972-73
Cogburn, Horace: 1904
Cogburn, W. S.: 1900
Cole, Bob: 1965-66-67
Cole, Gordon: 1959-60
Coleman, John: 1968
Collie, Larmar: 1948-49-50
Collins, Bob: 1963-64-65
Colson, Keith: 1973-74, 1976
Coman, Herbert: 1940-41-42
Conway, Mike: 1988-89
Cooley, Scott: 1990
Cooper, J. F.: 1925-26, 1928
Cooper, Jimmy: 1950, 1952
Cooper, John: 1989
Cooper, Robert: 1907
Cooper, W. A.: 1899
Corley, Chris: 1981-82-83-84
Cornett, Ben: 1976, 1978-79-80
Correll, Allen: 1930-31
Correll, Ernest: 1930-31
Costen, Jim: 1959-60-61
Couch, Henry: 1944-45
Couch, Jack: 1946-47-48
Courson, Steve: 1973-7475-76
Covington, Dick: 1953-5455
Cox, Cary: 1943
Cox, Steve: 1962-63,1965
Crabb, Greg: 1969-70-71
Craft, Fred: 1933-34-35
Crafts, Everett: 1960-61-62
Craig, Larry: 1935-36-37-38
Craig, Tom: 1932-33-34
Craig, Wallace: 1938
Crawford: 1911
Crawford, George: 1941
Crawford, L. C.: 1898
Crawford, W. P.: 1919
Cregar, Bill: 1972-73-74
Crews, John: 1937-38-39
Croft, Edward: 1903
Croft, Theodore: 1907

Crosby, Henry: 1959-60-61
Crouch, J. E.: 1907
Crouch, James T.: 1916, 1920
Crowley, Harry: 1955
Crumpler, Rich: 1976
Culp, Heyward: 1929-30
Cunningham, Leon: 1951-52-53-54
Currier, Bill: 1974-75-76
Curtis, Ray: 1964
Curtis, Scott: 1976

D

Danielowski, Cas: 1981-82-83
Daniels, Ricky: 1984-85,1987
Dantonio, John: 1975-76-77-78
Dantonio, Mark: 1976-77-78
Dargan, Alex: 1907
Darling, Dennis: 1963-64-65
David, Fred: 1977-78-79
Davies, Bo: 1969-70-71
Davis, Bundy: 1902
Davis, Fitzgerald: 1983-84-85-86
Davis, Robbie: 1971
Day, Dick: 1960-61-62
Deal, A. M.: 1899-1900
Deal, C. F.: 1901
Dearth, Ralph: 1936-37-38
DeBoer, Rob: 1990
DeCamilla, Dave: 1968-69-70
DeFore, Joe: 1952-53
Delaney, Shannon: 1977
DeLoache, Harry: 1947-48-49
DeLuca, Sam: 1954-55-56
DeMasi, Dickie: 1989-90
Dendy, Thomas: 1982-83-84-85
DePasquale, Kerry: 1974-75-76
Derrenbacker, Jim: 1935
Derrick, D. C. ("Casey"): 1928-29
Derrick, Jack: 1928-29-30
Derrick, Julius: 1955-56-57
Derriso, Ken: 1958-59-60
Desmond, Jim: 1983-84-85
DesPortes, U. G.: 1911
Destino, Frank: 1956-57
DeVaughn, Redding: 1929-30-31
Dew, Ed: 1946-47-48
Dial, Dan: 1897
Dick, H. M.: 1911
Dickens, Bill: 1964-65-66
Dickinson, Sonny: 1963-64
Dietz, Emmett: 1951
Diggs, Shed: 1984-85-86-87
Dingle, Mike: 1988-89-90
DiVenere, Pete: 1962-63-64
Dixon, Ernest: 1990
Dixon, Gerald: 1990
Dixon, King: 1956-57-58
Dobson, Alex: 1972
Dockery, Bob: 1947,1949
Dodgen, San: 1980
Dorflinger, Jack: 1936-37-38
Dorr, Jack: 1951
Dorsett, John: 1956,1958
Dorsey, Steve: 1976-77-78-79
Dowling, Geddes: 1904
Doyle, Joe: 1978, 1980-81
Drawdy, Bobby: 1951-52-53
Drost, Bob: 1959-60-61
Dubac, John: 1971-72
Duckett, Fred: 1950-51-52
Duke, Troy: 1989-90
Dukes, Arthur: 1923

Dukes, John: 1923
Duncan, Dale: 1972-73
Duncan, Hayden: 1974
Duncan, Jimmy: 1957-58-59
Dunham, Earl: 1941-42, 1946
Dunlap, Jerry: 1983-84-85
DuPre, Billy: 1968-69-70
Durham, Burl: 1936
Durham, Earl (Big): 1936-37-38
Durrah, Mike: 1980-81-82
Dyches, Danny: 1968-69-70
Dyches, Tim: 1980-81-82
Dye, Marty: 1988-89-90
Dyer, John: 1965

E

Eades, Bud: 1945
Earley, Don: 1950-51-52
Edens, H. H. (Hap): 1928-29-30
Edmunds, Blake: 1922-23
Edwards, Brad: 1984-85-86-87
Edwards, Buck: 1921
Edwards, Marion (Buddy): 1947-48
Edwards, Van: 1937
Edwards, W. G.: 1911
Efird, Dwight: 1973-74-75
Ehrich, Lou: 1902
Ekimoff, Len: 1946-47-48-49
Elliott, Ricky: 1980-81
Ellis, Phil: 1979-80-81-82
Ellis, Todd: 1986-87-88-89
Elston, Arthur (Dutch): 1939, 1941
Epps, Carl: 1902
Epps, H. V.: 1919
Epps, John: 1932-33
Ericsson, Rich: 1954-55-56
Erwin, Mac: 1944
Estes, Bill: 1947
Evans, Pete: 1933
Evans, Tracy: 1982-83-84
Evans, W. B.: 1898
Evat, Spec: 1940-41
Ewing, John: 1963-64-65
Ewing, Kent: 1930-31

F

Fagan, Dick: 1947-48-49
Fair, Mike: 1965-66-67
Faress, Al: 1943, 1946-47-48
Farina, Deron: 1985-86
Farmer, Bob: 1958-59-60
Farnam, Thomas Curry: 1936-37
Farr, Ed: 1930
Farr, J. S., Jr.: 1927
Farr, Quay: 1978-79
Farrell, Kenny: 1990
Farrell, Mike: 1972-73-74
Farris, George (Chesty): 1944-45
Felder, William: 1901
Feltz, Jay: 1979
Fendley, William: 1902-03-04-05
Fennell, J. B.: 1935
Fennell, W. W.: 1924-25
Ferguson, Ricky: 1989-90
Fewell, Sam: 1958-59-60
Field, Ed: 1955
Files, Neville: 1970-71-72
Findley, Dean: 1960-61-62

Gamecock Lettermen

Finklea, G. W.: 1911
Finney, Chuck: 1979-80-81-82
Fitch, Francis Burt, Jr.: 1927
Fleetwood, Mark: 1981-82-83
Fleming, Astor: 1931
Fletcher, Ladd: 1983, 1985
Floyd, Bill: 1954-55-56
Floyd, Norman: 1986-87
Ford, Dennis: 1970-71
Ford, Morris: 1935
Forston, Nelson: 1931-32-33
Fosnacht, Rick: 1976
Foster, Cansen: 1896-97-98
Foster, C. A.: 1899
Foster, Ralph: 1902-03
Fowble, Dean: 1931-32-33-34
Fowble, Dean, Jr.: 1960
Fowler, Larry: 1977
Fralic, Mike: 1976-77
Frantz, Dick: 1946-47-48
Frazier, Derrick: 1986-87-88
Freeman, Billy: 1969-70-71
Freeman, Bob: 1933
Freeman, Harry: 1930-31-32
Freeman, R. L. (Bob): 1899-1900, 1902
Frick, Buddy: 1954-55-56
Frierson, Larry: 1977
Frye, Jay: 1983-84
Frye, Jerry: 1958-59-60
Fryer, Mark: 1986-87-88-89
Fuller, Bobby: 1990
Fuller, J. D.: 1979, 1981-82-83
Fulmer, Red: 1927-28
Fulton, Hewitt: 1922
Fusaro, Tony: 1967-68-69
Fusci, Dominic: 1942-43,1946

G

Gabryelski, Marcellus: 1965
Gadsden, Jake: 1980-81-82
Gaffney, Paul: 1935-36
Gaines, Corky: 1953, 1956-57-58
Gallo, Lenny: 1977-78
Galloway, Benny: 1965-66, 1968
Gambrell, Billy: 1960-61-62
Ganas, Rusty: 1968-69-70
Gargano, Vince: 1949-50-51
Garner, Tom: 1981-82-83-84
Garnto, Ben: 1965-66-67
Garrett, Lance: 1975-76-77
Gaskin, Nelson: 1930
Gaston, W. H.: 1896
Gatling, Jimmy: 1983-84-85
Gause, O'Neill: 1950
Geer, A. Eugene: 1914
Genoble, Richard: 1968
George, Robert: 1940-41
Gettel, Steve: 1978,1980
Gibbes, J. Heyward: 1907
Gibson, Robert: 1987-88-89
Gibson, Tommy: 1961-62-63
Gil, Kenny: 1981-82
Giles, Bobby: 1945-46-47
Gill, Larry: 1962-63-64
Gillespie, Tim: 1978, 1980
Gilliam, Marcus: 1983
Gilliard, Bryant: 1982-83-84
Gilmore, Bill: 1930-31-32
Giovanis, George: 1951

Girardeau, Ted: 1911-12-13-14
Girardeau, Ted: 1959
Glass, Johnny: 1965
Gobble, Jimmy: 1965-66-67
Godfrey, Dwaine: 1960-61-62
Godwin, Curtis: 1988-89-90
Going, H. R.: 1915
Going, Otis: 1913-1415
Gomes, Joe: 1958-59
Gordon, John: 1958-59-60
Goodrich, Joel: 1960-61-62
Goodman, Martin: 1919
Gosnell, Larry: 1953-5455
Gowan, Charles: 1985-86-87-88
Graham, R. E.: 1928
Gramling, John: 1951-52-53
Granger, Spec: 1950, 1953-54
Granoff, Irving: 1937-38-39
Grant, Bernard: 1976-77
Grant, Dave: 1966-67-68
Grantz, Jeff: 1973-74-75
Graves, Jerry: 1964
Graydon, Clinton: 1907-09-11
Green, Harold: 1986-87-88-89
Green, John: 1975-76-77
Gregory, Johnny: 1966-67-68
Gresham, Gregg: 1979
Gressette, R. E. "Bob": 1928-29-30
Gressette, Tatum: 1920-21
Gribble, Steve: 1972-73
Griffin, Buddy: 1953
Griffin, Drufus: 1928
Grossman, Dobby: 1972
Grotheer, Bill: 1974
Grygo, Al: 1940-41
Grugan, Joe: 1939-40
Guarino, Ralph: 1926-27-28-29
Gunnels, Bob: 1963-64-65
Gunter, Guy: 1902-03-04
Gunter, Kim: 1976
Gunter, Robert Neal: 1923, 1925
Guyton, Tony: 1983-84-85

H

Habnicht: 1907
Hagan, Harold (Bo): 1946-47-48-49
Haggard, Mike: 1970-71-72
Hagler, Scott: 1983-84-85-86
Hagood, Kent: 1981,1983-84-85
Hagood, Lee: 1896-97-98
Hagood, Rickey: 1980-81-82
Hajek, Chuck: 1931
Hall, Deane: 1970-71
Hall, Jack: 1955-56
Hall, N. C.: 1926
Halminski, Bob: 1975
Halsall, Walter (Mouse): 1942
Hambright, Fred: 1931-32-33
Hamilton, Harry: 1932
Hammett, Lamar G.: 1958
Hammond, James: 1909
Hampton, Frank: 1916
Hamrick, Doug: 1968-69-70
Hamrick, Hal: 1989-90
Hanna, Mac: 1961,1963
Hanna, Zip: 1939
Hannah, Tom: 1959-60
Harbour, Randy: 196465-66
Harmon, Paul: 1965

Harmon, Terry: 1965
Harper, Garry: 1978, 1980
Harper, Steve: 1976
Harralson, Dan: 1944-45, 1948
Harrelson, Louis: 1951
Harris, Bob: 1965-66
Harris, Dick: 1969-70-71
Harris, Ike: 1987-88-89-90
Harris, J. B.: 1898
Harris, J. B.: 1915
Harris, Leon: 1989-90
Harris, Melvin: 1960
Harrison, Claude (Red): 1947-48
Harrison, James (Skimp): 1942-43-44
Hart, H.: 1911
Hart, Oliver: 1935
Hart, Roy: 1983-84, 1986-87
Hartel, Harold: 1937-38
Harvin, Will: 1947-48
Harwell, Randy: 1986-87-88
Haskell, C. T.: 1897-98
Haskell, F. H.: 1898
Hassen, Gary: 1977-78-79
Hastings, Andy: 1978-79
Hatcher, Doug: 1958-59-60
Hatkevitch, Joe: 1938-39-40
Hawkins, Alex: 1956-57-58
Hawkins, Brian: 1989-90
Haynes, Albert: 1988-89-90
Haynes, Kenny: 1986-87-88-89
Haywood, Carlton: 1971
Hellams, Tyler: 1968, 1970-71
Helmly, Hook: 1945
Hempley, Gus: 1939
Henderson, Hal: 1980-81
Hendricks, Wes: 1987
Hendrickson, Vic: 1946
Hendrix, Kevin: 1985-86-87-88
Henry, Mario: 1990
Henson, Doug: 1946
Henson, J. B.: 1936, 1938-39
Henson, Lucius: 1938-39
Herbert, R. Beverly: 1897-98, 1900
Herdegen, Charles: 1944
Hering, Lance: 1988-89
Hertwig, Ed: 1962-63-64
Heterick, Gene: 1950
Heyward, Dan: 1912-13-14
Heyward, N. B.: 1904-05
Hicks, N. B.: 1931
High, Curt: 1988-89
High, Tim: 1987-88-89
Hill, Carl: 1984-85-86
Hill, Curtis: 1983, 1985-86
Hill, Luke: 1911-12-13-14-15
Hill, Tommy: 1976
Hill, Willie: 1983,1985
Hillary, Ira: 1981-82-84
Hinton, Patrick: 1987-88-89-90
Hipkins, Rick: 1969-70
Hodge, David: 1985, 1987-89
Hodge, Lynn: 1966, 1968-69
Hodge, Wilbur: 1964-65
Hodges, Ralph: 1943-44
Hodgin, Jay Lynn: 1972-73-74
Hoffman, Bruce: 1976
Hogan, Ben: 1990
Holcombe, J. R. (Buster): 1925-26-27
Hold, Mike: 1984-85

Gamecock Lettermen

Holland, W. T.: 1923
Holler, Ed: 1960-61-62
Holloman, Rudy: 1967-68-69
Holmes, Homer: 1904
Hopkins, James Porcher: 1933-34,
Horton, Tate: 1933-34-35
Howell, W. R. (Pop): 1936-37-38
Huffman, Ken: 1945
Huggins, Carl: 1960-61, 1963
Huggins, Lide: 1962-63-64
Hughes, Jerry: 1936, 1938
Hughes, J. G.: 1898
Hughey, Curran: 1929-30-31
Humphreys, Sam: 1960-61-62
Hunnicut, Jim: 1943
Hunter, Ford: 1934
Hunter, Jimmy: 1959-60
Hunter, William: 1899
Hursey, John: 1901
Huskey, Freeman: 1931-32-33-34
Hyde, Tristram: 1905
Hyder, George: 1984-85

I

Injaychock, Tom: 1977
Inman, Jerry: 1990
Isom, Buck: 1945

J

Jabbusch, Harry: 1948-49-50-51
Jackson, Ed: 1948
James, Jack: 1967
James, Jimmy: 1913
Janus, Bill: 1977-78
Jarrett, Jim: 1952-53-54-55
Jascewicz, Alexander: 1923-24-25
Jeffords, W. R.: 1923, 1925
Jenkins, R. W.: 1933
Jennings, Charles: 1899-1900
Jerry, Bill: 1957-58-59
Jeter, Leroy: 1989-90
Jetton, Charlie: 1971
Johnson, A. W.: 1952
Johnson, Bob: 1935-36
Johnson, Charlie: 1955-56-57
Johnson, David: 1985-86
Johnson, Don: 1955-56-57
Johnson, Earl: 1982-83-84
Johnson, Jim: 1962-63
Johnson, Joe: 1931-32-33
Johnson, Karey: 1980-81-82
Johnson, Mike: 1964
Johnson, Roy: 1935-36
Johnson, Thad: 1984
Johnson, W. W. (Hootie): 1950-51-52
Jones, Allen: 1905
Jones, Carroll: 1970-71
Jones, Clyde (Tubby): 1955
Jones, Harold: 1959-60-61
Jones, Howard (Butch): 1971
Jones, Jack: 1943
Jones, John: 1960-61-62
Jones, Kevin: 1986-87-89
Jowers, Jeff: 1963, 1966
Joye, Walter: 1927-28
Joyner, Buster: 1927-28
Juk, Stan: 196465-66

K

Kahle, Bob (Moose): 1950-51
Kalmback, Lyn: 1937
Kaney, Bob: 1976
Kanian, Leonard: 1939-40
Kater, Walt: 1980
Kavounis, Alex: 1949-50-51
Keels, George: 1926-27
Keely, Pete: 1943
Keenan, Jack: 1942
Keith, Dwight, Jr.: 1956-57-58
Kelly, Fant: 1921-22
Kelly, Vincent: 1936
Kendziorski, Jeff: 1977,1979-80
Kerr, Dick: 1914-15-16
Kerr, Gayle: 1952
Kight, Duke, 1961
Kilgore, Benjamin: 1916
Kilgore, Curtis: 1985-86-87
Killen, Jay: 1990
Killen, Jimmy: 1965-66
Killoy, Bill: 1947-48-49-50
Kilzer, Paul: 1962
Kincaid, Billy: 1947
Kincaid, James (Blackie): 1949-50, 1953
King, Bob: 1950, 1952-53
King, Heyward: 1957
Kinney, George: 1943
Kirkland, Chris: 1985
Kirkpatrick, Mike: 1961
Kiss, Frank: 1936
Kittredge, Bill: 1976
Kline, Brad: 1973-7475
Kneece, J. P. (Jake): 1944
Knight, J. Arthur: 1910-11
Kohout, Pat: 1969-70-71
Komoroski, Joe: 1964,1966-67
Kompara, John: 1956-57-58
Kopec, Gene: 1951-52-53-54
Kopian, Steve: 1958-59
Korn, Bob: 1950,1952-53
Krivonak, Joe: 1939-40-41
Kroto, Leo: 1938,1940
Kuldell, Curly: 1944
Kuritz, Russ: 1970
Krokos, Paul: 1974,1976

L

Lamb, Ronnie: 1963 64-65
Land, Jake: 1947-48
Landry, Mike: 1990
Lane, Bill: 1976-77-78-79
Lane, Pete: 1945-46-47
Langston, Felix: 1912-13-14
Lasse, Bill: 1984
Latimer, James: 1986-88-89
LaTorre, John (Lip): 1950-51-52
Laval, W. L., Jr.: 1929-30-31
Lavoie, Phil: 1957-58-59
Lawhorne, Ernie: 1943, 1946-47
Laws, Henry: 1973-74i5
Leardo, Pat: 1929-30
Lee, Augustus W.: 1902-03-04
Lee, Dozier: 1905-06
Lee, Gus: 1902-03
Lee, Marion: 1951-52
Lee, Stevie: 1978
Legat, Dan: 1963-6465
LeGrande, Glenn: 1982
LeHeup, Andy: 1973-74
LeHeup, John: 1970-71-72

Leitner, John: 1940-41-42
Leopard, Eddie: 1977,1980
Leslie, Tommy: 1972
Lester, Ken: 1960-61-62
Leventis, Andy: 1972-73
Lewis, Alex: 1913
Lewis, Crosby: 1953-54-55
Lewis, Harold: 1953-54-55
Lewis, Joey: 1986
Lewis, Quinton: 1982-83-84
Lightsey, H. M.: 1919-20-21-22
Lillard, J. E.: 1923, 1925
Linder, Jon: 1963-64-65
Lindsey, Gene: 1965
Lindsey, J. E.: 1943
Little, Derrick: 1985-86-87-88
Little, Dick: 1937-38
Logan, Phillip: 1974-75-76-77
Logan, Reggie: 1960
Loggins, Mark: 1980
Lomas, Richard: 1960-61-62
Lonchar, Tommy: 1937
Long, Bobby: 1958
Long, J. C.: 1923-24-25
Long, Julian: 1942-43
Long, Kevin: 1974-75-76
Long, Leonard: 1937-38-39
Love, Byron: 1985-86
Lovell, Harry: 1951-52-53-54
Lowry, Billy: 1939-40
Lucas, Dave: 1967-68-69
Lumpkin, Hope: 1903
Lyons, Jack: 1935-36-37
Lytle, Frederick: 1940

M

McBride, Bobby: 1960
McCabe, Mike: 1973-74-75
McCallum, C. J.: 1898-99;1901
McCarthy, George: 1969
McCathern, Jack: 1962-63-64
McClain, Carroll: 1955, 1957
McClain, Johnny: 1955
McCrady, Shack: 1933
McConnell, Vic: 1986-87-88
McCord, Toy: 1966-67
McCormack, Brendan: 1984-85-86-87
McCullough, Charles: 1940-41
McCutchen, Thomas E.: 1900-01-02
McCutcheon, Kevin: 1982
McDaniel, Donnie: 1980-81
McDougall, Allie: 1932-33-34
McDonald, George: 1943-44-45
McDonald, Keith: 1988-89-90
McFadden, Sam: 1935
McGee, A. H. (Buddy): 1921-22-23
McGhee, John: 1902
McGovern, Jim: 1959-60
McGowen, W. B.: 1911-12
McGregor, Joe: 1975-76-77
McIntee, Willie: 1983-84-85-86
McIntosh, Jim: 1897-98
McKay, Douglas: 1903
McKee, A. H.: 1923
McKernan, Matt: 1985-86-87-88
McKie, James: 1980
McKinney, Zion: 1976-77-78-79
McKissick, C. L.: 1910
McLaughlin, Chann: 1988

Gamecock Lettermen

McLauren, Gary: 1972-73-74
McLaurin, C. H.: 1894-95-96
McLaurin, Roy: 1957
McLendon, Lockhart: 1950-51
McLeod, Yancy: 1933
McManus, Henry: 1931-32-33
McMillan, John: 1920-21-22-23
McMillan, Mack: 1914-15-16
McMillan Van: 1972
McMillan William: 1940, 1942-43
McMillen, John: 1938
McNair, P. R.: 1910-11
McTeer, G. M.: 1913
McWhirter, E. F.: 1899
Mace, James: 1910-11
Mackie, Collin: 1987-88-89-90
Mackovik, George: 1937
Magill, Tom: 1927
Maginn, "Maggie": 1945
Major, Chris: 1983-84-85-86
Mann, J. H.: 1899
Manzari, Russ: 1974-75-76
Marino, Bobby: 1973-74-75
Marion, W. F.: 1919-20
Marion William: 1905
Markle Eric: 1987-88
Martin, Frank: 1936
Martin, George: 1953-54-55
Martin, Jim: 1963
Martin, Paul: 1982
Massey, Ben: 1946
Matheny, R. P. (Bull): 1928
Matthews, Monty: 1971, 1973
Mauney, Harold: 1932-33-34-35
Mauro, Bob: 1967-68
Mayfield, Buddy: 1957-58
Meadow, Dave: 1966
Medlin, Wally: 1967-68
Meeks, Bryant (Junior): 1945-46
Meers, Dave: 1931-32
Melton, W. H.: 1898
Merck, Hugh: 1950, 1953, 1955
Merck, Jimmy: 1956-57-58
Metts, A. W.: 1910-11
Meyer, Frankie: 1921-22-23
Meyer, F. O.: 1923
Middlebrooks, Harold: 1940-41-42
Miller, Corey: 1988-89-90
Miles, Don: 1959-60
Miller, Danny: 1983-84
Miller, Eddie: 1988-89-90
Miller, Othel: 1897-98
Milner Bill: 1941-42
Mills, James H.: 1899
Mills, J. D.: 1909-11
Mills, J. L.: 1925-26
Mills, John: 1911-12-13
Mimms, Chuck: 1970-71
Mims, Dru: 1984-85
Mincevich, Frank: 1952-53-54
Minton, Skip: 1982-83-84
Minus, R. W.: 1898
Miranda, Bob: 1970
Mitchell, Allen: 1983-84-85
Mitchell, Jack: 1949
Mitchell, Jim: 1969-70-71
Mitchell, Wright: 1990
Mobley, Marion: 1909
Monaco, Ron: 1984-85

Mooney, Kevin: 1970
Moore, J. H. (Dummy): 1917-18
Moore, Jack: 1929-30
Moore, Paul: 1903-04-05
Moore, Spratt: 1918
Moree, Bobby: 1955
Morehead, Arthur (Buddy): 1931-32-33
Morrell, Buddy: 1952
Morrell, John: 1986-87
Morris, Bob: 1967-68
Morris, Bob: 1971
Morris, Glenn: 1971
Morris Jack: 1959-60-61
Morris Otis: 1982, 1984-85-86
Mortimer, Jim: 1944-45
Moss, Jim: 1960-61-62
Mote, Kelly: 1942
Mott, Garry: 1973-74-75
Moye, Richie: 1969-70-71
Muir, Warren: 1967-68-69
Muldrow, Eddie: 1972-73-74
Mullis, Norris: 1951-52
Mulvihill, Jim: 1965-66-67
Munn, John, 1932-33
Murdaugh, Alex: 1923
Murdaugh, Randolph: 1907-09
Murdaugh, Randolph: 1935
Murray, Hazel: 1935-36-37
Myers, Glen: 1936-37-38
Myers, Woody: 1985-86-87

N

Nash, Jimmy: 1969-70-71
Nater Marcos: 1986
Neely Jimbo: 1976
Neeley, William: 1942
Neil, W. A.: 1900
Nelson, Andy: 1973-74-75
Nelson, Billy: 1964-65-66
Nemeth, Brian: 1975
Nemeth, Jim: 1959-60
Newman, Wilbur: 1949-50
Nicholson, W. H.: 1902
Nidiffer, David (Buddy): 1955-56-57
Nies, Billy: 1962-63
Norman, Chris: 1980-81-82-83
Norman, Doyle: 1941,1946
Norman, Mike: 1988
Norton, Ken: 1959
Norton, Kirt: 1938-39-40
Nott, T. E.: 1911
Novak, Steve: 1940-41, 1946
Nowak, Stan: 1939-40

O

O'Connor, Tom: 1984-85
O'Dell, Firpo: 1932
Odomirok, Paul: 1975
Oglesby Marvin: 1987
Oglesby R. C.: 1911
O'Hagan, Larry: 1976
O'Hara, Bobby: 1942,1946-47
Oliver, Gene: 1900-01-02-03
Oliver, Len: 1979
Ollic, Walter: 1954-55
Orkis, Bob: 1976-77-78
Orrel, Wally: 1966-67-68
Osborne, Rut L.: 1915,1917

Overstreet, Charlie: 1961
Owens, Edgar E. (Mgr.): 1956-57
Ozburn, John (Red): 1946-47-48

P

Padgett, Benny: 1968-69-70
Parker, Bill: 1968-69-70
Parker, Daren: 1987,1989-90
Parler, J. D.: 1922-23
Parlor, Anthony: 1988
Parrish, Britt: 1976-77-78
Parrish, R. L.: 1899
Parrott, V. A.: 1907
Parson, Ron: 1972
Patrone, Joe: 1939-40
Patrone, Tony: 1944
Pasky, Ed: 1947-48-49-50
Passailaigue, Edward: 1911-12
Patrick, Neal: 1959
Paul, A. M.: 1911
Payne, Johnny: 1972
Payne, Ricky: 1974-75, 1977
Peacock, Gleen: 1984-85
Pender, Bru: 1990
Penny, Tony: 1977-78
Pepe, Jim: 1986-87
Pepper, Tony: 1972-73-74
Perkins, Andrew: 1916
Perkins, Less: 1911
Perlotte, Robert: 1978, 1981
Perrin, L. W.: 1907
Perry, Gerald: 1984
Perry, Mac: 1965
Pettiford, Jahmal: 1990
Phares, Kirk: 1957-58-59
Phiel, Dick: 1950
Phillips, Ashley: 1948-49-50
Phillips, Grahl: 1973-74
Phillips, Paul: 1964-65-66
Philpot, Greg: 1983-85-86-87
Pickett, Bayard: 1948-49-50
Pierce, Hyrum: 1966-67
Pilcher, Tommy: 1960-61-62
Pinkerton, Jim: 1947-48-49-50
Pitchko, David: 1989-90
Pitt, Jack: 1958-59-60
Pitts, Ed: 1957-58-59
Platt, Carl: 1987-88-89
Poinsett, David: 1984-85-86-87
Poole, Eric: 1982-83-8485
Poole, Jimmy: 1965-66-67
Pope, David: 1961-62-63
Pope, Jimmy: 1968-69
Porter, Jerry: 1911-12-13-14
Poston, Jimmy: 1968-69-70
Prater, Gary: 1985
Prehodka, Joe: 1961-62-63
Prezioso, Chuck: 1949-50-51
Prezioso, David: 1975-76-77
Price, Rodney: 1986-87-88-89
Price, W. R. (Monkey): 1925-26-27
Prickett, Dalton: 1981
Prickett, Mackie: 1954-55-56
Pringle, Wes: 1988
Privette, Jimmy: 1971-72-73
Proctor, Phillip: 1980-81
Proctor, Rubin: 1980
Provence, Andrew: 1980-81-82

Gamecock Lettermen

Provence, Jerome: 1974-75-76-77
Pruitt, Bobby: 1953

Q

Quarles, Buddy: 1984-85,1987

R

Rabune, Rick: 1983-84
Rabune, Ron: 1985-86-87-88
Raby, Nolan: 1931-32
Ragin, Mike: 1964-65-66
Rambo, Tony: 1981
Ramsey, Skip: 1978
Randle, Cat: 1918
Rawl, A. F.: 1909-10
Rawl, Jacob: 1911
Reaves, Joe: 1988-89-90
Reed, Aubry: 1955
Reed, Richard: 1903
Reese, Kenneth: 1977
Reeves, Dan: 1962-63-64
Reeves, J. B.: 1907
Reeves, Percy: 1979, 1981
Reeves, Roy Don (Butch): 1965, 1967-68
Regalis, Joe: 1969-70-71
Renfrow, Billy: 1950-51
Reuhr, Fred: 1900
Reynolds, James: 1938
Reynolds, Robby: 1971-72-73
Reynolds, Tommy: 1933
Rhame, Crip: 1929
Rhame, H. B.: 1922-23
Rhame, Lee: 1960
Rhino, Tim: 1979,1981
Rhodes, Tommy: 1971
Rice, Billy Ray: 1969-70-71
Rice, Glen: 1940,1942
Richards, James P.: 1920
Rietkovich, Ty: 1982-83
Riggs, Buddy: 1944-45
Rivens, Antoine: 1989-90
Rivera, Lennie: 1984
Rivers, Billy: 1954-55-56
Robbins, Andy: 1986
Robbins, Bob: 1931-32-33
Robbins, Roddy: 1951-52
Robelot, Paul: 1935-36
Robertson, Arthur N. B.: 1935
Robinson, Dave: 1920
Robinson, Gene: 1935,1937-38
Robinson, Kenneth: 1982-83, 85-86
Robinson, Robert: 1985-86-87-88
Robinson, Stacy: 1989-90
Roe, Bob: 1971-72-73
Rogers, Bill: 1924-25-26
Rogers, Bobby: 1950
Rogers, Don: 1956-57-58
Rogers, E. Power: 1926
Rogers, George: 1977-78-79-80
Rogers, Jim: 1957
Rogers, Jim: 1963-64-65
Rogers, Lawton: 1956-57-58
Rogers, W. M. (Power): 1925-26-27
Rose, Donnie: 1966
Rosen, Marty: 1962-63-64
Roskie, Ken: 1940-41-42
Ross, Ken: 1968
Rossomano, Jimmy: 1924-25

Rowe, Thad: 1971-72-73
Rowland, John: 1934
Rucker, Larry: 1961-62-63
Ruehr, Fred: 1900
Runager, Max: 1974,1976-77-78
Rush, George: 1988-89-90
Rushing, Lyn: 1971
Russell, Rusty: 1981-82
Rutledge, Bill: 1946, 1949
Ryan, Gary: 1983
Rytienburg, Charles: 1901

S

Sadler, Shaun: 1984
Saldi, Jay: 1973, 1975
Salley, John: 1902
Sally, Ken: 1985-86-87
Sanders, E. D.: 1923
Sanford, Rick: 1975-76-77-78
Sarrocco, Bill: 1979
Satterfield, Steve: 1957-58-59
Saunders, John: 1957-58-59
Schechterly, George: 1978,1980
Scheutzner, Jack: 1949
Schmidt, Ira: 1945
Schwarting, Gene: 1966-67-68
Schwartz, Bob: 1953-54
Scott, Mitchell: 1947-48
Scott, Willie: 1977-78-79-80
Scruby, Frank: 1945
Seabom, Colie: 1916-17
Searingen: 1898-99
Sears, Len: 1963-6465
Seawright, James: 1981-82-83-84
Sehulster, Don: 1954
Seideman, S. S. (Si): 1924-25-26
Senter, Doug: 1963-64-65
Shand, Monroe: 1899
Shand, W. M.: 1928-29-30-31
Sharpe, Sterling: 1983, 1985-86-87
Sharpton, B. T.: 1909
Shaw, Joe: 1943
Shea, Walt: 1950-51-52
Shealy, Bobby: 1954
Shealy, John: 1976
Shiflet, Harvey: 1958-59-60
Shifiet, Wayne: 1958-59
Shinn, Dick: 1931-33
Shinn, Joe: 1931-32-33
Shively, David: 1984
Shivers, Paul: 1985-86-87-88
Shope, Greg: 1976
Shue, Zeb: 1973-74-75
Shugart, Bubba: 1974-75-76
Silas, Joe: 1952-53-54
Simmons, Tommy: 1969-70-71
Simmons, T. R.: 1923
Simpkins, J. E.: 1909
Simpson, Bill: 1937
Simpson, Trent: 1988-89-90
Simrill, Frank: 1916
Sims, Lana: 1916
Sinclair, Fred: 1977-78-79
Singieton, Tim: 1976-77-78-79
Sistare, Byron: 1969-70
Sizemore, W. C.: 1920-21, 1923
Skelton, W. A.: 1950-51-52
Skinner, Benny: 1949-50
Skinner, Roy: 1947-48-49-50
Skinner, Rube: 1919
Skipper, Harry: 1979-80-81-82
Slaughter, Chuck: 1978,1981

Sligh, C. E.: 1909
Sligh, Thomas: 1905
Sligh, Waldeck: 1911-12-13
Smith, Anthony: 1983-84-85-86
Smith, Bamey: 1928
Smith, Burney: 1919
Smith, Danny: 1984-85-86-87
Smith, E. Z.: 1973-74-75
Smith, Ed: 1918-19-20
Smith, George: 1982
Smith, Horace: 1978, 1981
Smith, Joe: 1975
Smith, Jule: 1964-65
Smith, Larry: 1949-50-51
Smith, Sydney: 1902
Smoake, Tommy: 1980
Snell, Fred: 1939
Snider, Robert: 1937
Snipes, W. E.: 1921-22-23
Snoddy, Fred: 1942
Snyder, Tom: 1959-60
Sohm, Howard: 1959-60
Soles, Jerry: 1963-64, 1966
Somma, Don: 1965-66-67
Sossamon, Lou: 1940-41-42
South, Dan: 1958
South, Harry: 1981-82-83-84
Sowell, Dave: 1959-60-61
Sparks, Dave: 1948-49-50
Spears, Stan: 1957-58
Spinks, Randy: 1973
Staley, Frank: 1959-60-61
Stasica, Stan: 1941
Stephens, Billy: 1949-50-51
Stephens, Calvin: 1987-88-89-90
Stephens, Paul: 1949-50-51
Stephens, Stevie: 1975-76
Stevens, Al: 1978-79
Stevenson, Scott: 1983
Stevenson, Tom: 1942-43
Steward, Charles: 1989-90
Stewart, Don: 1974, 1976-77
Stewart, Harry: l949-50-51
Stillwell, Ed: 1935, 1937
Stillwell, Robert: 1935,1937
Stirline, Mike: 1971
Stoddard, Bob: 1927-28
Stoddard, Hugh S.: 1928-29
Stokes, Earnest Weston: 1935
Stone, Mack: 1970-71
Stoney, A. Burnet: 1912-13-14
Strickland, Bishop: 1947-48-49-50
Strickland, W. L.: 1957-58-59
Strobel, Jim: 1944-45
Stroud, Heber (Rock): 1937-38-39
Stroud, Roy: 1931-32-33
Strowder, Steve: 1986-87-88
Suggs, Tommy: 1968-69-70
Sumpter, James: 1981-82-83-84
Surratt, Cedric: 1989
Suttle, Ben: 1944
Swearingen, G. T.: 1898-99
Sweet, Richard: 1989-90
Swinehart, Steve: 1979
Swink, Marion: 1923-24-25
Swink, W. W. (Red): 1925-26-27

T

Talley, Andrew: 1917

Gamecock Lettermen

Tandy, Al: 1976-77
Tanner, John: 1980-81-82
Tarbush, Tami: 1975-76-77
Tarrer, Bill: 1954-55
Tate, Bruce: 1941-42
Tayloe, Hinton: 1982-83-84
Taylor, Benjamin: 1935
Taylor, Conley: 1959-60-61
Taylor, David: 1988-89
Taylor, Lorenzo: 1935
Taylor, Sam: 1984-85 1987
Taylor, Zack: 1950-51
Teague, Jeff: 1983-84
Teston, Randy: 1979, 1980
Tharpe, Mack Lee: 1968-69-70
Theusen, Dick: 1955
Thomas, Brad: 1976
Thomas, Floyd: 1925-26-27
Thomas, Jim: 1982
Thomas, Scott: 1973-74-75
Thomas, Skeets: 1987,1989
Thomas Troy: 1980-81-82
Thomas, W. Harris: 1919-20
Thompson, Buck: 1972-73-74
Thorman, Phil: 1965
Thornton, Fleming: 1943
Thrash, Pat: 1943-44-45-46
Timmerman, John: 1959
Timmons, Neal: 1978-79
Timmons, Herbert: 1919
Tisdale, Mike: 1976-77
Tobias, Ashley (Pat): 1935-36-37
Todd, Joe: 1985-86-87
Tolbert, Mike: 1987-88, 90
Tominack, John: 1944
Tomlin, Donald: 1935
Tope, Jeff: 1970
Townsend, Scott: 1965,1967
Toy, Roger: 1971-72-73
Trevillian, Tom: 1969-70
Troup, Bill: 1972
Truby, Dave: 1963,1965
Tucker Wayne: 1964-65
Tumer Fritz: 1935-36
Turner, Jim: 1980
Turner, Park: 1960
Turner, Pat: 1986-88-89
Turner, Roy (Rabbit): 1931-32

U

Urban, Alex (Jeep): 1938, 1940
Urban, Frank: 1936-37-38
Urbanyi, Arthur: 1936
Urquhart Jim: 1933
Usher, Al: 1968, 1970-71

V

Vargo, Mike: 1980-81
Vaughn, Timmy: 1981
Veal, Dylan: 1990
Veal, Nat: 1977-78
Vella, Pat: 1949
Verner, J. S.: 1926
Verner, Jim: 1897-98
Vickers, Sammy: 1956-57
Vogel, Paul: 1981-82-83-84
Von Kolnitz, Alfred H. (Fritz): 1911-12

W

Wade, Chris: 1982-83-84
Wade, Scott: 1978-79
Wade, Steve: 1971-72
Wadiak, Steve: 1948-49-50-51
Wagnon, Gene: 1943
Waite, Alex: 1919-20-21
Walker, Antonio: 1988-89-90
Walker, Bucky: 1957-58
Walker, Joe: 1943
Walker, Max: 1946-47
Walker, Rodney: 1985-86
Walker, Tony: 1982
Walkup, Ken: 1968-69-70
Wallace, J. W.: 1923
Wallace, Phil: 1971-72-73
Walsh, Jim: 1980, 1982-83-84
Waring, Clark D.: 1916-17-18
Waring, Clark: 1959-60-61
Waring, Robert: 1916
Waring, Wingate: 1909
Warren, Phil: 1943
Warren, Tom: 1943
Watson, George: 1926
Watson, Gillis: 1929-30
Watson, Hoyt: 1911
Watson, Ken: 1988-89-90
Watson, Pat: 1967-68-69
Watson, Roscoe: 1976-77,1979
Watts, Jeff: 1976
Weaver, Emanuel: 1980-81
Webb, Kenneth: 1939
Webb, Roy: 1961
Webb, Tanny: 1912-13
Wehman, E. E.: 1913
Wehmeyer, Bob: 1966
Weir, Jim: 939
Welch, Greg: 1985
Welch, Tony: 1946
Wessinger, Chalmers: 1907
West, Carl: 1980,1982
Weston, Bill: 1953-5455
Weston, Bully: 1917-18
Weston, Nelson: 1955-56-57
Wheat, Ken: 1969-70-71
Wheeler, Joe: 1920-21-22-23
White, Homer: 1904
White, Kevin: 1984-85-86-87
White, Roger: 1955
Whitecavage, Leon: 1975
Whitman, Mike: 1990
Whitner, W. C. (Crip): 1909-10-11
Wilburn, J. R.: 1963-64-65
Wilburn, Terry: 1990
Wilds, John: 1902-03
Wilds, S. H.: 1903-04-05
Wilkes, Del: 1980-81,1983-84
Willard, Henry: 1931-32-33
Williams, C. R.: 1903
Williams, Charley: 1961-62-63
Williams, Clarence: 1974-75-76
Williams, Curtis (Cooter): 1965-66-67
Williams, Gerald: 1988
Williams, Irving (Buck): 1943
Williams, J. B.: 1935-36-37-38
Williams, Jimmy: 1959
Williams, Mike: 1978
Williams, Paul: 1980
Williams, Randy: 1970

Williams, Rex: 1937
Williams, Stephane: 1987-88-89
Williams, Vemon: 1965
Williams, W. T.: 1978-79
Williams, Y. S. Yates: 1928-29-30
Wilson Brice: 1976
Wilson C. A.: 1972-73-74
Wilson, Ed: 1952-53
Wilson, Eugene: 1977
Wilson, Gene: 1951-52-53
Wilson, Kurt: 1986-87-88, 90
Wilson, Roger (Red): 1946-47-48-49
Wimberly, Bob: 1925-26-27-28
Windsor, Scott: 1986-87-88-89
Windus, Mike: 1927,1929
Wingfield, Emmett L., Jr.: 1925-26-27
Wingard, Carl: 1929
Wingard, Joe: 1968-69-70
Wingard, Ted: 1965-66
Wingard, Tom: 1966-67
Withers, H. N.: 1899-1900
Withers, John: 1902
Witherspoon, James H.: 1899
Witherspoon, Jerry: 1972-73-74
Witt, Gene: 1951-52
Witt, Gerald: 1972,1974
Wohrman, Bill: 1952-53-54
Wolf, Grayson: 1931-32
Wolf, Harry, Jr.: 1927-28
Womble, Carl: 1983-84
Wood, Robert: 1972
Woodard, Theartis: 1987-88
Woodlee, Tommy: 1950, 1954
Woodson, Albert: 1922
Woodley, Glenn: 1983-84
Woodrow, McMaster: 1911
Woolbright, Cecil: 1947-48
Woolbright, Marty: 1971-72-73
Woolbright, Roger: 1974,1977-78
Wright, Frank: 1981-82-83-84
Wright, George: 1948-49
Wright, Jack: 1923, 1925
Wright, Jake: 1969
Wright, Johnnie: 1977-78, 1980-81
Wunder, John: 1990
Wyman, Benjamin: 1903
Wyman, James: 1903
Wylie, J. A.: 1930

Y

Yancey, Hogan L.: 1900
Yoakum, Randy: 1968-69
Yonce, Walker: 1932-33
Young, Jackie: 1970-71
Young, Steve: 1973-74-75

Z

Zanders, Zip: 1986
Zeigler, Fred: 1967-68-69
Zimmerman, D. M.: 1899
Zipperly, Tom: 1972-73-74
Zobel, Edwin: 1927-28-29

This list represents football lettermen since South Carolina began football in 1892. The sports information office will appreciate your assistance in correcting any errors.

Gamecock Lettermen

New 1991 Lettermen

Brandon Bennett	Antwan Jackson
Hank Campbell	Eric McDowell
Toby Cates	Asim Penny
Rocky Clay	Konata Reid
Vincent Dinkins	Kevin Rosenkrans
Ernest Dye	Chris Rumph
Kenny Favors	Marty Simpson
Larry Foster	Bryan Thomsen
Keith Franklin	David Turnipseed
Norman Greene	Tony Watkins
Roderick Howell	Terry Wilburn